# M ND GAMES

## Understanding Trafficker Psychological Warfare

Dr. Deena Graves
and Derek Williams, a former 32-year child sex trafficker

With foreword by Denise Williams, Derek's longtime victim and bottom
and creator of the *My Life My Choice* program

## M³ Transformations
### PUBLISHING

2

M³ Transformations Publishing
An imprint of M³ Transformations, Inc.
P.O. Box 919
Crowley, Texas 76036

M³ Transformations
PUBLISHING

Copyright © 2022 by Dr. Deena Graves and Derek Williams
Foreword by Denise Williams
Edited by Cheryl R. Welch

Library of Congress No. 2021925882
Library of Congress
US Programs, Law, and Literature Division
Cataloging in Publication Program
101 Independence Avenue, S.E.
Washington, DC 20540-4283
ISBN: 978-0-578-33399-1 (paperback)
ISBN: 978-0-578-33508-7 (eBook)

Includes bibliographical references and index.

Visit https://www.m3transformations.com/mindgames for more about this book. Contact media@m3transformations.com for press inquiries. For information about purchasing *Mind Games* in bulk quantities, please contact mindgames@m3transformations.com.

Please understand that this book does not replace a medical or mental-health expert for individuals reading it or for those they work with. Physically, psychologically, or emotionally traumatized children and adults should be under the care of a physician, licensed therapist, psychologist, or psychiatrist. The information, tools, and resources shared in this book are not intended to supersede professional supervision. Neither the individual authors nor the publisher is responsible or liable for trauma, loss, pain, or damage allegedly stemming from the material contained in this book.

## Dedications

For the many individuals whom I victimized. My sincere prayer is that you can forgive me, and that God would be glorified through me now. When all else failed, Jesus healed and transformed me. ~ Derek

We also dedicate this book to abused-and-neglected children around the world and to those who've devoted their lives to helping them. May all who read it find within these pages solutions with hope.

# Additional Resources

Thank you for your passion for our abused-and-neglected children. Visit www.m3transformations.com to download the M³ *Delivering Hope* Catalog, which details our 40+ trainings and consulting services. We provide in-depth trainings on many of the topics discussed in the *Analysis With Dr. Deena Graves'* sections of this book and also develop custom trainings. Our consulting services include:

- Treatment planning based on the specific dynamics of a child or teen's trafficking.
- Identifying the unique trauma bond a trafficker has over a teen.
- Curriculum, protocol, and multidisciplinary team development.
- Court preparation.

Join our mailing list at www.m3transformations.com for updates on new M³ trainings, resources, and tools.

# Contents

6

# Foreword

I had two addictions for a good deal of my life. One was drugs, and the other was Derek Williams.

I did whatever I had to for both. I'm not sure which was harder to beat. Probably Derek. When I beat the drugs, I immediately threw away everything remotely related to them. Long after I worked up enough strength to leave Derek, on the other hand, I proudly kept the tattoo that declared, *"I love Derek."* Even he was surprised when I finally covered it up. I kept it for years after we parted ways **because it gave me hope**.

That's how completely a trafficker takes over your mind.

I still clearly remember the day I got that tattoo. I was so excited because it inked the deal – just Derek and me against the world. It didn't matter to me that 10 other girls sported the same tattoo and the same pipedream that Derek secretly loved them.

You see, loving a trafficker becomes a way of life just as much as heroin or crack. When addicts catch a whiff of their drug of choice in the air, they can close their eyes and get lost in the utopia of a remembered high. I could close my eyes and get lost in the scent of Derek. **HE** smelled like utopia to me. I'd stare at him for hours while he slept. He looked like the dream always just out of my reach.

That's because he had meticulously etched that dream into my mind. Traffickers cunningly manipulate you into falling in love with everything about them. They make you believe you are the most remarkable thing on earth. You get in over your head, and you can't dig your way out. Your heart is persuaded they're in love with you, but in reality, they're in love with what they can get out of you. Pimps get as much as they can, as quickly as they can, because they know your body and emotions can only hold up so long before they collapse under the weight of all the trauma.

Derek wasn't the first person to sell me a dream. I fell for another trafficker's "undying love" at 13. That's where my most urgent warning for youth was born. Don't listen to even the first word. If you listen for 15 minutes, it's probably over. That's all it takes for a trafficker to hook you. Their hook impales you as surely as it does a fish biting on a shiny lure. They're both flashy and appealing. They look good from a distance, but once you take the bait, it snags you into something you had no idea was waiting for you.

My first trafficker didn't bother to tell me that clients would stick a gun in my mouth and other body parts. I would never have believed pimps who said they loved me would bang my head against the wall or kick my insides out. It's funny. You see the buyers for precisely what they are, but you routinely blame yourself for what your pimp does to you.

I did with Derek even as I watched him grow into full-blown pimp mentality. I chose him because I noticed a sensitive side to him on the track. My other pimps had been aggressive, physical, maniacal. Derek wasn't … at first. The more money I made him, the harder his heart grew and the more violently his gator-clad foot came down. It hurt even more because my body paid for those shoes.

Everything a trafficker says to you is to make money. Period. It's a false lifestyle. Everything about it. There's nothing sincere.

As our story unfolds in the pages of this book, you'll see that although Derek stole my identity, I had the blessing of helping propel him into his true identity. The same way I saw his heart harden with each day in the game, I've seen it melt more and more the longer he's been out of the game. Believe me, Derek knows how to get money. He walked away from hundreds of dollars a night. Now, changing lives is his greatest payout.

As for me, I've found my true identity, too. We'll talk more about that later, in my book. For now, dig deep with this book, and you'll walk away with a new arsenal of tools to keep youth from what the game does to your mind, whether you're the trafficker or the victim.

Denise Williams

Derek's victim, long-time bottom
(known as Sparkle in the game), and ex-wife
Creator of the *My Life My Choice* Program

## Prologue

**From the Heart of Derek Williams**

Make no mistake. You *do not* want your child to cross even the peripheral vision of someone like I was. Once a girl caught my eye, her eyes told me all I needed to know about her vulnerabilities. The challenge was on. Only it wasn't much of a challenge. I whipped out my charm, or should I say manipulation savvy, quickly bending her still-developing mind to my iron will. She was a lost cause after that. To you. Not to me. In the span of a conversation, I manufactured my next product.

There's an army of people like my former self out there luring our kids into their arms for their own profit and pleasure. They lurk inside your child's cell phone. They smile at your child in the mall. They sit behind her in school. They talk her up at parties.

If you think your teen is too smart to fall for the tricks, traps, and lures of a child sex trafficker, let me encourage you to think again. They weaponize teenagers' brains against them – their scientifically proven heightened need for risk-taking, the rollercoaster that hijacks their emotions, their inability to logically think through the consequences of one out-of-character choice.[1] They don't stand a chance against a street-smart trafficker if we don't arm them with the proper knowledge and tools. Traffickers and other predators launch fiery darts at them like incoming torpedoes. The explosion of excitement, adventure, anticipation, mystique, secrecy, and confusion leaves them defenseless. Therefore, we must fortify them to head off the incoming attack.

That's where I come in. My name is Derek Williams. I am a war criminal, so to speak. I tricked more than 150 teen girls – starting with my 14-year-old girlfriend – and women into selling their bodies for my profit and pleasure. I am a master of psychological warfare. My purpose in writing this book is to equip you and your kids, whether they are your children or you work with them, with an "anti-torpedo system." Youth cannot protect themselves from a trafficker's mind games without understanding them. Neither can you.

Traffickers wage an all-out war for the mind of a child. The money is too good, and the chances of getting caught too slim, not to. They typically don't come to the battlefield with guns or knives. They rarely take them captive through kidnapping. They don't have to. They ambush their minds and emotions through intentional and methodical manipulation.

I could meet your teen in a mall and walk out 30 minutes later with her not just willing but elated to do anything for me. So can a lot of other people.

You won't find excuses in this book. I know what I did is one of the most despicable things one human being could do to another. Especially a child. When I looked at another human in those days, I didn't see a person. I saw my ticket to the easy life. I saw my next drug fix, dinner at the most expensive restaurant, a new ride, a more luxurious gold chain. I didn't care how it destroyed every fiber of their being. I only cared about how it gratified mine. There's no excuse for that. But a lot of people feel that way.

I knowingly, intentionally, and meticulously decimated bodies, minds, and souls. I sold them in every state, Canada, and Europe without so much as a thought about their well-being. As you read these words, multitudes of children around the world are in the hands of people who are just like I was. Hopelessness holds countless other kids captive, making them an easy target for a skilled predator or an incubator for a trafficker in the making.

I share my story so that we might take these children back and prevent endless more from falling into the psychological prison and physical hell of a pimp, a pornographer, or other predator.

To be clear, then, I'm not justifying what I did. My goal is not to gain your sympathy, empathy, or forgiveness. Rather, it is to give you an in-depth, behind-the-scenes tour of the recesses of a predator's mind, a deep dive into the psychological manipulation they use to systematically dismantle their victims.

I also want to prevent today's youth from growing into the monster I was. With that in mind, I will unpack my story. It starts with a little boy who was determined to protect his mom from an abusive dad. It evolves into a man who didn't blink an eye at inflicting even worse torture on females than he did. I will take you on the journey of a good student who wanted to grow up to be a lawyer but instead willingly chose pimping as a career. I'll give you insights into how a young boy with big dreams of helping the helpless grew into a man who unleashed nightmares on the powerless. We need to take our children back from that, as well.

By unfolding my story, I hope to give youth and those who work with them tools to detect those incoming torpedoes and divert the attack. Traffickers stick with proven tactics. I'll dismantle those for you, and Dr. Graves and I will fortify your defense against them with strategic countertactics.

While I can never make restitution for all the lives I ravaged, I long to prevent the destruction of more of our children. I understand you might disdain me as you read my words. Many of you will have a hard time getting past the fact I didn't serve a day of jail time for trafficking such a substantial number of people. That's another fact I hope to open your eyes about. I trafficked people, including kids, precisely because I knew I *wouldn't* serve jail time. Although it is changing, we have a long history of sending victims to juvenile detention or jail, while the traffickers and buyers walk away with money and satisfaction. We still have work to do in our mindset toward teens who become victims. For example, law requires mandated reporters to report *all* known or suspected cases of child abuse or neglect. Yet, almost 60 percent of mandated reporters in a 2017 study said some youth "choose to be prostitutes" and "reporting depend(s) on the situation."[2]  I can guarantee you from 32 years of firsthand experience that *all* trafficked youth endure *devastating* abuse and neglect.

I'm not going to try to change your mindset toward me. That's not my purpose. You might not ever be able to forgive me. I had a hard time forgiving myself and only did after years of therapy, tears, and grieving. During that process, saving children from people like I was became my passion and is now my life's purpose. I hope you can forgive me, and we can work together for the sake of our children. If you can't, I pray you still can find valuable information within the pages of this book to take our children back from predators and trauma. I'm willing to take the hit for that possibility. I am not willing, though, to chance people I already hurt suffering more trauma because of me. Therefore, all names other than my family and Denise, who chose to use her name, have been changed to protect identity and privacy.

Let me warn you. To give you an accurate picture of what our children live in the arms of a pimp, I must use words and descriptions that will disgust you. They nauseate me now, too. We can't escape the fact, though, that they are entrenched in the world we are talking about. Traffickers don't speak to their victims like they would another person. They don't even talk to them like they would a dog. If we gloss over them, our strategies and protocols to help the children who live them will fall flat. We can't truly help them if we don't understand the psychological and emotional debris left behind by that incoming torpedo.

**From the Heart of Dr. Deena Graves**

I recognize this book causes mixed emotions because, frankly, I had to go through a process to get there myself. If anyone had told me when I started doing this work that I would one day work with a former trafficker, I would have laughed. I have nothing but repulsion for such heinous crimes.

However, I've been doing this work for more than 13 years and grew frustrated at our lack of progress. If we take an honest assessment of where we are in preventing victims, keeping them from running back to their pimps, and helping them heal, we must admit we haven't made a tremendous amount of progress despite years of raising awareness and enacting laws. Yes, we've taken baby steps, but traffickers are still leaps ahead, torturing an inexcusable number of children. And, many of those children choose them over us when offered a way out. That is not acceptable. It tells you, and evidence-based research backs up, that at-risk youth across the country have not been kept safe from traffickers and those victimized have received inadequate treatment strategies for their unique and complex trauma.[3,4]

I asked myself: ***What are we missing? What are we not seeing? What do we need greater clarity about?*** I realized a gap existed in the conversation. Only someone who has waged the psychological warfare of a child sex trafficker can help those of us in the fight analyze how they do it. We can only develop an effective game plan to combat their reign of terror when we understand their mindset. It's an unnatural and despicable way of thinking to us, so we must learn its dynamics. We are in a war for our children, and to win a war, you must understand your enemy.

A passage from an ancient Chinese book on military strategy shines revelation on that with the following quote. As you read it, think about the battles you've waged for children against an unseen predator and how this quote applies.

> *"If you know the enemy and know yourself, you **need not** fear the result of a hundred battles. If you know yourself **but not** the enemy, for every victory gained, you will also suffer a defeat.* (I personally know this one well.) *If you know neither the enemy nor yourself, you will succumb in every battle."*[5]

So again, if we don't understand how traffickers think and execute, we will continue to suffer defeat after defeat. And, our children will continue to pay the consequences.

With that in mind, I hunted for someone who could help me understand how the enemy thinks. Of course, the search could not lead to just anyone. It had to be someone who had not only been out of the game a substantial amount of time but whose actions in that time proved he is a truly changed man.

My pursuit led me to Derek. Anyone who preyed on other people for 32 years has extensive insights into the full-fledged war traffickers wage against our children and the weapons they employ. What sets Derek apart, however, is his remorse and his humbleness. He didn't serve time behind prison bars, but he did serve agonizing time – and a great deal of it – coming to terms with what he did.

I want to caution you before you continue reading: Consider if this book is right for you. Take care of yourself if you decide to proceed. The child sex trafficking or Commercial Sexual Exploitation of Children (CSEC) subject matter and the need to understand their specific complex trauma requires the inclusion of information that is difficult to read. It can cause people with a history of trauma to trigger. I've known people without trauma who wanted to make a difference shut down out of fear for their own children. However, we cannot prevent victims or help them heal if we don't understand the unprecedented dynamics of what they live, and Derek is extremely transparent about what they lived at his hands. It is a crucial conversation because of that eye-opening and worth-repeating research that has overwhelmingly exposed that across the United States:

- At-risk youth have not been kept safe from traffickers.
- Trafficked youth have not received adequate treatment strategies for their unique, complex trauma after living CSEC.

*We are losing the psychological war for our children. This book will help change that.* But, it is a hard read. With that said, I wish I could have read it before the first time I looked into the eyes of a trafficked child telling me what she had lived. Nothing can prepare you for that, but I believe the information in this book would have made it easier for me before hearing it from a child the first time.

I had worked with some of the most tortured youth on the planet by the time I met Derek. Kids who were the victims of ritual abuse. Preteens forced into despicable acts by gangs and transnational crime syndicates, including committing murder and baby sacrifices. One child had to choose who would live between her mom and dad. I could go on and on. And, yes,

I am talking about American children on U.S. soil. I learned a tremendous amount from each of those youth and continue to learn from survivors.

But from Derek, I learned what I had not from any other source. Only someone who has been a trafficker can help us peel back the layers of a trafficker's psyche. He takes us inside the inner workings of a predator's mind and gives us revelation that we have no other way of learning.

As Derek said, there is an army of people out there just like he was luring our children into their traps. In this book, we take you into the thought process of these predators, giving you unique insights to help the youth you work with, whether trafficked or at risk of trafficking. We are real with you because our children desperately need us to be real.

Derek and I believe we can create exponential change by strategically partnering his insider knowledge of this destructive industry with my evidence-based, award-winning experience with at-risk and trafficked youth and those who work with them. To that end, at the conclusion of each chapter, you will find a section titled, **Analysis With Dr. Deena Graves**. This section makes crucial connections between the events in Derek's life in that chapter and what could have led to different outcomes. These eye-opening connections that explore the "what if" ready us to transform what is happening to our children. With the unprecedented revelations, we can rewrite that research that shows we are not keeping our children safe from traffickers and that treatment strategies are not only not working but leaving our children spiraling even years later. Crucial components of the analysis include:

1. Cutting-edge brain science.
2. Notable research findings.
3. How that research lines up with Derek's experiences as a child and as a trafficker, including what he observed in his victims and other traffickers.
4. My insights from working directly with trafficked youth, including obtaining dozens of detailed disclosures within an hour of meeting youth and helping put traffickers behind bars where they can't decimate more children.
5. An examination of these components through the lens of strategic foresight, systems dynamics, and anticipatory management.
6. Our recommendations for leveraging the pivotal analysis and our innovative leadership tools to intentionally and strategically create a different future for our children.

This section will give you, the warrior, solutions infused with hope. That's what our organization, M³ Transformations, does. We design solutions with hope. It's time to move beyond awareness. It's time to stop force-fitting "solutions" that weren't designed for the unique, complex trauma of child sex trafficking.

It's time to take our thinking to the next level, and that's the aspiration of this book.

I hope you, as I have, will challenge your thinking as you gain a deeper understanding of trafficker psychological warfare and what leads a person to that mentality. Doing so forges creative and powerful change. With that in mind, you'll find a question titled **Two-Minute Introspection** after the **Analysis With Dr. Deena Graves** section. The question provides an opportunity to pause and reflect on the contents of the chapter, thinking about how you can incorporate the insights, research, and tools into your work to:

- Join us in shaping a different future for children.
- Influence those you work with.
- Energize yourself.

We would love to hear your ideas! Email them to us at mindgames@ m3transformations.com. Our collective brainstorming *WILL* result in strategies to give our children their identities and destines back. That brainstorming isn't truly exhaustive without Derek's voice, the voice of a man committed to protecting youth from what he did to them and from preventing them from becoming *what* and *who* he was. He's not asking us to forgive him, just to hear him and weigh for ourselves if the information he shares will save lives.

I choose to do both. I hope you will, as well.

# PART 1. DEREK'S CHILDHOOD

# 1 If These Walls Could Talk

It was a slow death.

So gradual that no one even noticed the life draining out of me. Not my teachers. Not my uncles. Not my sisters. Not even my mom, Helen, who tried her hardest to be a good mother. Life's hardships just overwhelmed her.

That slow death sucked the innocence of childhood entirely out of me. A budding monster who cared only about his self-gratification took root in the ashes of my innocence.

You see, there's never a solitary moment in a child's life when he decides to hand his body over to the carnage of drugs. There's no such thing as a split-second decision to make the streets his home. It's not a single, recognizable thought that leads a kid to commit his first armed robbery. There's no one tick of the clock when a teen says, "It's time to make a career out of demolishing lives." Not really.

It's a series of moments. Repeated heartbreak. A sequence of events that pile on top of each other. Finally, the child crumbles under the weight of them all. He's looked, to no avail, to adult after adult to dig him out of the obliteration. He's searched in his home, in his school, everywhere he can think of. With no help in sight, he finally loses his ability to shoulder the weight alone. His frantic search for relief, for someone to help him breathe, leads him to adults more than happy to help. They might not take the burden off him, but they know how to dull the pain. They're not too hard to find, either. They hang out patiently in the streets, knowing a steady stream of desperate kids will make their way to them. The drug dealers, the drunks, the murderers, the gang members, the robbers, the pimps – all happy to take a protégé under their wings. They don't have to work for it. Trauma already finished the job; they just reap the rewards.

It's not a path to evil in a 10-year-old's mind. It's merely a path to survival.

I fought for survival as long as I could. In reality, I **endured** survival until I was 10. That's when enough moments collided to make me fight for it. My dad, Tyrone Williams, ran out the clock. I'd stomached all his violence

I could take. Not for me. For my mom. Maybe turning 10 had emboldened my courage. Perhaps I had a death wish. Whatever it was, I hit my breaking point watching him slap her around one day when something random set him off.

"You're not hitting my mom anymore."

I picked up a broomstick and hit him as hard as I could. Not that 10-year-old boys, especially small ones like I was, can swing that hard – or that men three times their size can't grab the broom out of their hands. Instead of stopping the broom, though, he let me hit him. It gave him the excuse to ball up his fist and punch me as hard as he would've a drunk in a bar brawl. He knocked me about eight feet across the room into the wall, leaving an indention as easily as fingers molding Play-Doh.

His fist in my face wasn't anything new. Only my resolve was. Yeah, in hindsight, that was the last straw – my turning point. I didn't consciously decide in that moment to become a pimp who also terrorized the powerless. However, I did make up my mind to never again *be* powerless, no matter ***what it took***. I didn't realize then that all the abusive moments suddenly colliding inside me caused an implosion that radically changed the way I looked at the world … and other humans. My emotions, my humanity, laid lifeless somewhere among the shrapnel of my bruised and battered body and mind.

Trauma buried a tenderhearted little boy that day and gave root to a sadistic trafficker.

Something was born in my mom that day, too. Like me, she'd finally had enough. I guess seeing your baby, whose only crime was trying to protect you, fly across the room and crash into a wall does that to you.

I had 75 cousins in Boston, so we didn't think anything about it when Mom sent us to one of my aunts' houses after I picked myself up off the floor. We frequently spent the night with one of them when our dad flew into a drunken rage. She'd let him sleep it off, and we'd go back home the next day, acting as if everything were normal. That's just what you do in the hood – because it is normal.

That particular weekend, though, my older cousins didn't walk us home. They walked us to a set of row houses we'd never seen. That's where Mom told us she'd given our dad the boot so that he couldn't give us a foot in our guts any longer. Elation welled up inside of me. No dad was better than an abusive dad. No one in my neighborhood had a dad anyway. The few who had an actual father figure couldn't hang out with those who didn't. We didn't want them to, either. Having a dad made you stick out in the hood.

I loved my mom for trying to get her life together for us. Until she told us we had to change schools, that is. Worse yet, I had to take the bus to get there.

More moments collided. I didn't grieve my dad, but in one weekend, I also lost my school, my friends, my neighborhood, and the little bit of security I had in life. My mom tried to take my freedom, too. She gave us strict orders to come straight home after school, forbidding us from going any-where after we got home. My sisters obeyed. I didn't. I snuck out regularly in search of relief from all the loss. My mom never noticed.

I was the man of the house now, so I was on my own. Her job was to feed us and make sure my sisters didn't get pregnant. I started roaming the streets, desperate to find a place to fit in. Back then, I just thought I was kicking it. I was cool. I was doing the hood thing like all the other boys in both my old and new neighborhoods. Boys a little older in both hoods drank and smoked weed, so, at the ripe old age of 10, I took my first drink and smoked my first joint the same day. I thought they might stop my freefall through the cracks since no adults in my life had.

Sure enough, they deadened the pain and made me fit in. Like a dentist's numbing shot, though, they quickly wore off, so I made them a daily habit. I got them anywhere I could. Low self-esteem taunts you into doing stuff to try to make yourself feel better, bigger, so I even snuck some wine from behind the altar while carrying out my altar boy duties. Why not? None of the adults in my life noticed that I was no altar boy now, so why should I act like one? I quickly developed a tough-guy image to gloss over the lost kid who couldn't even pass as a knock-off of whom he was born to be.

My mom went missing in action, working long hours to support four young children and going to night school to try to dig us out from under the despondency of poverty. I lost both my dad and my mom in a matter of weeks. Moments started to crash into each other again.

I found a new addiction – girls. They stroked my ego, giving me another source of temporary relief from the trauma that followed me everywhere I went. Trauma had become my shadow. I messed around with every girl who came across my path. As a preteen, I wasn't quite yet talking them into sex, but I bumped and grinded my way into believing I was the man. Girls made me feel like I mattered. I didn't realize it, but I was surrendering any lingering self-worth.

When the drugs and alcohol wore off, my insignificance popped back up. I doubled down, finding all the trouble I could at 10, 11, 12. My grief wrapped tighter and tighter around my heart like a python, constricting it until it shrunk to the size of the Grinch's heart.

My heart might have been tiny, but my head was huge.

## Analysis With Dr. Deena Graves:
### Fatherlessness

A strong father figure, or even a weak father figure, would have empowered me to make many different decisions, decisions that didn't harm other people or me. I didn't believe anyone cared about me, so I developed a forget-it attitude. I didn't care if I lived or died. I just existed.

I'm not alone in yearning for a nurturing relationship with my father or another strong father figure. Fatherlessness decimates children.[6] It takes a toll on the child's development but doesn't stop there. It has the potential to wreak lifelong psychological havoc.[7] It's not surprising, then, that it hampers the ability to form healthy relationships and escalates the risk of drug and alcohol abuse, delinquency, violence, and other criminal behavior.[8] I eventually worked my way into all those categories.

One study found that children who grow up in a home without a father have a 279-percent higher likelihood of packing a gun and selling drugs than children who grow up with a father in their home.[9] No wonder boys growing up in a single-parent home are more than twice as likely to land behind bars than boys who have both parents.[10]

Like me, kids without a healthy father influence hunt everywhere for self-worth, including in risky sexual activities. Left to figure out sex alone without the benefit of a father's guidance, boys often develop more aggressive behaviors and think nothing of objectification.[11]

And, when you grow up watching a man get results by physically overpowering a woman, you start *believing* that's the way to get what you want. It wraps its tentacles around your brain and squeezes out basic human decency. You never realize there's another way when your earliest memory is watching your mom cower and jump at your dad's every command. Your dad, stepdad, or the latest in a long line of boyfriends slugs your mom enough times, and she's like the dogs in Pavlov's experiment. She becomes conditioned to respond before he even pulls his fist back because she doesn't want her body or her kid's body to leave an imprint in another wall. Results.

When I started my family – my sex trafficking family – I was determined to leave the hood and all my childhood memories behind me. That meant I needed results. I turned to the only way I knew to get them: Controlling women through the threat and use of violence. I saw it work unconditionally in my home. I knew I could slap females down, and they would do what I said. If I let them get away with something, they'd pull more stunts. So, I nipped it in the bud at the first significant offense and every offense thereafter. Violence worked. Sadly, later in the book, you'll see how effectively.

At least it works for little boys who don't know how to grow up into caring men. I had no idea what a true man, a loving husband, a devoted father, looked like. Tyrone Williams *was* real in his own way – an undeniable, towering 210-pound, almost 6-foot-tall *man* torturing a 5'6"-tall, 125-pound woman and little children with brute force when things didn't go his way. Why would I find it unacceptable or wrong, then, for a pimp to control his girls through violence? That thought didn't even flicker across my mind. Remember, I didn't have any positive male role models. An evening-and-weekend alcoholic who used my mom's face as a punching bag when she didn't bring him a drink quickly enough was my role model.

We talk about the astronomical problem of domestic violence, especially in October during awareness month. Honestly, though, everything has an awareness month. How much attention do people *really* pay when one awareness month fades into the next year after year? Thankfully, we protect women and children in domestic violence shelters when given the opportunity and the resources. Researchers conduct studies that open our eyes with evidence-based proof of all the potential consequences for children who live with or witness domestic violence. We shouldn't be surprised, then, when a new generation of domestic abusers grows up. Research warns us their violent homes serve as a breeding ground.[12] Yet, we shake our heads and sigh at the latest alarming stats, wondering where things went wrong.

As I said, it went wrong for me because no one taught me differently. I didn't see another option. It's time for men to rise up and make sure every little boy has a healthy role model. We cannot expect boys who watch the females in their house get routinely beaten to magically treat women with dignity and respect. Or, for that matter, to treat anyone or anything, including society, with dignity and respect.

We have a little more than 37.8 million boys in the United States.[13] Almost 101 million males over 18 live in the U.S.[14] That's nearly three men per boy. What if each of us found a young boy who needs a role model?

## Two-Minute Introspection

What would the future of every young boy look like if they all had a healthy male role model? What would the future of our society look like? How do we engage more men in the battle for our little boys and the future of our society?

# 2  Road to Nowhere

By 12, my mom saw hell when she looked at me. When I looked at her, I saw someone who I thought had handed me over to hell.

I am so proud of my mom now. In retrospect, I know she did the best she could. She didn't mean for me to slip through the cracks. As I alluded to, the mindset that boys should be men, stand on their own two feet, permeated the Black community in the hood. She tried here and there to get me on the right path; she'd even occasionally call my dad to threaten me. She had no idea, though, what all I was up to. She was too focused on working to better our lives and keeping my sisters from adding another baby to our struggling family.

Resolve pumped through my mom's veins. She juggled four young children, her job as a secretary, *and* night school. Eventually, she worked her way up to become the judge's right-hand person as the assistant chief of the Boston Housing Court. She served the court for 20 years before retiring. She worked her way off welfare and bought a house while navigating all that. That's almost unheard of. My mom held tight to the identity deprivation tried to steal from her. To this day, she is a go-getter. She's 80 years old and going strong, serving people in three ministries. I think, like me, Mom feels she has some things to make up for.

It took many years to pull herself out of welfare *and the poverty mindset, though*. Years of living on peanut butter and rice, drinking powdered milk, and gagging down powdered eggs hijack your brain. I can still vividly see those gallon-sized silver cans with bold, black writing on them: USDA. We'd crunch foil around the top of the cans to keep the food from tasting any staler than it already was. Something about a diet of government-supplied powered food ridicules you into believing you don't have much worth, no matter how hard you work.

Working hard in the hood usually doesn't translate into an escape from welfare, despite how desperately you want it to. Welfare is just as much a hand-me-down from generation to generation as passing on a faded, stained T-Shirt and ripped jeans to a younger sibling. Not the kind of jeans you buy ripped. Tattered jeans from making the rounds among 10 to 12 kids. You might say we inherited welfare. My mom's parents existed on it and passed the expectation down to their kids. That's just what you did. When you got old enough to have kids, you went down and applied for your own welfare without even thinking about it.

It's the American way in some neighborhoods. We still have it today. I call it financial segregation.

For me, financial segregation felt as if I was trapped in a giant ocean wave that suddenly grabbed me and sucked me under. I couldn't even tread water. My grandparents, mom, and one of my uncles not only treaded water, they worked hard. They had determination. Despite the odds, they tenaciously fought to carve out a better life for their children and their children's children. My grandparents moved their 11 children to Boston in hopes of that. My grandfather got a job in the shipyard, but he started with less than nothing. With 11 hungry mouths to feed and 11 constantly growing bodies to clothe, they couldn't right their sinking ship. Hopes faded into acceptance. They simply couldn't make enough to keep their heads above water, so they still depended on the government for survival.

So did my mom. Government assistance helped feed us. It provided us with medical care. Despite her long hours and sheer willpower, it always loomed over us, impacting how we saw ourselves. Welfare plays mind games with you, telling you that you have no value. It strips you of your self-esteem, gnaws away at your self-respect. If you can't respect yourself, you have little, *or no*, capacity to respect others.

When people ask me how I became a trafficker, I tell them I learned some of it from our government. The government and traffickers think alike in some ways: Why would I let you get up and not be dependent on me? If I can keep you dependent on me, I can keep you working for me. You're going to do what I say.

As a society, we created an entrenched mentality that says you don't have to do anything if you are on government assistance. The government supplies your food, housing, medical care. Many people are cool with that. They don't have to use their intellect. It's easier just "to be" when hopelessness weighs you down like an anchor.

I played on that mindset as a trafficker. I looked for girls with the same vacant look in their eyes as mine. I'd put them up in a hotel room, feed them fancy dinners, buy them nice stuff, take them fun places. I gave girls just enough to make them feel they had it made. They got used to getting taken care of without having to exert the energy to think about it. It's hard to think when despondency takes up all your brain space.

See the similarity between trafficking and government assistance? Victims, like welfare recipients, just have to get up, do what they're told, go through the motions of life without putting thought into it, and the rest is taken care of.

If you need me, you can't revolt against me. That's how you stay in power – whether you're the government or a trafficker. If you're hungry, and I'm feeding you, you're going to vote for me. If you're hungry, and I'm feeding you, you're going to keep laying on your back for me.

That's where the government gives traffickers a foot up, though. The government gives her family food stamps to eat. She has to go to the store, buy the food, and suffer the mortification of paying with food stamps. Then, she has to go home, cook, and clean up. It's a lot of work and humiliation. Plus, she's limited on what she can buy. After she eats, her dreary life goes on with little to brighten it up.

A trafficker, on the other hand, *TAKES* her to eat. She's sitting in a nice restaurant for the first time in her life. He buys her a drink and lets her order whatever she wants. He gives her his full attention while they're eating, making her feel special and worthy. He tells her they'll go shopping afterward, maybe to the movies, to a concert one day. He whips out a wad of cash to pay the bill, making sure to flash the diamond ring on his pinky.

He goes in for the kill – I'm going to take care of you. You won't have to worry about anything. I'll feed you better than you've ever eaten. Dress you. Buy you wigs and makeup. Give you a place to stay where you don't have to clean up after yourself. You'll travel with me. You can even drive one of my cars sometimes. I might buy you one eventually. It's not complicated. She's thinking she already has sex with people to feel better about herself, or someone in her house is molesting her, raping her night after night. She might as well get paid for it.

The trafficker neglects to say that he's going to keep her broke and emotionally dependent on him, so she doesn't leave, just like the government doesn't explicitly say it will keep you broke and mentally dependent, so you can't leave.

Welcome to the pimp mentality.

## Analysis With Dr. Deena Graves:
### Dependence on Welfare

Like all children, I was helpless to change my dependence on welfare or the emotional games it wreaked with my identity. Government assistance told me I could never measure up. No matter how hard I tried, I was mentally doomed to failure. After all, I saw my grandfather toil day after day in the shipyards just to stay deflated by his inability to escape reliance on the government. I watched, frightened, as my mother drove herself to utter exhaustion trying to singlehandedly claw our way out of poverty just for life circumstances to keep yanking us back in.

Welfare and other adverse childhood experiences whispered lies in my ear. I searched my unresponsive home, the apathetic halls of my school, and the crime-riddled streets of my neighborhood for my identity. It alluded me at every turn. It felt as if I were constantly bumping into my distorted reflection in an endless house of mirrors. I ran headfirst into unbudging dead ends again and again as the demoralizing image mocked me. I couldn't find an escape from the twisted image it reflected. Reflections don't lie, after all.

Tragically, not much has changed in the 50 years since I was 10. If anything, it's gotten worse. Our children live the same story I lived, ensnared in generational poverty, with the same deadly results. Why is that? Why have we not made more progress in 50 years?

Today, more than half of our children live in homes on government assistance.[15] Research suggests that prolonged dependence on welfare chips away at a child's passion for learning and achievement, eroding self-esteem.[16] Some researchers argue that the depths of poverty that I grew up in engulf children like a tsunami, leaving in its wake hopelessness, paralysis, feelings of incompetence and unworthiness, and both a reliance on and a disdain for society.[17] Hunger does funny things to your mind, too, causing kids to withdraw into themselves, especially as lack of food security often makes the child susceptible to adults who release their stress through violence.[18]

We need to conduct more research, but you get the picture. Poverty and welfare turn destinies into desolation. You begin to believe that's just your lot in life. Something as simple as the sound of the ice cream truck screams, "There's no way out." You watch as the kids not on welfare stand in that inviting line on a hot summer day, laughing and talking, enjoying the small things in life. When you can never have something, it's not a small thing. You believe you're not invited to the ice cream party because you're not worth an ice cream. Some kids *never* get anything from that musical truck, even though it drives through their neighborhood day after day. I can still remember how it used to feel when I heard the music a few streets over. The same old song taunted me every time. I knew better than to ask, though. My mom struggled just to keep the lights on. She couldn't cater to my craving for a Popsicle.

My hunger for ice cream opened my eyes to how to satiate my appetite. I learned a little about the inner workings of my neighborhood through that musical truck. Our next-door neighbor sold drugs and worked in prostitution. She always had people at her house, including pimps. They would throw their change on the floorboard of their flashy cars and let us climb in to get it when the ice cream truck rolled around.

I made a mental note that a pimp could buy me ice cream, but my mom couldn't. It didn't slip by me, either, that they never seemed to work while she worked day and night. I noticed the people who appeared to be doing well weren't the ones going to work every day, pulling long hours at two or three jobs, and supplementing it with welfare. No. The ones with expensive stuff, the ones with the money to buy me a Popsicle, were the ones raking in the dough without barely lifting a finger, the ones pimping, selling drugs, breaking into houses.

The ice cream truck screamed I wasn't worthy. The pimps made me feel I was.

I made sure to buy kids ice cream once I became a pimp.

I knew they felt less-than everywhere they went. Kids try to stuff the shame down when they're doing everyday life. Like sitting in the lunchroom pulling a hard, crusty sandwich out of a plastic bag while non-welfare kids pull cookies and an apple out of their shiny, character-painted lunchboxes.

That's why we must create a different future if we want to turn traumatized children's desolation into destinies. Otherwise, people like I was turn children's desolation into their own profit and pleasure. I'm speaking from experience when I say we can't let welfare and the streets beat the hope out of our children.

## Two-Minute Introspection

What would it take to free families from generational dependence on welfare?

# 3 Betrayal of Trust

As bad as my dad was, he was still my dad.

Or so I thought.

Nothing could have prepared me for the next moment that collided break-neck into all the others. How can you be ready for your world to turn upside down at 12, especially when it's already fallen apart multiple times?

By this point, I was starving for attention. I didn't know it then, but I know it now. I was so hungry for people to notice me, to care about me, that I did whatever I could to grab the spotlight. I've always been a showoff. To say I was the class clown is an understatement. I wore a trail between my classroom and the principal's office. Trouble and I became good friends even before my mom kicked my dad out, such good friends that I got suspended in the third grade.

My mom's dogged determination to change our plight didn't stop with night school. She sacrificed whatever it took to provide my sisters and me with the best education possible. She enrolled my sisters in an inner-city program that bused them to a highly rated public school in a nearby middle-class neighborhood. With assistance, she kept me in a private school during my early elementary years. The Catholic Church established the school in our hood to provide advanced educational opportunities for low-income students who worked hard and kept their grades up. She'd buy my uniform – blue slacks and shirt with a tie – at a bargain basement store.

All my teachers were nuns. My third-grade teacher was harsh. She called me to the front of the class one day for disrupting her. The teachers used their wooden pointers to punish us. Maybe they call them pointers because they usually pointed them straight up in the air and swung down, hitting our hands. That day, for interrupting her class, she swung it all the way back behind her like she was chopping wood. She flung it down to hit my hand, but I was too fast for her. I jerked my hand out of the way. She hit herself in the leg with all the force meant for my small hand. My classmates lost it. The nun didn't think it was quite as funny as they did. She saw to it that I got suspended for three days.

I wasn't about to tell my mom, so I got up every morning, got dressed, and headed off to school. Well, at least that's what I told her. As soon as it was safe, I snuck back home and hung out, having fun while my family was at work and school. Turned out one of my classmates either missed me or was curious about what happened. I still remember her name: Angela. Either way, she made it her business to find out what was going on. She called my house, and, as luck had it, my mom answered the phone. Angela asked my mom if I was okay. My mom was like, "Yes. Why?" She told my mom I hadn't been in school for three days.

I was sleeping when Angela called … but not for long. My mom woke me with a good flogging. She tore me up. Mostly, she was mad at me because she would have to miss work to take me to school the next day.

She was mad at the school, too. Mad they didn't call her instead of hitting me, and mad they didn't call her when they suspended me. The following day, she took me to school and gave them a good tongue lashing. Mom left no doubt in their minds they had better not ever put their hands on me again. She laid down the law. Told them if they had a problem with me, they call her. Black parents don't like you to put your hands on their kids.

I can remember it like it was yesterday. You might think I have such a clear memory because I was embarrassed. Not at all. It made me feel good. It gave me something I had never had before that point – I never felt my mom cared. Made the whipping worth it.

My mom quickly squashed any expectations I had, though, that she was finally ready to show me the ongoing attention I craved from her. She went back to work and school and watching over my sisters in the little spare time she had. I felt like I could see the hope slipping through my fingers.

To make it worse, I also faced more exasperation at school. My teacher and principal weren't just agitated with me. They were upset with my mom, too. Back then, people of color did not go to a Catholic organization and raise hell. I guess my mom didn't understand that. Nor did she understand that even if they didn't hit me anymore, I'd pay the price for her outburst in other ways.

I turned to the only coping mechanism I knew for school – upping my clown act. Of course, that went over like a lead balloon. Nor did it satisfy my need for attention. I was starving for attention from anyone. I guess emulating sex with a bunch of girls and smoking weed didn't fulfill that deep-down yearning I had to feel I mattered. I might have believed I was "the man," but the little boy in me was still desperately searching for the kind of nurturing I had never known. You know, the kind all kids long for. So, with nothing else filling the void, I decided to try my hand at acting in sixth grade. Maybe mesmerizing a crowd would satisfy my hunger. If I could wow a crowd of not just other kids but adults, surely, I would prove my worth, my value. Maybe my mom would even come watch me.

I landed a solo speaking part in the school play. There I was, center stage. Just where I liked to be. All eyes on me. Everybody fixed on what I had to say. I ate it up. I've always been a showoff. Nothing like having an audience – even if my mom wasn't in it. Someone else was, though. I had my own private audience. An audience of one. An audience I knew nothing about.

She approached me after we took our final bow. It was almost as if she was lying in ambush for me, although I know today her intentions were pure. She waited outside and pulled me aside from my friends for a moment, a moment that froze in time. A moment in time that made all my other moments feel astoundingly insignificant.

She hugged me and then handed me $10. Wow. Who was this lady? I must be an even better actor than I thought if some woman I'd never met was willing to shell out dough for my performance. Maybe she might want my autograph, too. I was awfully proud of myself at the thought. Bravo. I had finally found a way to get the attention I hungered for from adults. Anyone willing to reward my newfound talents with $10 had my full attention.

Only she wasn't there for my acting. She was there to unleash more unprovoked trauma in my life. She came without so much as a warning – to me or my mom. She told me calmly, matter-of-factly, unemotionally, that she was my auntie, my father's younger sister. No, not Ty's little sister. Jimmy's. Nothing like learning outside a crumbling-down school auditorium surrounded by a sea of unfamiliar faces that your dad is not your dad. Nothing like learning it from a complete stranger. Talk about sucking the air out of my big night – the night I had finally earned positive attention. No way. She just wished she was my aunt because she was so dazzled by my acting skills.

Wait, though. She's telling me where I live. She's talking about my birthday coming up in a couple of weeks. She says my mom's name and mentions my uncles.

All kinds of questions ran through my 12-year-old mind in a split second. Where was he? Why did he leave us? What did I do wrong to make him not want me? Didn't he love us? ***Did my mom know?***

Mixed in with the shock and barrage of questions piercing my heart like a flaming spear was a slight glimmer of hope. Did he realize he'd made a big mistake and sent her to find the son he couldn't live without? Wouldn't he be proud of me if he had seen me in the play? Why didn't he come watch? When could we throw a ball around together? When could he answer all my questions about girls? What was he going to teach me about life? When was he going to move in and be my full-time dad? What would he do to my fake father when he found out how he beat us? Wouldn't my mom be ecstatic I found him? Maybe he was an attorney. That'd make sense since that's what I'd always wanted to be.

I couldn't wait to get out of there to get answers to the questions whirling around my mind like an EF5 tornado. My heart was already racing home to celebrate with my mom, but I waited patiently as my new rich Aunt Bernadette gave me her address and told me to come by. I smiled politely as she hugged me and kissed my cheek. I even hung around to talk to other people a few minutes after she slipped away. I needed to look cool, after all.

Then I ran home as fast as I could.

Only there weren't any answers waiting for me there. None. Just more questions. Why wouldn't my mom answer me? Why was she brushing me off like a fly buzzing around her head? Couldn't she just give me a "yes" or "no"? Why was she acting like I wasn't there? Why wasn't she excited?

I wasn't mad at her, though. I felt too betrayed by her to be angry.

## Analysis With Dr. Deena Graves:
### Parental Betrayal

Like many kids, I stuffed the pain of betrayal so deep down inside that I didn't even realize it was there. It was like a shadow, always with me but something I didn't pay attention to. I believe that's why I stayed in the game so long. It wasn't until I quit pimping at 48 and sought help from a therapist that it came bubbling up inside me like the sudden fizz of a popped-open can of soda.

Trust flies out the window when you feel betrayed by a parent. You build a wall – a thick wall – of protection around you with bricks made out of alcohol, drugs, sex, pornography, or whatever else you can find to take the pain away, however temporary it is. That's why so many kids get in trouble. They have bottled-up anger from feelings of betrayal. Either no one is listening to them, or they don't feel they have anyone they can trust to talk to.

I might have gone down a different path if somebody had explained that my mom didn't have the tools to deal with what she was going through. Ignoring my questions about my new revelation was her way of coping with it. No one was there to explain that to me. As a child, I sure didn't have the tools to deal with what I was going through, so I built that prover-bial wall.

Betrayal Trauma Theory argues that traumatic events suffered at the hands of a parent can propel a child on a path to several psychological and rela-tional struggles. Both researchers and clinicians have concluded numerous traumas at the hands of someone children trust can influence their:

- Behavior and ability to think through the consequences of actions.
- Mastery of emotional responses.
- Ability to develop trusting, healthy relationships.
- Cognitive aptitude.
- Somatic reactions.

Stunted psychological development, or a developmental trauma history, buries the child in humiliation and stigma, which cripples their ability to flourish socially. Some scholars contend that the feelings of shame and guilt can erode children's identity and lure them into believing it's their fault, catapulting them into pathological actions.

Multiple betrayals at the hands of someone children should be able to trust are linked to increased dissociation. Dissociation makes it possible for them to tolerate the relationships they are dependent on by blurring out the traumatic actions perpetrated against them and keeping any good aspects in sharp focus.[19]

I certainly am a textbook example of the ravages of betrayal trauma. That night changed my relationship with my mom. It changed the way I looked at her and felt about her. It took a long time and a lot of tears in therapy years later to get over it. I carried it inside for decades, unaware of how it ate away at me, not realizing how excruciating the buried pain was.

My therapist encouraged me to talk to her about it despite all the time that had passed. It was something I had to do for **myself**. My therapist warned me not to expect a response but to openly and honestly share my feelings regardless. I'm glad she told me not to expect a response because I got little – just like on that life-changing day almost 40 years before. This time, I had someone to help me work through it, though. My therapist had me write down how it made me feel, including the blank face looking back at me as I poured my heart out. Since I didn't get the long-hoped-for answers from my mom, I poured all those bottled-up feelings onto paper. I mulled over them. I worked through them with my counselor.

Then, I burned them.

I understand what I understand. As for the things suppressed inside my mom, I made peace with the fact I'll never know. I choose to be free from that bondage instead of stuffing it as I did for so many years.

That freedom and the grace of God allowed me to build a strong relationship with my mom. We talk two or three times a day now.

As I said, I wish I had someone to talk to when it happened. That might have changed the entire trajectory of my life – and the lives of so many I hurt in a vain attempt to erase my heartache. Let's change the way we respond to betrayed children. We can't expect them to just get over it. They don't. Believe me. We must make it a priority to incorporate it into our treatment plans. Don't just make it a formal thing, though. Our children need mentors and role models they can confide in.

## Two-Minute Introspection

Besides therapy, mentors, and role models, what other creative measures can we implement to help children process feelings of betrayal?

# 4 Character Assassination

Since my mom turned her back on my need to know, I decided to hunt down the answers myself. Besides, answers might come with an added benefit: My new aunt's pocketbook. I took her up on her offer to visit. What better day than my birthday, I reasoned. How much money would she give me on my special day if she'd give me $10 for no reason at all?

Honestly, the thought of a few bucks in my hand far outweighed a potential relationship – with anyone. Rapid-fire trauma over the course of my short life left my emotions tattered. A father and an aunt were just two more bullets aimed directly at my heart. Another $10, on the other hand, would buy me a bit more notoriety with my weed-smoking, wine-sipping friends. If everything went right, she'd hand me $10 more. We could not only buy marijuana, but we could talk one of the guys loitering in front of the liquor store into buying us wine.

Aunt Bernadette's surprise visit had already gained me a fleeting celebrity status. My friends were like, "You really don't know these people, D, and she just came to the play and gave you $10?" Even so, the spotlight doesn't stay on anyone in the hood too long. Everyone has stuff like that going on in their lives. It was just like "the saga continues." I needed to give it a little boost in the arm if I wanted to keep playing it.

Not to mention, I was nervous about dropping in on this stranger who called herself my aunt, so I talked my friend, Jamal, into walking to her house with me. I had a little excitement mixed in there, too. It was like a seesaw, really, with nerves and excitement teetering back and forth. My nerves eclipsed my enthusiasm, however, crashing inside me over and over like waves pounding the shoreline. I can feel the tension even now. I didn't know what to expect as we walked up to the three-story tenement house, so I steered the conversation to where we would buy weed. We decided on the place with the fatter bag.

The sun streamed down outside, but the narrow hallway didn't have lights, so it was dim, gloomy, like my hopes. I saw stairs to the left and her door to the right. I hesitantly tapped on it. I had no clue what lay on the other side of that door. Apprehension welled up inside me and smothered any other feelings.

My Aunt Bernadette opened the door. "Oh, you came," she looked surprised but smiled excitedly. "I wondered if you would."

I introduced her to Jamal. "Hi, Jamal. How are you doing?" She waited for his reply. "Fine." He looked apprehensive, too.

I couldn't see past the door that stood between me and my self-proclaimed family I knew nothing about, so I almost turned and ran when she invited us in.

I saw them when she swung the door shut behind us. An older woman and a man. I wondered, "Who are *these* people?"

She must have read my thoughts. "This is your Grandmother Renee and Abraham, a friend of the family."

I had a Nana. As a matter of fact, I already had two grandmothers. Confusion danced around in my head as I stared at another surprise relative. I didn't know what to think.

I sat down. Awkward. They wished me happy birthday. Asked me about school and my mom and sisters. Talked to Jamal. Told me my father would love to see me, but he was in the hospital. After a few minutes of stilted conversation, the gentleman made a hasty exit.

I felt naked, exposed. These people I knew nothing about seemed to know everything about me.

I was the firstborn grandchild, so my new grandmother was elated to meet me. Her excitement turned to tears when the phone rang. She didn't say much. She stared at me as she listened. Her smattering of words still rings in my ears, "You will never believe who I am looking at. It's Derek."

She thrust the phone at me. I didn't know what else to do, so I reluctantly took it. I had no idea who I was saying "hello" to. The faceless voice on the other end said "hello" back. He told me it was my birthday like I hadn't figured that out.

"How do you know?" I asked the voice. And who are you, I wondered. I was tired of being the only one in the dark.

"Because I'm your father."

"You're my father?" I repeated, stunned.

"Yeah. My name is James. They call me Jimmy."

My stomach turned. I didn't know what to feel about that or how to respond. For once, I was at a loss for words. A fog enshrouded my brain for
the umpteenth time. Years of trauma and $10 had upstaged anything my
aunt told me after my play, so it was almost as if I was hearing it for the
first time.

I guess Jimmy wanted me to realize he knew me even if I didn't know
him. He started ticking off stuff I already knew, like my mom's name, her
mom's name.

"Hey, is your Uncle Danny still doing hair?"

"Is your Uncle Thurman still at the news station?"

It felt like some stranger had been snooping around in my life. He tossed
around my family members' names like he knew them.

We only talked a few minutes, but it felt like an eternity. He did most of
the talking. My side of the conversation consisted mostly of "Yeah" and
"Uh-huh." I got that feeling in the pit of my stomach I had years later
when police interrogated me. They knew all my business, and so did this
stranger who called himself my father. The thought crept into my per-
plexed mind that there had to be something to this.

How could there not be? This man who I didn't know existed had been
thrust upon me as suddenly as the phone. I didn't have any idea what to
say to him, but he was chatting away like it was the most normal thing in
the world, spouting out all these details like he'd known me my whole life.

I squeezed my eyes shut, trying to picture him while he rattled on. My
aunt and grandmother had raved about how much I looked like him, so
I tried to envision an older me. It didn't work. He was just some random
man in my mind. Could have been someone I passed on the sidewalk.
Maybe I had.

He'd eaten up enough of my time anyway. I did not work up the courage
to go there to waste my time talking to someone on the phone. He couldn't
help with my immediate need. I'd gone there with the sole intention of
showing off my cuteness to manipulate more money out of my aunt for my
birthday.

I told him bye and handed the phone back to my grandmother. I felt terrible about her being caught in the middle of this and everything. She wiped her eyes.

"Are you okay?" I asked her. I didn't want to be the one responsible for making some old lady I'd just met cry, especially if she really was my grandmother.

"Just happy," she reassured me.

If my Grandma was happy, Aunt Bernadette must have been overjoyed. She ran and grabbed a photo of this man who called himself Jimmy; I guess she wanted to convince me I looked like him. I remember thinking he wasn't a bad-looking guy, but, to me, I didn't look like him, and he didn't look like me. Their over-the-top excitement must have made them see things.

We just sat there.

No one knew what to say.

I needed to make an escape. I tried to catch Jamal's eye. I mouthed for him to say he had to get home or something, but he ignored my signals. He had witnessed enough – he was enjoying this too much. I had to come up with my own plan before he heard much more.

Luckily, my new Uncle Butch, Jimmy's younger brother, walked in, providing me an out. He was hungry after a long day at work. I made my getaway as soon as we got the obligatory introductions out of the way.

Not before I accomplished my original mission, though. My uncle pulled out a $5 bill and told me, "Happy birthday." My aunt and grandmother each gave me $10. We left there loaded. The money also deflected the attention from me when we walked out the door. I knew Jamal was chomping at the bit to pepper me with questions. However, he completely forgot his burning questions when he saw them hand me a small fortune. The allure of drugs and wine won hands down over a few details that weren't anything unusual in the hood.

We stopped by the store for chips and soda before we caught the bus to buy weed. We could afford to splurge.

We started joking around about my new family to cover up any uneasiness. We joked about how the guy sitting on the couch dressed and how my grandmother reached inside her bra for the $10. He decided to venture into the phone call.

"They're saying he's my father," I reminded him.

"What about the other guy who says he's your dad?" he pressed.

"They say he's my father, too," I shrugged.

He had the same questions I had. Our questions weren't so much about me having two dads. As I previously mentioned, that was the norm in our neighborhood. Four out of six neighbors had the same thing going on, *but they weren't hiding it.*

In the haze of my confusion and Jamal's curiosity, my mind drifted to my mom. Surely she would clear it all up for me now that I had talked to Jimmy. Kind of hard to ignore that. Evidently, she'd had a secret relationship with him – at least secret from me. Everyone else seemed to know about it. My brain couldn't think straight, but my heart reminded me she'd ignored my questions about his sister two weeks prior.

Feelings of betrayal flared again. Why would she hide the truth from me about my flesh-and-blood dad?

Suddenly, the answer hit me. Terror flooded me.

What was so bad about him or *ME* that she couldn't even tell me he was my father?

## Analysis With Dr. Deena Graves:
### Lying About Biological Parent

A significant, abrupt shock, such as learning who you have always been told was your dad is not, jolts a child's reality and identity. It can lead to "intense psychological and existential issues,"[20] with anguish and animosity churning underneath the surface. It also can throw family dynamics into a tailspin.

Tragically, little research exists about the far-reaching consequences of lying to children about their biological parents. I urge child scholars to close this gaping hole in child-development research. My identity died a quick death that day. I no longer knew who I was. I no longer knew who my family was.

Countless teens and children today wonder, like I did, who they are but are unable to find themselves. They search for identity on social media, in the streets when they run, or in a mix of fentanyl or other drugs. When they don't find purpose, they often come to a fork in the road that leads them down one of two paths: victim or victimizer. Or both.

As you see in my story, I internalized it as something was wrong with me. I can assure you they do, too. They probably also try to laugh it off as I did. Jamal and I bought weed and kicked it back with our friends. Jamal told them all about how I scored the money and him finding out I had another father. He couldn't resist telling them I had another grandmother who keeps her money in her bra even when she's in her own home. They were clowning me, so I laughed it all off.

On the outside. On the inside, bewilderment and panic raged.

Even high, I couldn't wait to hurry home to get answers. Surely my mom would see how scared I was and answer my questions this time.

The words spilled out as soon as I rushed into the house.

"Remember that lady I told you about a couple of weeks ago? The one who came to my play? The one who said she was my aunt? I went to her house today, and I talked to a guy on the phone who told me he's my father. He knew stuff about me."

No eye contact. No answer. Just silence.

And birthday cake.

We ate cake and ice cream, and my mom and sisters sang *Happy Birthday* to me like nothing had changed.

My mom's lips were sealed. Sealed so tight we never talked about it again. Ever. In her mind, there wasn't a point. I knew who my father was. That was way more than I needed to know. Periodically, I'd tell her I visited them. She'd dismiss the subject: "Oh, yeah."

That was it.

For her, at least. For me, when I blew out those 13 candles, my wish was to know what was so bad about me that no one wanted to claim me. My wish never came true.

Many children today share the same wish that never comes true. They internalize adult problems as their fault, just as I did.

If only I had known then that many adults stay mum about mistakes that they don't know how to handle. Maybe I wouldn't have become unlovable in my mind. Perhaps I wouldn't have become what I believed.

My mom's shame and guilt crippled her ability to see what her secrecy and silence did to my heart and identity. Many other parents fall into the same trap, the trap that snaps down on the child's self-worth, killing their ability to see their value.

I contend we can change the trajectory of many children by healing their parents of shame and guilt, as well as teaching them how to have positive conversations with their kids about painful facts. A simple dialogue with my mom would have cleared up a lot of anxiety and misconceptions I had about myself and life in general.

## Two-Minute Introspection

How might you help struggling parents learn to have crucial conversations with their children? How can we encourage society to embrace grace for others, rather than imposing and perpetuating destructive shame?

# 5 Name-Dropping

Who am I? The question played on rewind in my mind. Turns out I wasn't Derek Williams. I didn't have a drop of Williams' blood in me. Worse, I didn't know **anything** about the blood that was coursing through my veins. I wasn't who I always thought I was, but how could Jimmy be my real dad, either, when we didn't share the same last name or anything else in life except my mom ignoring us?

In one phone call, I went from years with an abusive father, to a couple of years with no father, to years of an absentee father – one I didn't even know was absent.

That was the day the streets became my father.

I was wandering in the wilderness now. I could have gone any direction before that. The betrayal and bombshell loss of my core self hot on the heels of all the other trauma settled my direction. It sent me scurrying to the streets like a rat in search of food. Up to that point, I went to school. I made good grades. I participated in school activities. I starred in the school play. Sure, I acted out for attention and did a little weed and alcohol to soothe my pain, but I still cared. How could I care now? I had something so wrong with me that two dads tossed me out like garbage. And my mom left me on the curb to rot.

I could still feel a couple of all-consuming emotions, though. Like anger. Fury welled up in me like a volcano ready to erupt. All this time, I thought I shared this abusive guy's DNA. All those times he knocked my mom around. All the times he hit me like a man – and he wasn't even my father. And I wasn't his son.

Not by blood, at least. I later found out I was born Derek Toon, my mom's maiden name gracing my birth certificate. She married Ty, my concocted dad, when I was about 3. He adopted me and my older sister, who had a different dad. It's kind of ironic, really. I had seen myself in their wedding pictures at my grandmother's house, but it never registered with me. I thought we were one big, unhappy family. The photos formed part of the fog that gave cover to all the moments that had been colliding since the day my parents conceived me.

We shared the same last name and a few family photos. That didn't give him the right to use me as his punching bag.

It really wouldn't have mattered which family I was born into, though. Yes, my stepfather was abusive and a weekend drunk. At least he could control his drinking and hold down a job. Any glimmer of hope that the unfamiliar voice on the phone might become a role model quickly gave way to more disillusionment.

The hospital discharged my biological father a couple of weeks after the call that ambushed my life. My new aunt and grandma asked me to come back when he got home, so I dropped by one afternoon. Alone this time.

I would say it was a shock to meet this man who said he was my father, but that wouldn't do my feelings justice. I had an in-depth Q-and-A session with myself on the way over there. Will I like him? Why had he never tried to contact me? Did he even know his sister had hunted me down? Why was I deceived all those years?

Don't get me wrong. I didn't harbor ill feelings toward him. No, all my animosity had one target: My mom. We shared a relationship. All kids believe their moms care, that they'll protect them. The worst part of the deception to swallow was that she made me call that abusive man "Father" for all those years, knowing my real father was out there.

I didn't have any hostility toward my dad, but I was nervous. I had no idea what would happen when we came face-to-face. I headed straight over after school to get it over with. I'd be myself to see if that was enough for him, and I'd find out who he was.

Aunt Bernadette opened the door. She was like, "Mmmm, Jimmy? It's your son." Then she told me to go say hi to my father.

My grandmother was sitting on one couch, and he was on the other. He stood up and said, "Hey, son. Come give me a hug." Like I had just gotten home from school or something. I walked over apprehensively. I still didn't see the resemblance except for our shade of skin. His brother was dark-skinned. Jimmy was fair-skinned like me.

He hugged me and then started making small talk. Asked me about school. About my mom and sisters. I stuck around for a couple of hours and had dinner with them. My Uncle Butch made it home in time to eat, and we all sat around the table and talked and joked and laughed like a family.

I joined in the banter, but I was baffled. What was this? I was sitting around with this family – my family – but I didn't feel like I was part of them. How could I? They dropped into my life after I called another man dad for 13 years. I didn't meet them sooner because my real father made no effort. Aunt Bernadette cared enough to find me, not him. Did my father even want me there?

Sure. We shared a genetic makeup, but I felt like an outcast even as I listened to them tell me things about myself. Stuff they couldn't have ticked off so naturally without knowing me. That's a weird feeling when you don't know anything about someone. When you only just learned they exist. My father even mentioned the company where my stepdad – that word sounded odd in my mind – worked. Really? He was talking about the person who took his place. My fog thickened.

I have no idea how long I stayed. All I knew was these people were saying they were my family. I had mixed emotions because we sat down and ate like a family. I felt the love they extended to me, but I felt powerless to return it. I was too wary and dazed. Their stories sounded like Charlie Brown's teacher to my befuddled brain: "Wah wah woh wah wah."[21]

I was a little upset when I left, too, because they didn't give me money this time.

My agitation grew as I walked home. To get there, I had to pass by where my stepfather lived with his new girlfriend. The first time I left my new family's house, I felt too numb to have feelings. My mind was too fixated on buying weed for my friends. Truthfully, that was just an excuse. I wanted the weed to take my pain away.

This walk was different, though. My new family made me feel welcome, part of them, even though we just met. They genuinely seemed to love me, and now I'm walking past this abusive man's house. The man who had masqueraded as my father. Who I had **never** felt love from. He made me feel like an outcast in my OWN family.

## Analysis With Dr. Deena Graves:
### Physical Abuse and Domestic Violence

We could talk about so many things regarding creating change for our children in this chapter. Let's focus on the domestic violence that beat the hope out of me, and we'll talk about the others in later chapters.

It's funny how people justify things. Like when you leave someone for knocking you and your kids around, again and again, you'd think you'd be done with that person. Not my mom. She still called Ty to set me straight when I acted out. He'd come tear me up or threaten me. I feared him, so the thought never crossed my mind to disrespect him. I took whatever he dished out.

My mom even sent me to live with him and his girlfriend the summer I turned 14 because she could no longer control me. That was actually one of his threats: "You keep doing what you're doing, and you're going to come stay with me. You don't want that."

He was right. I didn't. No child wants to live with someone who roughs them up. Yet, according to one study, almost 40 percent of children in the United States endured two or more violent acts in a one-year period, and one in 10 experienced five or more violent attacks.[22]

I did, and my mom couldn't provide the emotional and physical protection I looked to her for. Children do not have the mental maturity to defend themselves, and they don't understand when people who should protect them don't. The resulting fears can lead to:

- Distrust and an inability to form positive relationships.
- Poor grades and dropping out of school.
- Impaired brain development and cognition.
- Health issues.
- Self-harm or suicide attempts.
- Behavioral problems, including aggression, substance abuse, pregnancy, conduct disorder, delinquency, bullying, violence, and other criminal offenses.
- Depression, low self-esteem, anxiety, isolation, shame, fear, guilt, Post-Traumatic Stress Disorder, dissociation.[23,24]

As this book unfolds, you will see I can put a checkmark by most of those bullet points. There's a profound difference between reading a bulleted list and living it. Many children today are living it. And, as in my case, the violence in their families often goes unreported. That's why we must methodically look for it as adults responsible for the well-being of children.

I didn't know how to treat women, let alone form healthy relationships. I modeled what I lived. I had a front-row seat to the results violence produced: My stepfather didn't have to raise a hand to get whatever he wanted from my mother, sisters, and me; he merely had to ball a fist. We kowtowed to his every desire so that he wouldn't succumb to every trigger. I **learned** you get what you want by controlling people. I used it on the streets, and I used it in all my relationships before I learned differently in therapy.

You can't do **what you don't know**. I didn't know I could deal with my anger or hurt feelings without lashing out. Most violence erupts out of anger or hurt.

Therefore, we must teach children who experience violence in their homes how to relate to other people rather than operate out of learned survival skills. They need highly relational therapy where they feel safe.[25]

I know that from experience. As a young, impressionable teen, I had **highly relational** counselors who made me feel not only safe but valued – street counselors. I did what all kids do who think no one sees them, no one listens to them. I found adults who were more than happy to lend me a listening ear, adults who love having an audience. It adds a little excitement to their seemingly irrelevant existence. It's not that they don't care. It's that they don't know anything different than leading children down the same hopeless path they traveled. You know that saying, "Fake it until you make it"? In neighborhoods like mine, you fake it until you break it.

Other than those street psychologists, most adults talked at me, not to me. So, I listened intently to those I believed cared about what I thought. Way before I became a career trafficker, they taught me never to put my heart into a relationship with a woman. Females, they explained, were nothing but sex toys, and you always want to play with more than one toy. They seemed to know what they were talking about.

When you tire of a toy, you toss it. When your toy doesn't perform correctly, you take your anger out on it. When your toy starts to wear out, you find a new toy.

Say your toy – er, I mean the mother of your child – needs to feed your baby. She should have thought about that before she got pregnant. She needs to pay bills. Don't come looking to me; jump in the welfare line.

We had a term on the streets for men who gave women money: Sucker.

Society has terms for children who get their therapy on the streets: Delinquent. Throwaway.

Successful therapeutic work "recognizes that certain problematic behaviors tell you much more about what children may have needed to protect themselves from than assigning a label for who they are (i.e., oppositional, delinquent, naughty, withdrawn, etc.)."[26]

We need to let facts rip off the labels. Take the label "absentee dad," for instance. He's absent because he's never been taught he's supposed to be present. We can't expect boys to grow up to understand the responsibilities of caring for a family, or that it's right and honorable to treat women with respect, when they never saw those behaviors and qualities modeled. They saw just the opposite modeled their entire childhood. Think about a time you started a new job and didn't understand the culture. You don't know what's expected until you see it in action, or someone teaches you.

## Two-Minute Introspection

How do we negate the influence of street psychologists? What are the possibilities if we engage them in dialogue, as well? What are the crucial components of those conversations?

# 6 Following in His Footsteps

I threw myself into getting to know this man I supposedly resembled. Did I look like him on the inside, too? I needed to know. My identity hung in the balance. From what I had seen so far, his family loved one another. They treated each other with dignity and respect, not dismissiveness and violence. They never seemed too busy to notice me, to stop and talk to me. They appeared to care about what I cared about. Was I finally worth loving? Was I worth someone caring about me?

I started dropping by their house to find out.

I liked who I was in their eyes – the star in the Catholic school play, the good student, the polite grandson, the thankful nephew. It was like a Polaroid photo. The moment I stole the show, Aunt Bernadette's heart froze that image of me in time, and they all saw me through her description of that moment. I blurred out the rest of the picture, so they couldn't see the details.

I enjoyed sitting around the table with them, eating and joking. It enhanced my image of myself. Maybe, just maybe, I wasn't such an awful person after all. How could they so willingly accept me into their family otherwise?

I liked getting to know my dad, too. We'd sit on the porch and talk while he smoked. Just two guys hanging out, learning about each other. No pressure. He didn't try to tell me what to do. He didn't yell at me or take a swing at me.

A few visits in, my dad said, "Come on and walk to the store with me." He must really enjoy my company. I jumped at the opportunity to spend quality time with him. Maybe he'd even buy me some candy or a drink.

He bought a drink, alright. Only it wasn't for me. He bought wine and cigarettes for himself.

Outside, he introduced me to the men lounging in front of the liquor store.

He knocked off the pint of wine while we stood around talking.

He didn't offer anyone a single sip.

I might have been just 13, but I knew he took me only to show me off.

And, I knew what it meant that he was so chummy with those he showed me off to.

Remember, the guys who stood in front of the liquor store in my neighborhood were the ones who went in and got the wine for my friends and me after we slipped them a dollar for their trouble. That's just how it is in the hood. Any hood.

And that's just how it was with my dad. The realization hit hard. I hadn't seen any other signs, but all the pieces came together on that fateful walk. Why he lived with his mom. Why he was in the hospital. Why he was not gainfully employed. Why he was on disability. Why he knew all those people at the liquor store.

My dad was one of those guys who hung out in front of the liquor store.

He most likely bought wine for kids like me.

He didn't want his mom to know that, though, because he warned me not to tell her on the walk back.

I left more at a loss than when I first met him. I was more confused than ever, and I was pretty confused before then. It took five of my friends and me a considerable while to down a pint of wine, but he gulped his down in the span of a short conversation – while he did most of the talking. He could obviously handle it, too, since he hid it right under his mom's nose.

A thought flickered briefly across my mind. Maybe this was why Mom didn't want me to know about him. Nah. That couldn't be it. She had alcoholic brothers, and she didn't hide them. I knew lots of other drunks in the neighborhood, too.

Nope. The betrayal wrapped itself back around my 13-year-old mind and dug its claws in deeper. To this day, I don't know if she was ashamed of him, embarrassed for herself, or frightened of his possible influence on me. The last one still doesn't make too much sense, though, since I was routinely exposed to people with drinking problems.

I felt like my life was on rerun. I had grown up with a drinking father. The only difference was my stepfather limited his heavy drinking to after work and weekends. He didn't let it interfere with work. My real dad, on the other hand, didn't let work interfere with his alcohol.

He'd stand in front of that liquor store, drinking all day. Right up until he died.

# Analysis With Dr. Deena Graves:
## Alcoholism

When I realized my biological father's flaws, it opened the door for me to tell him about my drinking and drug use. If somewhere in my young teen mind I thought he would do the fatherly thing and discourage it, I couldn't have been more wrong.

He, instead, encouraged it. Yep. A couple of visits after our first walk to the liquor store, my dad shared his alcohol with his recently discovered 13-year-old son. Maybe that's why he took me on that first walk so quickly after meeting me.

To be fair, I was a teen when we met, so maybe he thought it would be hard to step in and discipline me. Perhaps he was afraid of driving me away again. He probably figured I would do it anyway, so he might as well leverage it to connect with me.

It worked. We bonded over alcohol and those walks to the liquor store. I could be myself with my dad. I didn't have to hide it from him as I did from my mom and Ty.

My dad was a player but never a pimp. Nevertheless, I think I learned my pimp walk from him. He had a little pep, a little rhythm, in his steps, a self-assured nod to his head. I imitated that womanizing stride on our trips to buy wine. You might say I followed in his footsteps.

In more ways than one. It was like my dad handed me a license to drink. At 13, you don't realize alcoholism might run in your genes.[27] In hindsight, I realize how vulnerable I was. If it didn't run in my genes, it certainly ran in my mind. I felt my chances for a strong, positive role model slipping through my fingers. Life had just handed me another toxic role model.

Parental approval can increase risky drinking.[28] Further, research suggests that socially disadvantaged parents are more likely to give their children the okay to drink.[29]

Whether poor or wealthy, parents who try to bond with their children over alcohol aren't just poisoning their bodies. They're poisoning their minds. As I said, it ran in my mind.

Let's talk about people with money first. They have a bad day at the office, come home, pour themselves a scotch, and throw it back. They're telling their children, "Here's how you handle stress." That's what the child sees. Have a problem? A drink makes it feel better.

Same concept with people in a different type of neighborhood. It just plays out differently. When Ty got pissed off about something, he'd slam down a beer – and beat us. That made him feel better.

Or think about losing a job. When middle- or upper-class people get laid off or fired, it's not the end of the world. Sure, they might take a day or two off to drown their sorrows and regroup. They might feel sorry for themselves or mad at their boss. But they get back out there again.

A different scenario plays out in a poverty-stricken neighborhood. The plant closes, and people give up. They're stuck in a victim mentality. Those guys you see every day on your way home from school were there when you went to school. They've been there all day, drinking and smoking weed on the corner. Hearing their sob stories encourages you to get bogged down in your own. They keep each other down. There's no one on that corner saying get off the street and do something with yourself.

Rich, poor, middle class, they're saying, "Where do we get our next drink to forget our troubles?"

All three sets of children get the same message: Alcohol makes life's problems easier to shoulder. A teacher disciplines them, or a parent says I don't have the money for the ice cream truck, or you can't drive the Ferrari tonight, and they think, "A drink will make this go away."

We need to teach our children the dangers of alcohol and the benefits of short-term coping skills. Children face tremendous pressure in today's high-tech, constantly changing world. Their everyday schedules brim with stress. Research shows their ability to positively handle stress significantly influences their mental well-being. Multiple studies, in fact, point to positive coping skills as a firewall between anxiety and psychological disorders.[30]

Engaging the five senses helps relieve stress. Try a peppermint. How many of the five senses does it activate? Think about it for a moment before continuing.

1. Touch. You feel it in your hands and in your mouth.
2. Taste. Peppermints have a robust, distinctive taste.
3. Smell. They also have an engrossing scent.
4. Sight. Their bright red-and-white stripes pull your eye to them.

5. Sound. You hear the wrapper crinkling and the peppermint
   crunching in your mouth.

It's a simple, convenient tool to help soothe anxious feelings.

## Two-Minute Introspection

What other coping skills can both children and stressed parents employ for the mental health of themselves and their families?

Advertising routinely exposes children to alcohol. What conversations can we have with children about the dangers of alcohol? What conversations can we have with socially disadvantaged parents about the dangers of allowing their children to drink?

# 7 Lead by Example

Since I couldn't find a role model in either of my dads, I decided to look elsewhere.

I looked where any kid from my kind of neighborhood looks: The streets.

The houses in my neighborhood functioned like assembly lines, spitting out one abused-and-neglected kid after another. The dynamics of the home produced the prototype that the streets turned into the finished product. Drugs in the house produced drug dealers. Alcohol bred alcoholics. Violence begat abusers and gang members.

The people hanging out on the streets waited patiently to assemble the final product: Drunk, junkie, robber. The packaging might look slightly different, but the end product was usually the same: Destroyed life. No need for quality control. Results guaranteed.

Mine sure were. Boys like me who heard their "dads" habitually berate women finessed the art of verbally slicing and dicing females of any age.

I learned from the best.

Don't misunderstand me. I didn't hit the streets to become a pimp. I went in search of a father figure. All kids are looking for something elusive, a father, a mother, safety, identity, any escape from the nightmares playing over and over in their heads and in their daily lives. They're looking for direction and a bit of affection, however slight. The streets provide affection, even if it's false, and direction even if it's wrong. They don't have to act like they really care because they do. About their own profit and pleasure, covering up their insecurities, or whatever it is that kid will do for them.

The cycle continues generation after generation.

Escape is rare. It might be a passing fantasy. But you just know deep down inside that it's not a reality.

The reality is: I'm in the streets; I do what the streets do.

Otherwise, you don't survive the streets.

To survive, you set your mind like flint. That's not too hard. By the time you get there, you've learned that every time you see a tiny glimmer of hope, a little light at the end of the tunnel, and run toward it, someone jerks the light a little further away.

The distance between me and that little boy my mom left my stepfather for had grown into a chasm. On top of all the disappointments and hurts, my 13-year-old hormones raged out of control. The streets stoked their fire.

My new street "dads" threw kerosene and matches on the smoldering embers of my disillusionment and hormones. They were doing the things 17, 18, 19-year-old guys do when the streets raise them – binge drinking, overdosing, and having sex with as many girls as possible.

I followed their lead.

I didn't spend all my time partying in the streets, though. I was determined to be one of the rare ones who did escape. I decided to work my way up the career ladder, save up my money, and get out of that neighborhood. I took on a paid internship to accomplish my goals.

It started with 100 pills at $3 each. I just had to give my "internship" director $100. He called it "helping me out." I called it a nice little profit for barely any effort. I was hooked.

Once I waded in the shallow end, crime quickly became a lifestyle. Burglary. Robbery. Catching people in hallways with guns and knives. One of my first guns came from breaking-and-entering. We hid the gun behind a tiny mountain of debris where they cut out rocks to build houses.

My newly discovered "role models" didn't discourage me; they ***encouraged*** me as my dad had with drinking. I became their protégé. They taught me how to never worry about an allowance again. My plan to get out of the neighborhood took a backseat; we spent the money as fast as we "earned" it.

No worries. I knew how to keep money coming in, even at 13. I've always been an entrepreneur. Like the time I packed a shoebox with polish and brushes, scribbled 25¢ in black Magic Marker on the side, and strutted down to a bar a good distance from home – out of my mom's eyesight. I made a couple of bucks on a good day. Not too shabby for a kid who just wanted a little pocket money to go to the movies or buy an ice cream off the musical truck.

Or there was the time the older Caucasian man rolled into our neighborhood, packed us into his car, and drove us into an affluent area to sell candy bars. I sold so many that I won a ski trip to Maine. My mom wrecked that, though. I acted up in school, so she yanked the trip away as punishment. Kevin got to go in my place. That stung. It emotionally devastated me. He didn't even sell enough candy bars to earn the trip, yet my mom rewarded him instead of me. I needed that trip for so many reasons other than fun, but it felt like my mom never understood my desperate search for validation that I had a purpose.

Another blow. Until he came back with a broken leg. Somehow that made it a little better. He was the only one on the entire trip who had been skiing before, and he managed to break his leg.

Yeah, I laughed at the time. Just another bump in the road. Now, thanks to therapy, I know all those "bumps" added up to indifference; I *learned* not to care. Even if someone broke their leg. That's how you protect yourself from emotional devastation.

I guess not caring helped nudge me deeper into crime. I still remember the first time I stole something. We went to a convenience store to buy a soda. They stacked the candy bars right there on the shelf in front of the cash register, taunting us with how easy it would be to slip one in our pockets since we couldn't afford both a soda and candy. Peer pressure won that day. The fact it was so easy – and tasted so good to a kid not used to getting too many treats – made it all the more tempting to make it part of my daily routine.

We started going to the department store to see what we could sneak out with. My friends were braver than me. They'd roll up clothes and stick them and other merchandise in their pants. I was too scared to do that. I stuck to the small stuff – candy, trinkets, supplies for my shoebox store. Whatever I could fit in my pocket.

Speaking of pockets, mine were still fairly empty when it came to real cash. One of my "role models" taught me a new game to fill them up – pick other people's pockets. He grabbed my hand, and we headed to downtown Boston. You could tell people we passed admired that he held his "little brother's" hand to make sure he stayed safe. While I diverted their attention with my cuteness, he'd empty their pockets or slip into their pocketbooks.

Impressive. I wanted to know how to do that, so I practiced on my sisters. I'd have them put their purse on their arm and turn their backs.

"Could you see me do it?"

"Could you feel it?"

Eventually, I talked my "teacher" into letting me give it a try. I explained I had been practicing and could do it without a hitch. I proved myself to him on the first attempt. It was euphoria, like an accomplishment, a rite of passage, another thing to put on my "resume."

He saw I was a natural, so we started tag-teaming it. We picked pockets in turnstiles, department stores, crowded trains. You name it. If there was a pocket to be had, we were happy to pick it. Before long, I became the "role model," taking younger kids, 9, 10, with me so that I would be inconspicuous.

Now I was getting somewhere. I could get my own money. I had two profitable hustles – a legal, if not risky, shoe-shining hustle that my mom disapproved of and an intoxicating illicit hustle that my mom didn't know of.

No reason for her to know. All I had to tell her was that I was saving my shoeshine money.

What *I* didn't know was that my mom had her own "hustles" going on. Hers were all legit, though. Night school, hard work, and sheer determination gave her that usually unobtainable leg up out of our neighborhood. She landed a job at the courthouse and moved us from our *lower* lower-class neighborhood, Roxbury, to the nearby *upper* lower-class neighborhood, Mattapan.

## Analysis With Dr. Deena Graves:
### Behavior Modification Therapy

Too bad I was so angry at my mom for hiding my birth father that I couldn't see her striking accomplishments – she should have been my role model all along. Too bad she was so busy achieving them that she couldn't see my anger and trauma. I have all the respect in the world for my mom *now*. She singlehandedly pulled my family out of the pits of welfare like a ferocious momma bear pulls her young cub out of the mouth of a rabid wolf. But, as a highly traumatized teen, that had no meaning to me. It didn't register psychologically or emotionally.

Sure, we ate peanut butter out of a jar instead of a can now. Suddenly, we had a lid that screwed on and off instead of struggling to keep plastic or foil snug over the top of a can to keep peanut butter fresh. Only in hindsight do I realize that's a notable difference in the level of poverty.

Of course, she took pride in upgrading our school clothes to ones that didn't have holes and stains, ones that actually fit. What mom wouldn't?

But what I needed wasn't fresh instead of stale peanut butter. It wasn't slightly better clothes. My mom was so busy trying to give her kids a better life that she couldn't see the life had been sucked out of me. Her desire to keep me on the straight and narrow blinded her to the fact that taking a ski trip away fueled my bad behavior. The promise I felt at winning the trip crumbled into more profound hopelessness.

Her punishments were always stiff because she could only see my behavior, not the trauma that birthed and nurtured the behavior. She'd even slap me around from time to time in her desperation to get me on the right track. But I was almost her size by then, so I'd just grab her hand.

That's what I needed. Someone to grab my hand. Someone, anyone, to understand that my behaviors masked the trauma raging inside of me. Think of my actions like a beginning swimmer pulled under by an unexpected undercurrent. Arms and legs flail as waves pound him, pulling him under over and over. He's gasping for breath, running out of strength, getting sucked down into a murky, dark world where he can't breathe anymore.

And then a lifeguard swims out. The exhausted swimmer sees the life preserver over the lifeguard's shoulder and manages to tread water as the hope of survival swims toward him. To his shock, though, the lifeguard doesn't throw the life preserver over his head and swim him to shore. He beats him over the head with it, telling him his strokes are all wrong. He's got to change how he swims if he wants to make it to the surface and out of the ocean. Then, he turns and swims away, leaving the worn-out, inexperienced swimmer on his own to battle the relentless swells of water.

Too tired to fight anymore, he lets the surf yank him back under, and he becomes part of its underworld. That's what untreated trauma does to a kid.

Unfortunately, my mom is not alone in focusing on behavior instead of trauma. We can prevent kids such as I was, kids who want to grow up to be attorneys who instead grow up to be career criminals, by ensuring they get the right kind of therapy.

For example, the go-to modality for abused-and-neglected children often is Trauma-Focused Cognitive Behavioral Therapy (TF-CBT), which is focused on precisely what my mom was focused on: Behavior modification. Instead, we must throw the life preserver over that inner nightmare forcibly pulling the child under, and get the child to safety.

Don't get us wrong, TF-CBT is an effective therapy … when used at the right time. The right time just isn't when waves of trauma are crashing over a kid. When the internal has not changed and the external pressure is removed, they can easily relapse.[31] Think back to the *Groundhog Day* movie or watch it if you've never seen it. It's an excellent metaphor for how trauma holds our children captive. Bill Murray's character lived a single day over and over. That's what it's like for a traumatized kid. They're battered nonstop by those memories. Trust me, when you tell youth who feel like someone is cracking a baseball bat over their head every day that they need to change their behavior, crime gets a new best friend. It's a coping mechanism, a desperate cry for help.

No wonder, then, that up to 75 percent of youth prematurely terminate from TF-CBT. The ones most likely to terminate? Kids like I was: Abused and neglected, minority status, lower-income, multiple traumatic events.[32]

## Two-Minute Introspection

I tried to flee my trauma by running to street predators; countless numbers of kids today fall into the hands of predators or other life-threatening situations as they try to outrun their trauma. How can we help those who work with traumatized children better understand trauma?

# 8   Happy to Indulge

We moved just a few miles away and a slight income bracket up, but it might as well have been to a different country. Their ways were foreign to me.

The streets on that side of the track operated by a code I never knew: Honor and respect. On our side of the tracks, we grew up learning not to care what anyone thought.

If people chose to walk in front of us smoking weed, for example, we'd blow it in their face. They made the choice, not us. The guys in my new neighborhood had too much respect to do that. They were classy. They *hid* their weed.

They didn't desecrate the neighborhood. They spoke to neighbors who walked by, "How you doing, Ma'am?" They even put their trash *in* the trash barrels. In my old neighborhood, we got high and knocked the barrels over.

In Roxbury, you didn't struggle; you gave up. In Mattapan, you didn't give up; you struggled. Although it was still the hood, it wasn't as hood.

People had respect for themselves and others. Government assistance wasn't a way of life. Dilapidated projects didn't dot the landscape. Instead, semi-well-kept, three-family tenements lined the streets. Typically, the owner lived in one unit and rented out the other two. We moved above our landlord. Yep, my mom was advancing in stature and trying to make sure her kids did the same. So, I packed up all my street knowledge, and off we went.

I didn't understand the new culture she dragged us to, but I went along with it. It was merely a matter of adapting to how highly traumatized youth did the streets on the new side of the tracks. My address changed, but my I've-got-to-make-this-happen-on-my-own mindset didn't. Lucky for me, my new role models shared a somewhat similar philosophy; they just disguised it. They also executed it differently, more cunningly. It was nothing but a temporary slowdown for me. I quickly caught onto their way of clandestine crime. I had to. It was the honorable, the respectable, thing to do.

They taught me how to play the cemetery, for instance. We crept up and grabbed pocketbooks out of cars while people put flowers on graves or snatched them as they walked from the graveside.

I effortlessly changed with the times. Surprisingly, this "noble" way of committing crime made life easier, more doable.

You might be wondering why. Why would kids turn to crime when their parents had jobs and halfway decent houses? Why would they turn to crime if they understood manners and held esteem for other people? I can sum it up in one word: Hopelessness. That made the move with me to Mattapan. Good thing. It lived with the kids there, too. They were just better at camouflaging it like their crime.

Let me explain. My mother couldn't help but settle into a false sense of security, of hope for her children. She went from abusive relationships, a subsidized house, two jobs, night school, and sheer physical and emotional exhaustion to a decent-paying job, a tolerable neighborhood, a modest home, a new opportunity for her children, and the pride of accomplishment. That light at the end of the tunnel might still be far off, but she could see the glimmer.

The same old struggle still blinded me, on the other hand. It blinded most kids on that "better" side of the tracks. Our parents might have jobs that afforded us a little more of the essentials, but they still didn't have disposable income. Roller skating, playing pool, and girlfriends cost money. So did our weed and alcohol habits. In our case, crime did pay.

It paid even more when we made our way over to the middle-class neighborhood butting up next to ours. Instead of snatching a lady's bag as she got off the bus, we snatched a lady's purse when she got out of the car in her driveway.

Talk about more effortless. The ladies in Roxbury and Mattapan stepped off the city bus looking around, clutching their pocketbooks under their arms like someone might grab them or something. The ladies in the middle-class neighborhood didn't even pay attention. They naively dangled their purses off their shoulders or in their hands – an open invitation to snatch them.

And these pocketbooks actually had money in them.

Their houses had one lock instead of three. One kick and we were in. Sometimes we didn't have to bother kicking because they trusted enough to leave them unlocked. Bars didn't block our way in through windows. Yeah, definitely easier. My days of sneaking around to the back door or hunting for a window with a few missing bars were in the rearview mirror.

Something else caught my attention in this novelty of a neighborhood. I saw how the other half lived. Where I came from, we had no idea another half existed. I watched the middle class in fascination, learning about an entirely different way of life. I had never considered the possibility of a hopeful lifestyle, but middle class seemed achievable. That whole candy-bar-selling thing with the Caucasian man had made me lose hope for more. Those houses weren't another way of life. They were another world, an unobtainable world. Not one Black person opened the door when we knocked in that world – unless they were the maid or another servant. In the middle-class neighborhood next to Mattapan, even Blacks could attain. They didn't seem to understand they were supposed to struggle and be hopeless.

I became obsessed with obtaining. How could I seize the life I was only stealing bits and pieces of?

It became clear fast. My new cash flow made acquiring the things I wanted much easier. Take drugs, for instance. Money made them more accessible. Not just weed, either.

Let me back up for a minute and introduce you to my new "role models," the ones who understood and lived by honor and respect in their nefarious dealings.

I grew up near several basketball courts in Roxbury. Basketball helps you pass the time in the hood, so I was pretty good at it by the time we moved to Mattapan. That made it easy to make new friends. My mom could see the basketball court in the park across the street from our new house, so I didn't have to go in when it got dark like a lot of kids. The lights came on, but the darkness covered up what was going on besides basketball. We smoked weed and took girls in the bushes. By day, we'd sit on the wall, playing cards for money and drinking. My mom was at work, so she didn't see. Plus, they taught me how to hide it from view. They were experts at concealment, after all.

I met one of my older role models, James, when he started dating my sister. He had a basketball goal at his house, so I hung out over there. Before long, I started dating his 14-year-old sister, Gabrielle. Kids flowed in and out of their house, visiting them or one of their other six brothers or sister.

I came and went with the rest of the stream of kids. Sometimes, I'd sleep in their attic. I stayed up there until their parents went to work the following day so Gabrielle wouldn't get in trouble. I spent the night with friends a lot, so I didn't get in trouble with my mom, either.

I didn't have much choice. My mom wouldn't let me have a key to our house because I woke them one too many times coming home from the park late. I'd stay with one of my friends, so I didn't disrupt the whole house. She didn't think anything, then, about me not coming home the night at 16 that changed my life forever.

My friend, Robert, and I needed weed, so we decided to break into a law office. Blue Hill Avenue, one of the primary roadways, ran through my neighborhood and the middle-class neighborhood we frequented. Both neighborhoods used this law office. We figured we might as well, too.

We stole two typewriters. Electric typewriters with the little spinning balls with letters on them had just come out, so we knew we stood to make good money, at least 60 or 70 dollars. We carried those bulky typewriters around with us on the streets all night. The streets had been my father for three years, but that was the first time I made them my home for the entire night.

We woke James up early the next morning. We needed him to help us sell the typewriters. We'd worked hard to get them, and I was excited about the weed and alcohol we were about to score.

I was smaller than James and Robert, so I fell behind as I juggled a typewriter. We'd been talking about splitting the money and what we were going to do. I didn't have reason to believe they'd changed topics. It took me a long time before I realized what they started talking about once they maneuvered out of my hearing.

James took us to two places to sell them. The first place bought one; an auto garage purchased the other. Once we had the cash in hand, they told me we needed to make a quick stop before we hit the liquor store. We strutted down the street full of our accomplishment and ourselves. I was surprised when we stopped at a bar. It was still early, so it wasn't open, but a lot of people milled around in front of it. They told me to wait on the corner. I was tired and trusted them, so it was no big deal. I knew they wouldn't steal from me. We were tight. They always had my best interest at heart.

Curiosity got to me, though, when I saw them making some kind of veiled transaction.

"What was that all about?" I asked when they sauntered back up.

"We got something to get high. Come on. Let's get out of here." Their rush should have tipped me off.

They walked swiftly because, I now realize, it was a drug-infested area. It was only 9 or 10 in the morning, and all these people were hanging out in front of an unopen bar.

I can see us scurrying down the street like it was yesterday. I don't even know what my thought process was. I just followed along. I had weed. I had my share of the leftover money. Sure, they used part of my money for this purchase, whatever it was. I hadn't asked any questions. I was a follower then. I had snorted cocaine a couple of times and thought they had bought some of that. No big deal.

James told us to wait while he ran into his house. He hurried back with a bag of something.

We headed to an abandoned house. I can still see that house as clearly as I can see us bolting away from the bar. My life changed profoundly – forever – in that house, so I'll never shake the memory of it.

I consumed weed and alcohol like they were candy by that point. I'd played around with cocaine. I hadn't played with fire yet, though. They pulled out something no one had ever offered me. I had no idea what it was – or what it does to you. People who shot heroin didn't broadcast it like they did weed or cocaine. You shot heroin once, and you were taboo even among junkies. Weed and cocaine are mental addictions. Heroin takes you physically captive. Your body becomes so sick without it that you'll do anything to get it. Rob. Steal. Even kill.

I didn't know all that when they handed a bag my way. I was hesitant, a little apprehensive, because I had never done it. I pushed my fears aside, though. I knew these guys. Like I said, I trusted them. Besides, I was "street" inquisitive. If someone said, "Let's," I said, "Go." Probably because I was addicted to more than weed and alcohol. I had become addicted to the streets and what they had to offer me. I was willing to try just about anything to get my hands on the life on the other side of that law office.

James pulled out the "works" – a one-piece hypodermic needle and syringe combo and a bottle cap. They had bought three $10 bags of heroin. I pushed my bag back to James. "No, I don't want all that." James was the kind of friend who always had your back. He offered to do half my bag for me, leaving me $5 worth. That seemed harmless enough. After all, I'd smoked countless bags of weed and sniffed my fair share of cocaine. Half a bag was nothing, or so I thought. People on the street call half a bag of heroin a "G Shot." Not even enough to get a junkie high; merely enough to keep dope sickness at bay.

I watched James and Robert, who was 16 like me, shoot theirs. I liked what I saw. Their mood and demeanor instantaneously changed. That had to be some good stuff for that kind of swift reaction.

It was my turn. I didn't have a clue. Oh, I thought I did. I thought I was smarter than the streets. Now I know I was a naïve, trusting, hopeless kid, looking for escape but about to land in captivity.

I might not have realized how naïve I was, but James did. He knew better than to let a newbie shoot up himself the first time – or for months afterward. He injected it for me, mainlining 10 ccs directly into a primary vein to send it rushing to my brain for an instant high. A pro at work. Professional junkies don't mess around. They go straight for results. Looking back, I wouldn't quite describe it as results. More like thankfulness I didn't die.

I can still feel the sensations pulsing through my body. Heat seared through me; sweat beaded up on my skin. My head fell, its sudden heaviness making it impossible for me to hold it up. My eyelids drooped. My nose itched. My heart rate decreased. My words crept out in slow motion. We'd been dashing around from place to place for a couple of hours; instantly, my body movement slowed, sluggish but smooth. It was like a record player that suddenly scratched from 78 RPMs to 33. Calm instantly settled over my whole being.

Calm wasn't the only side effect that came in a flash. The sickness came on like a freight train. Everything in my system came back out. They handed me a Grape Fanta. I gulped it down. It rushed back up. I can still remember that taste, too. Heroin and trauma are alike in that regard. They leave a lasting imprint on your brain.

My body laid down on its own.

I could think, but not rationally.

I managed to think half a bag was too much.

Throwing up helped. I felt a little less intoxicated each time because I got rid of more of that half-bag with each heave.

After a while, I could walk, but my body still wanted to lie down. I decided to go with them to the bowling alley across the street from the law office. We hung out for a bit before Robert decided to go to school. I knew I couldn't go around anyone; they would know. It was written all over me. I made my way to the park across from my house and stretched out on a bench for four or five hours. I could have gone home since my mom was at work and my sisters at school, but I didn't have a key.

I pulled myself up from the bench when kids started coming home from school. I was still intoxicated, but I could function. Better yet, I could still feel the high. And now it felt good. I could enjoy it, so I headed back to the bowling alley and played pool. I chatted people up. I relished in the fact the high lasted all day. If only I had known it was just for that first time.

I went home a different person that evening. While the streets had given me many role models, I had a new best friend: Heroin.

## Analysis With Dr. Deena Graves:
### Poverty or Survival Mindset

My body moved to a new neighborhood with my mom and sisters; my mind stayed in the old neighborhood. It's tough to mentally escape the hood. The tentacles of poverty wrap around your brain and squeeze the life out of you. Survival becomes your purpose, your way of life, taking over your thinking, your decisions, your behaviors, your actions.

Survival is, after all, a moment-by-moment endeavor. You can't think about the future, or a new socioeconomic bracket, when all you've known is hand-to-hand combat with trauma. It's like you're in a time warp, living in the moment because you aren't too sure another moment will come. When your mind is in a fog like that, it's almost impossible to think through decisions logically. You make decisions on the fly based on your feelings and your desperation to make it to that next moment.

Think back to the lady getting off the bus, clutching her pocketbook, eyes darting back and forth, scanning the horizon to make sure someone isn't creeping up on her. That's a survival mindset. You're constantly on the lookout for a threat to your safety. It stems from a dangerous home or a dangerous neighborhood. Mine, like many of our children today, stemmed from both.

The tentacles don't fall off just because you get a new address … or a new placement.

It doesn't matter who you are. Your neighborhood and your societal class define how you dress, how you talk, where you work, how you think, your values. That value system is etched into you as deeply as the colors on a priceless painting. You're like a "fish out of water" if you try to jump to another class – even if it's a minuscule jump like mine was.

My mindset didn't have the capability **on its own** to adjust to my family's beefed-up socioeconomic status. My mom moved up and on, dragging my sisters with her. I stayed trapped in the poverty mindset of the streets. She expected me to appreciate and settle into the new lifestyle she had worked so hard to achieve. But, I needed someone to show me how to fit into it. If they had, my story might be different.

Like my mom, we often expect foster youth to appreciate a better house and more opportunity and settle in. We're surprised when they don't. We don't understand it when they say, "I don't belong here," because we're offering them something they've never had. It's the same concept as my move into a neighborhood with a different way of doing things. They don't know how to fit into our middle-class homes or middle-class ex-pectations.[33] Think of a time when you've felt conspicuously out of place. Maybe you weren't dressed like everyone else, or you didn't know which fork to use. Or you didn't know how to fit into their conversation. How did you feel? Now, put yourself in the place of foster children regularly going into situations where they feel out of place.

## Two-Minute Introspection

What assumptions do we need to test or challenge in our thinking about how we interact with abused-and-neglected youth who have their own ingrained thinking?

# 9   Always On My Mind

My mother and sisters had no idea a different person sat down at dinner with them that night.

Really, I didn't either.

Nor did I realize that was the day a savage pimp was born. He had been simmering inside me for years, smoldering in the embers of trauma and hopelessness. There was no turning back now, though – unless someone noticed quickly and diverted me off that track.

No one did. As aforementioned, my mom, enjoying the fruit of her new standing in the world, thought she had saved her kids from what our old neighborhood condemned us to.

My teachers didn't see past the good grades and clown act sitting in their classrooms. My truancy, nodding off in class, and other tell-tale signs failed to catch their attention.

My father – the streets – took pride in a job well done. My two other fathers paved the way. I was growing up to be just like all of them. That's what most fathers want.

I crawled into bed in love with a new high. Weed and alcohol demanded I keep it up all day to maintain the high; heroin proved less exacting – for now. One injection early that morning, and the euphoria slid underneath the sheets with me late that night. This wasn't a child's high; heroin was for men. Now I knew. And it didn't kill me. Only 16 and another notch in my dope belt. Another milestone on my path to becoming a career trafficker. I had never experienced anything like it before. I was on top of the world, only I didn't know how dark that world was.

Granted, I still itched and threw up a little here and there, but my head no longer weighed me down. My voice might still be raspy, and I might still be moving slower than usual, but I could function.

It hit me. I had merely done too much. ***That's*** why the physical symptoms lingered. All I had to do was dial it back a few CCs to get the euphoria without the physical side effects.

Long-term consequences or costs never crossed my mind. Neither did the thought of getting physically addicted or going to jail. Despite years of use, I wasn't mentally addicted to weed or alcohol. I could have easily laid them down given the right help, the proper understanding of why I should. I didn't have access to them every day, so I enjoyed them when I could. I didn't get depressed or fall into a bad mood without them. Really, in my mind, they were just what you did when you got a little cash and hung out with friends. No different than going to the movies or playing pool. We call it normalized today.

I woke up the next morning with heroin on my mind. I hurried to James's as fast as I could. I needed some advice.

"I think I did too much," I explained to him. "I was sick all day, but I was fine after I slept it off on the park bench."

"Yeah, you probably did too much," he shrugged, not too worried about the consequences my body suffered.

Based on how long my physical reaction lasted, we reasoned I should've stuck to a trey bag. About $3 worth, we calculated. Not important now. He hadn't wanted to cheat me out of my fair share. I appreciated that.

We bought another bag with the money I had left from my typewriter profits. He injected $3 worth in me, and he shot up the other $7. The euphoria instantly swept over me again, but this time I felt like I did the night before *after I slept off the excess*. Problem solved. Weren't we clever?

My spirits soared so high I headed to school. My head came back down a little once I got there.

My body ached, worn out from the abuse, and my grades had suffered. Two days of hard drugs and several days of backbreaking crime had taken their toll. I needed a breather. Besides, I'd blown through the typewriter money, with most of the reward going to someone else. If I spent the little I had left on heroin, I'd have to split it with James since I didn't know where to get it or how to inject it. I settled on investing my leftover cash in weed since it lasted longer, and I could keep it all for myself. It wasn't a hard decision; my body wasn't craving heroin yet.

That's not to say I didn't think about it. I thought about it *a lot*. I thought about the electricity that bolted through my body when the needle slid in. I thought about how long the elation lasted. Mostly, though, I thought about what people would think about me if they knew. How they would look down on me. How livid my mom would be. I didn't think about how much it would hurt her; I just thought about how much she would hurt me if she found out. She'd probably kick me out. Heroin came with a stigma. I knew junkies had a reputation for stealing from their families, and my mom had a lot more to steal now, including her reputation at the courthouse.

I dabbled with heroin off and on for a few months. I'd give in whenever the thoughts of the euphoria outweighed the thought of my mom. I'd run over to James' when I got a little extra cash, and we'd head off on a dope run. Then we'd find somewhere to get high, the attic in his house, an abandoned building, the park. Sometimes we just shot up right there in the hallway of the projects where we scored it.

I didn't mind too much when James wasn't free when I went to get him. I'd head off for weed and alcohol instead. They lasted days instead of a day, anyway.

I was in control. At least in my mind. My body started lurching out of control without me noticing. The more I dabbled, the more my body started physically aching for heroin. Occasionally shooting up morphed into frequently shooting up, and, somehow, I missed it. The same amount wouldn't cut it anymore, either. My mind followed along with my body – I wanted that same level of euphoria I got initially, but it eluded me. My body demanded more and more of the bag to find that high from the first day.

That meant I had to cut James out of the picture. I had to stand on my own two feet, or at least find heroin with my own two feet. James didn't mind me cutting him out of my dope runs. That's how it goes when newbies evolve into junkies.

I watched how he interacted with the drug dealers in front of the bar, at an auto garage, and in the hallway of the projects. They knew me on the dope scene now. I was one of them. I no longer had to wait across the street. I stood proudly by James's side as he used my money to make the purchases.

I analyzed every move when James prepared the needle and injected me. I asked tons of questions. Why did he always flick the needle before he stuck it in my arm? Why did he squeeze my arm? Why did he pull a little blood up first? I wasn't afraid of needles, but I knew there had to be a science to it. If something went wrong, I couldn't rush home and tell my mom I messed up my dope. I had to comprehend what I was doing before I went solo.

I knew one wrong move and the needle could cause a lot of damage. If it missed the vein or went all the way through, it could cause bruising, an infection, or an abscess. The vein could collapse or the needle break off and float through my bloodstream. Inexperience could lead to blood clots, paralysis, amputation, or even death.

I didn't know all that the first time James stuck a needle in my arm. Even after I learned, I didn't think twice about trusting James. I was too far gone by then. He faithfully shot me up for about five months with his needle before I worked up enough courage to buy my own works. He hooked me up with an older diabetic woman in the projects not far from where we bought our Horse, also known as heroin. Miss Ronnell sold the needles she got from her doctor for $2 each. She made quite a tidy profit. I still wasn't daring enough to shoot up myself, so James used my needle on me and his needle on himself.

One day I went to get him, and he couldn't go. I had money. I had my works with me. I had the lust. The only thing standing between me and the euphoria was my fear. Craving welled up inside me, dwarfing the fear. I headed to the projects.

Nerves struck again. Major nerves. I'd never injected myself; some-one had done it for me previous to this. That always calmed my nerves somehow. I didn't want anyone watching or stumbling across me. That'd make me more jittery. That left out the hallway or an abandoned build-ing. I knew where I had to go to keep nerves from screwing it up. This job needed my full attention. I headed home. My mom was at work and my sisters in school, and my mom had finally given me a key. I could concen-trate and relax in the familiarity and privacy of my room.

I didn't give a thought to my family coming home early. The dope held my full attention. I wasn't taking any chances of spilling it, messing it up, pushing the plunger too far and sending the heroin flying into the air, shooting air into my vein, or jabbing the needle all the way through it, causing an abscess. The nightmare scenarios played over and over in my mind as I jaunted home.

I locked my bedroom door, pulled out the precious cargo, and carefully arranged it on my bed. I meticulously dripped water into the bottlecap. I coddled the Big H as I mixed it in. I adjusted the flame up and down before I slid it under the bottlecap, making sure it was just right so that evaporation wouldn't eat up any of my dope. I wasn't sharing this bag with anyone or anything.

I visualized everything James did, walking through his procedure step-by-step. I was a smart kid. Remember, I always made good grades even though I skipped school a lot. I followed instructions well when I wanted to. Not surprisingly, then, I cooked it to perfection. I flicked the needle like a pro. Luckily, I have prominent veins, so the needle slid in easily. I drew up some of my blood on the first try. I wanted to savor every moment, so I shot the dope in slowly, smoothly, like a skilled nurse. I gently pulled the needle out.

"I did it," I stated matter-of-factly but proudly.

A resounding success if I did say so myself. A triumphant first try. The beginning of unrelenting addiction.

I was in the big leagues now. I didn't need anyone. I didn't have to share my hard-earned money or my dope. I knew how to score it and how to use it. In a few short months, I mastered the art of die-hard addiction.

I cleaned up the mess, hid the works back under my mattress, and headed over to the park, a little more arrogance puffing my chest, to hang out just like any other day.

Only it wasn't any other day. I guess it was, in a way. Like many of my days, it collided with all my pent-up trauma. This day left much more in the wreckage, though. The collision didn't just leave a hardcore drug addict in its wake but the beginnings of a coldhearted trafficker.

## Analysis With Dr. Deena Graves:
### Heroin and Crime

Like I mentioned earlier, junkies are known for stealing from their families. It runs much deeper than that, though. Heroin and merciless crime go hand in hand. In one research study, 243 heroin addicts committed more than 473,000 crimes in 11 years. On average, they each committed almost 200 crimes – *every year*. They turned to robbery, forgery, assault, murder, and, like me, pimping to support their habit. The researchers estimated that 450,000 heroin addicts committed more than 50 million, often violent, crimes annually. Incarceration didn't tend to change the junkie's addiction or criminal behavior.[34]

We've talked about the epidemic of street youth in the United States. Hard drug use, including injecting dope, is rampant for these kids, just like it was for the kids I did life with on the streets. They're frantically looking for purpose but fall headfirst down a black hole that includes school suspensions and dropouts, health issues, psychological problems, overdose, and death.[35]

Heroin is a drug of desperation. It's also a drug of progression. Few people start at heroin. Let me use myself as an example. I first coated the ache of trauma with the high of alcohol and weed. Notice I said "coated." It's kind of like how Pepto-Bismol coats your stomach to give it relief from its own acid and "eases" the discomfort. Substances give you relief from your own mental anguish and eases the pain.

After a while, my body built up a resistance to the one-two punch of alcohol and weed, and I couldn't get enough of a high for the counterfeit "healing." There always comes a point where it's not enough, so you either add more or you add something new. I chose new. I started mixing in cocaine here and there. As time and trauma drug on, I needed a more significant high to get that same temporary relief from reality. So, I stuck out my arm for someone else to shoot me up with a brief reprieve. I'd looked everywhere else for someone to give me a respite and hadn't found it.

From there, I worked up the courage to inject my own break from the hurts of life; it wasn't that hard since trauma always looks better through a shot of dope. Heroin became a way of escape, a way not to feel.

Next stop: Sitting in a shooting gallery beside a guy with track marks running up and down his arm, interrupted by the occasional abscess, impatiently waiting for him to hand over the house needle.

No, the oozing sores on that guy didn't bother me. His bloated, boxing-glove hands – as junkies dub them – didn't faze me. By the time junkies hunt down a shooting gallery, all they care about is stopping dope sickness from ransacking their bodies.

If somebody had shown me those images *before* I let James plunge that first needle in my arm, I don't believe I ever would have. I didn't understand the horrors of drug addiction until I was too far into it. I didn't know I'd go from waking up from that first $5 shot of euphoria to a $100-a-day habit that I had to find a way to support. It would have been an extremely effective deterrent if someone had told me I'd have to get out there and hustle $100 *every single day* for 12 years just to keep from going to the bathroom all over myself.

I needed to understand the throes of addiction *before* I landed in its throes.

So do our kids today **unless we want them to become who I was**. They need to grasp the harsh realities of what awaits them on the other side of that first needle or possibly on the other side of that first gateway joint or drink. Instead, research shows that youth consider substances harmless behavior rather than something that puts them at risk.[36] I called that normalized earlier in the book.

We've helped it along. Anti-drug campaigns have been ineffective and sometimes led to higher illegal and dangerous drug use.[37] Look. Let me be real. If someone would've shown me one of today's anti-drug PSAs back then, I'd have laughed. I was feeling my way along the dark path of trauma avoidance. I needed someone to be genuine with me, not coddle me. Besides, I was a teenager. Teens are rebellious by nature. They are prone to taking risks, even ones who are not rebellious.[38] Campaigns that aren't authentic almost make kids **want to try them**. If they're thinking like I was thinking, and the odds are they are, they want to know what we're keeping from them. They see us talking about the risks of things like alcohol and then, as aforementioned, turning to it for our own stress relief. It makes it tempting, irresistible.

We're not even scratching the surface of helping them understand what will happen to them if they go down this road. We're instead plying them with cartoons and feel-good messages. We're prettying up the facts and then reacting in puzzled surprise when research comes back and says kids don't think drugs are dangerous. We must get real with them if we want to stop drug addiction and myriad other detrimental and criminal behaviors and activities. We must stop just talking to them or talking down to them in their minds. Kids see right through inauthentic. They see all this real-life stuff in movies, tv shows, video games, their school hallways, and on social media. Then we come at them with these sanitized, watered-down campaigns. They're rolling their eyes and laughing at us. They need to see the reality of track marks running down an addict's arm like a bad tattoo from years of jabbing at the vein. They need to hear the hideous stories of what they do to score the drugs.

Want to keep them from ever sticking their arm out for that first injection? Describe to them what it's like to go to jail and wake up the following day dope sick. It's all concrete, metal, cold, and dank in that jail cell. Dope sick gives you chills even in a sauna, so a jail cell is a rude – or should I say cold – awakening. The last thing you want to do is pull your pants down and sit on a cold metal toilet, but if you don't feed your body's drug appetite in the next couple of hours, it's either that or pooping all over yourself.

I get that it's a graphic and frightening subject. But would you rather kids learn from my experience or experience it for themselves? In hindsight, I would've much rather heard it from someone than lived it. I'd rather hold kids' hands through learning about the realities than hold parents' hands while we bury their uninformed children.

## Two-Minute Introspection

How can we get more authentic in our anti-drug campaigns?

# 10 What's Love Got To Do With It?

No matter how hard I searched, I never could find my self-worth. Every time I thought I had finally found it, it slipped through my fingers again. The surge of self-esteem I felt at shooting up myself proved short-lived like everything else I tried.

I started looking for it in sex. I had sex when, where, and with whomever I could. It's just another reality of growing up in a poverty-stricken neighborhood, another rite of passage for guys and girls. You try to find your consequence in relationships. It makes you feel better about yourself *until you come down from that high, too.*

I had gained a certain notoriety in the neighborhood. Other kids admired me as one of the cool guys. I could hustle. I usually had money. And I wasn't too hard to look at. It wasn't too difficult, then, to find girls to have sex with even if they knew my girlfriend.

Even if they hung out at my girlfriend's house. Gabrielle and I were sitting at her kitchen table one day when Lacy walked in. Her older sister, Vivian, dated Greg, Gabrielle and James's big brother. Lacy immediately grabbed my attention. We exchanged smiles. I kept catching her looking my way. I looked right back.

Turned out she lived between Gabrielle and me. Suddenly, I'd see her when I walked back and forth. I'd stop; we'd flirt. Before I knew it, I'd leave Gabrielle's and head straight to Lacy for sex since her mom wasn't an obstacle like Gabrielle's.

Lacy didn't have to live by the same rules as Gabrielle. She did whatever she wanted, and she wanted to do a lot – a real free spirit. Trauma plays out in people in different ways. Lacy went looking for it in the street, like me. Where I turned to crime, drugs, and a tough-guy image like most guys in the hood, she turned to her body like most girls in the hood. The attention of guys like me gave her a sense of identity that her father's abandonment had robbed. It'd stolen her mother from her, too. When her dad ran from his family, her mom bolted more frequently to a bottle. Alcohol drowns out the sound of the door opening and closing at all hours of the night, so her mother was clueless to Lacy's comings and goings, as well as mine.

Lacy's house became my haven because I could do whatever I wanted there. I would go over to chill at all hours of the night – whenever I got done on the streets. Her mother asked no questions, so I made no effort to hide smoking weed or having sex with her barely teenaged daughter. No way could I have pulled those stunts at Gabrielle's house.

As our relationship grew, so did my dope habit. The costs soared beyond my means; my craving soared beyond my control. I needed something with a higher return on my time investment. I couldn't count on picking random pockets to bring in enough cash fast enough. I headed downtown with some of the older guys. We had noticed men in the alleys who'd dropped their trousers down around their ankles or leaning their head back on the headrest of their car seat.

They kept their eyes closed, totally oblivious to anyone besides the girls with them.

We'd found a lucrative new hustle. We would walk around the Combat Zone in downtown Boston until we saw someone in a compromising position and make him our victim. We called it searching for a "Vic." We should have felt guilty. Talk about easy targets. These naïve guys from the suburbs came looking for quick sex, not understanding the brutal realities of the Combat Zone. They were out of their element. We literally caught them with their pants down.

It was mostly strong-arm robbery. They might be standing half naked in an alley doorway, and we'd grab them. If they were in the backseat of their car, we'd yank their car door open and jerk them out by their feet. Or we'd snatch their wallet through a rolled-down window or unlocked door.

The girls ran when that happened. They didn't need to. We never messed with them. They were always on the lookout, though – for pretty much everything: Police, pimps trying to elbow their way in on their pimps, buyers who might not pay or who would rape them. They had experience with all those things, after all. The buyers didn't have to worry about any of that. Even if the police came around, they arrested the girls. They knew they could freely head home or to find another girl. In retrospect, I'm glad we didn't ever take from the girls or even talk to them. That would have caused them problems with their pimps.

I spotted their pimps hanging around, but I didn't have a clue about their rules. My experience with pimps, as I stated, was limited to scooping up change out of their car floorboards to hit the ice cream truck. They cared about making people happy from my adolescent perspective. Their left-over coins couldn't compete with the wads of bills I watched the tricks dishing out to the girls, anyway. And we didn't have to ask them for it. We took it at will.

Their generous amounts of cash couldn't keep me from noticing, though, the extremely young girls with some of them. These guys were typically much older. They must have had lots more money where the money they flashed around came from. Many had nice clothes, fancy cars, expensive-smelling cologne. A thought took root in my mind the first time I realized that. This prostitution thing had to be lucrative because those girls were there every night. I knew the Combat Zone's reputation. Girls from both my neighborhoods dressed up and headed downtown. Bars and strip clubs lined the streets. We used to sneak down there and peek in to see the naked girls on stage. I learned through the years that the city was hot. A lot of money stood to be made down there. That's why we'd head down there to rob people. It's also what drew pimps from all over the country to work it.

I never noticed any pimps or buyers go to jail, only the girls, as noted, and the older guys I hustled with. They got arrested for robbery, drugs, and other crimes. Somehow, I evaded the cops' attention. My role models got caught while I was in school or with one of my girlfriends. Their cases began piling up, and, one by one, they landed in prison or drug rehab. Some went away for a long time.

That scared me. I didn't want that to be me. My luck was bound to run out at some point. Police upped their patrol. A couple of my friends even went to jail for snatching purses at the graveyard. Plus, I needed their help. My habit had grown too expensive for breaking and entering by myself. The progression escalated after I started shooting up myself. Once I got the hang of it, I was obsessed with it. It quickly became a way of life, and I was consuming two bags a day before I knew it. It took expensive items, such as large televisions, way too heavy to carry alone, to support that kind of habit. I didn't have a car, and I sure couldn't run around the neighborhood trying to juggle a bulky TV.

I needed a new cash flow. My mind kept flashing to the picture of the tricks handing fistfuls of cash to young girls in the Combat Zone. The thought that had taken root in my brain weeks before began to sprout. I couldn't see much of a downside. Even when cops arrested the girls, I saw them back on the street the next time I went down there. Seemed like a pretty reliable source of steady income.

My thoughts turned back to my first love: Heroin. I liked my girlfriends a lot, but I could do without them. Not heroin. It was the first thing I ever felt I couldn't do without. The thrill of doing it myself had become almost as addicting as the drug. Something about seeing my blood rush up in the needle and then feeling that warm sensation when I first shot it in intoxicated me almost as much as the drug itself. Heroin isn't just a way of life; it's a way of thinking.

It shoves out any thoughts not devoted to feeding it, rewiring your brain into one mode: Evil. In a few short months, a kid searching the streets for a father figure mutated into a beast prowling the streets for any means possible to satisfy an insatiable lust for heroin. Lust is the perfect breeding ground for twisted logic.

It stood to reason, then, that Lacy would want to sell herself for me. I knew she loved two things: Me and sex. She incessantly professed her love for me, and she wanted to have sex all the time. I, on the other hand, wanted to have heroin all the time. What better collaboration? I knew a place where she could get all the sex she wanted, and I could get all the money I needed. I'd be right there with her. If she wanted, she could always have sex with me, too, after she handed the money over. We'd both be happy. A win-win. My jaded view on love, taught to me by some of the finest manipulators around, my two fathers, was that if somebody loved you, you could get them to do anything for you, legal or illegal, even if it puts them in danger.

It didn't cross my mind that she might not want to have sex with strangers. She'd had sex with me when I was practically a stranger, after all. It hadn't taken me too long to figure out she didn't have a positive self-image, either. Again, that came with growing up in poverty, even upper-class poverty. She would do anything to be with me because it gave her a sense of worth that I wanted her body.

And, don't forget, she could come and go as she wanted. It all played into my hands as a wannabe trafficker. It seemed logical that she'd be my next hustle. Twisted logic.

I didn't think for a second about trafficking Gabrielle. I had more respect for her because she cared about herself, and her family stood between her and my plans. She couldn't get away with as much as Lacy. That doesn't mean I cared more about Gabrielle. I felt the same about both, as well as Evelyn, another girl I had sex with occasionally. They were fun, and I liked hanging out with them, but I wasn't capable of caring about anyone by this point.

The day I became a trafficker started like any other day. I woke up and went about my day as usual. I got high, went to school, hung out at the bowling alley. I was almost out of money, though. I knew I'd need to buy more heroin quickly to keep dope sickness from wreaking havoc with my body. That meant letting men wreak havoc with Lacy's body as soon as possible.

I'd been seriously formulating my plan for about a week. The time had arrived to put it in motion. I might have gone about my day as usual, but I thought about the plan all day. I woke up to it. My mind strayed to it during classes. I couldn't concentrate as we played pool. Finally, I decided to go to her house to pitch her the opportunity. As much as I had thought about the payoff for me, I hadn't thought about what I'd say to her. I'd just wing it. She loved me, and she thought I loved her. I didn't, but I told her I did.

I'll admit I was a little nervous as I walked to her house. I didn't know what she would think. Plus, I had no idea how to sell someone. I didn't know what a pimp's actual responsibilities were.

We'd figure it out as we went. That's what I did with school – and the rest of life.

"Lacy, I need to get money fast. I know a way I can get it if you'll do it with me. If you really love me like you say you do, you'll do this for me." It all came out in one breath.

She didn't ask me why I needed money, and I didn't tell her. She didn't know I shot heroin. I didn't do it in front of my girlfriends, and I was a functioning addict. Very few people knew. I could get high and go to school without anyone suspecting a thing, just like the first night I shot up and carried on a conversation at dinner with my family without them being any the wiser. I made sure never to leave any visible evidence on my body. I always went in the same spot in my vein to prevent track marks.

"It'll be really easy, Lacy. We can go downtown, and you can turn tricks. I'll be right there with you."

She knew what that was. We all did. We all knew someone who did it. Like her neighbor across the street.

Of course, she was a little taken aback at first. That was only natural. I sprung it on her out of the blue.

I turned the charm on. I pointed out how much fun it'd be to take random marks' money.

She stared at me reluctantly, unsure, "I don't know what to do." I could hear a little fear in her voice.

"Neither do I, but I'll be there with you," I reassured her. "It's not that hard. Guys come around, and you just get in the car with them. You do what you gotta do, and then they drop you right back off. Or, if they're on foot, you take them in an alley. I'll stand in the alley, too."

"It'll be alright. People do it every day. You're a natural at sex," I trotted out my biggest smile.

It didn't take much for me to win her over. She liked adventure, and, as I said, she loved me. I quickly laid out the plan before she had time to change her mind.

We'd catch the 10 o'clock bus the next night and then take the train that would drop us off in the middle of the Combat Zone. That was the extent of my plan. I didn't tell her what to wear. I wasn't that versed in the pimp world. I didn't know stuff like that mattered. All that mattered to me was the money waiting for me at the end of that train ride.

She dressed in regular clothes, a skirt she wore to school or when we went to the movies. She fixed her makeup like normal. The only thing she did special was wear one of her mother's wigs. Not to disguise herself. She wanted to look older. We didn't know the younger, the more money.

We drank some of her mom's vodka before we headed out. It calmed our nerves. Maybe that's why she never cried.

Once we got down there, I realized I didn't know how much to charge. I told her to mingle with the other girls and ask one of them. After they advised her, we settled on $25 for oral sex and $40 for sex in the car. Not that it mattered. No one approached her that first night. It was the middle of the week, and it was too early in the night for much activity. Another point of inexperience. She waved halfheartedly at cars, but she didn't really try. A few cars blew their horns back at her, but no one pulled over. They did for a couple of the more seasoned girls.

I didn't force her. I didn't even encourage her. She was game, but it was obvious she was anxious. We both were. To be honest, I was surprised we had made it this far, so I decided to focus on absorbing all I could that night.

She did, too. The other girls took her under their wing; it's like a secret society. "No, Honey. You don't want to do it like that."

"Watch out for those kinds of cars because that's the police."

They plied her with the dos and don'ts. I learned as she learned. I followed 10-15 feet behind them. I'd pull her aside every chance I got and ask her what they said. I felt nervous for her, afraid she wouldn't know what to do, that her first date would go badly, and she wouldn't like it. Gratitude welled up in me for their help. A lot rode on it: Money for heroin.

We only stayed a couple of hours. I didn't want to miss the last train back and use the precious little money I had left for a taxi. We debriefed on the ride home. She filled me in more on what the other girls told her. Ironically, everything I knew about being a pimp at this stage of my career came from my first victim.

We talked a little about how scared she was, but I didn't want to linger on that. I had something more important on my mind.

"We're going back tomorrow, right." I stated it as a fact rather than asking a question to make the chances of her saying "no" less likely. She nodded. Yes, we could try it again. I told her we needed to go a little later so there'd be more traffic. She could wear the same outfit.

It was settled. We got off the bus, went to her house, and had sex. We talked a bit more as she drifted off to sleep. She'd had a big day, so I decided to go home. I woke her up to say bye. "See you tomorrow," she murmured. Good. She was still in, even half asleep.

Conflicting thoughts raced through my mind on the way home. "Wow. I can't believe I did that. More importantly, I can't believe she was down for that." I was surprised and proud at the same time. For both of us. We had embarked on this new adventure together. So, we didn't make any money. She wasn't upset or angry. There were no bad feelings. She'd been afraid, but I had gotten her out there and exposed her to it, and she was willing to go back. That excited me. No regrets. No hesitation. Just great expectations.

I knew what I was doing now – or so I thought.

## Analysis With Dr. Deena Graves:
### Juvenile Sex Traffickers

Little research exists on juvenile sex traffickers. Most of the negligible amount of existing research is based on theories extracted from data on adult sex traffickers. I don't fit nicely into most of the limited research findings that have been unearthed on juveniles, such as "belongs to a gang." I also don't relate – and I would guess many of today's young male traffickers don't, either – to some of the hypotheses floating around, like not having a lot of friends. I had plenty of friends. The guesses go on:

- A drug dealer who knows people in prostitution.
- Has family members with police records.
- Likely has a problem controlling anger, which can be "explosive" and "aggressive."
- Sexually violent.

None of those things were me. I'm sure they apply to some juvenile traffickers, but I caution us not to fall into the trap of stereotypes or generalizations. The following theory, for example, is the exact opposite of what I was: "Does not sit at the pinnacle of running the business but is a key individual for such things as 'recruitment'" or a "pawn."[39]

I built my empire from the ground up. I *never* worked for another pimp. Many other young boys don't, either. You don't have to work for another pimp to learn the ropes; the streets teach you all you need to know.

Including how to stuff your emotions so deep inside you they go AWOL. That's a prerequisite for a trafficker. I mostly had that skill down; I'd learned it at home. My stepdad had one emotion – rage. My mom took good care of us physically, but she kept her distance emotionally. She grew up with 10 brothers and sisters and a working mom and dad. Needless to say, she didn't get a lot of attention herself as a child. When she married Tyrone, he beat all the emotions out of her except fear.

As a little boy, it shredded my heart to pick up my mom's emotions from the wreckage he left behind. I tried with all my might to carry them for her, but I didn't know how to hold up under the weight of them. They'd be on my mind when I'd go to school after a night of his fury, but I couldn't talk about them. That's an unwritten law in a house like mine. You don't dare mention what happened inside those four walls. You stuff it down and hold it there no matter how badly it tries to pry its way through your sealed lips.

My Grandmother Helen, my mom's mom, gave me the only emotional support I got for those first 13 years. She took a genuine interest in my well-being and my emotional growth. I acted like my emotions were growing just fine. I didn't want to say things weren't going well at home and then have to go home. I knew my grandmother would call my mom out, and I'd face the fallout.

By the time I met my biological father's family, trauma, weed, alcohol, and sex with random girls had already exhausted my emotions. They tried, but sporadic emotional support at 13 is too little, too late. If you showed emotions as a teen on the streets, people saw you as soft. Soft can get you hurt. Or killed. I couldn't let my guard down with my new family, or I might slip with my street family.

I have to give it to my dad, though. He might have been an alcoholic, but he tried to be an emotionally supportive dad the best he knew how. He hugged me all the time. Honestly, it was kind of awkward for a young teen boy. Besides, I thought a father's hands coming toward me meant a fist in the face, so I didn't know how to receive a hug from a different father. He'd reach out, and I'd stiffen up.

Those hugs and family dinners when I could make my way to his house somehow couldn't stop the feeling I was all alone in the world. My emotional void could have spanned the Grand Canyon.

I tried to fend for myself emotionally, and we see how that ended up.

Showing emotions became a sign of weakness. When my girlfriends started showing me the love I had longed for all those years, I wasn't looking for emotional support. I didn't want it. The only feelings I still could muster up were anger or excitement about sex. Of course, I told them I loved them. That's what manipulators do. It was nothing more than exploiting them to be what or whom I wanted them to be. At the ripe old age of 13, I did not possess the ability to form a deep, meaningful connection.

That's where I bring one of the research hypotheses about juvenile sex traffickers to life – "serious degree of intimacy deficit."[40]

That's the scientific term. "Deficit" means a shortage of something, an insufficiency. Those words don't adequately describe a pimp so that hypothesis might need a little work, as well. It might start as a deficit, but the words "intimacy" and "trafficker" are an oxymoron, with a chasm between them that also could span the Grand Canyon.

The word "emotions" often invokes thoughts of tame-sounding words, such as "happy," "sad," "calm," or "mad." Those words gloss over just how vital emotions are to how we interact with each other. Emotions impact everything about our lives, including our decisions, actions, our identity, our well-being.

"Adaptive emotions tell us what is important in a situation and act as a guide to what we need and want, but emotions can become problematic because of past traumas or because people are taught to ignore or dismiss them."[41]

Problematic is a nice way of saying a lack of emotions can lead to multiple issues and crimes, including depression, borderline personality disorder,[42] alcoholism, aggression, sexual violence, and, as I am a living example of, sex trafficking.[43]

To prevent our children from becoming traffickers, drug addicts, or other things that destroy them and others, we must intervene before they are 13. I'm not saying it's hopeless after 13, but we do have a much bigger hill to climb if we let trauma engulf them for 13 years.

I've said this several times already, but I can't emphasize it enough. One person could have prevented my destruction of myself and the more than 150 women and girls I trafficked. One person who saw through my mask, who saw through my clown act, who took a proactive interest in my well-being and my emotional growth might have prevented that. You could be that person for a child today. A child living an emotionally void existence needs a cheerleader. Anyone can be that for a child: A teacher, cafeteria worker, social worker, probation officer, mentor, crossing guard, grocery store clerk, the community center director, the parent of a friend. Anyone.

They often are left to their own emotional devices. Let me give you one more example from my childhood. When I made honor roll, no one praised me. Children need praise. They need to know their efforts matter, that someone sees them. They stop trying when they believe they don't. What's the use of going to all the trouble of making honor roll if no one notices?

Research points to emotional resources as the most crucial in helping them make the leap from a survival mindset and maintaining it. That means our most significant opportunity is to deposit into their emotional bank account. If they have been in survival mode, it will be in the negative. They'll have a negative emotional balance. It's overdrawn. We will have to do a lot to get it to a zero balance and then work it up where they can withdraw from it as needed.[44]

We also have to teach them to be their own cheerleader, to understand their value and their worth. I didn't know how to believe in myself. Neither did Lacy. I didn't believe I had *any* value or worth, so I went searching for it in the streets. So did Lacy.

Many children today are searching in dangerous places, as well. They have a lot more choices than we did, though.

## Two-Minute Introspection

Name three concrete ways we can invest emotionally in a child's life.

# 11 In the Money

I woke up with a clear conscience. My girlfriend loved me enough to help me out in my time of severe need. That was all there was to it in my mind. I absolutely didn't see myself as a child sex trafficker. Turning my selfishness into a career didn't cross my mind ... yet. I didn't know that was an option. Sure, I knew pimps and sex workers in my neighborhood. I'd seen them downtown. However, I had no idea they worked in an organized industry with people, including buyers, who made it a lifelong endeavor. At 16, I didn't grasp that pimping was a way of life.

A staple of life in the hood *was* manipulating people for personal gain. What I talked Lacy into was no different than talking her into sex. It fit the classic definition of love in the hood. Lacy was my girlfriend. She willingly did this for me because she loved me and thought I loved her. Love pure and simple – her hopelessly devoted love for me and my all-consuming love for dope.

I had no capacity to understand the psychological, emotional, and physical abuse my "love" inflicted upon Lacy. I don't think she did, either. I never considered my plan abusive. Abuse had been part of the daily routine for her and me our entire lives. It's hard to objectively see abuse in your own actions when it's woven into the very fabric of your existence. I'm not making excuses, but teenagers' brains are not fully developed. They can't logically think through the long-term, lasting consequences.[45] The combination of a lifetime of trauma, normalization of abuse, and undeveloped brain leads youth down disastrous paths without much effort.

I viewed it as simply another hustle for dope money, no different than breaking into someone's home or snatching a purse. I sure didn't think when I crawled out of bed that morning that the future of more than three decades of my life had been birthed the night before, especially since we hadn't scored any money.

Don't get me wrong. I wasn't discouraged by not turning a profit that first night. Just the opposite. I felt we both had achieved a new level of success. I had unquestionably executed my part of the job perfectly. I smooth-talked my girlfriend into walking the streets. She stood on the corner, waving at cars with the mission of selling her body for me. I was more than willing to invest the time to make it work. Hustling always takes patience. I'd broken into multiple houses that yielded no more than a dime-a-dozen 12-inch TV and a portable radio.

I didn't let that rattle me. It merely made me work harder for a better haul. I went back the next night and hit the house around the corner. I'd take Lacy back down the next night and hit the next guy coming around the corner. I *knew* there was money in this. I'd taken many a trick's money roll. I'd seen pimps sporting massive diamond rings and driving fancy cars. I could tell they got their hair done. I just had to learn the fine points of my girlfriend finding the money for me, so I didn't risk jail trying to get it myself.

It was on Lacy that she didn't bring me the money that first night, anyway. Understand that clearly – in a pimp's mind, even a fledgling one – his job is to get his victim out there. Once he does, what happens from there is *her* responsibility. It doesn't matter if she has a profitable night, gets arrested, raped, killed; it's all on her. It's out of the pimp's hands. When you sink to the level of selling other people for your own profit and pleasure, you're way past emotions such as guilt or shame. Of course, by the time you grow your business to three, four, five girls, you know you must do product control if the money's not coming in. I was a new business owner, though, and I knew I had put an appealing product out there.

It just takes a little time to market it.

Like any new business owner, I was excited to see what kind of customer response I'd get on Day 2. Despite my great anticipation, I played it cool. I went to school. Hung out at the bowling alley afterward. Shot a little pool. I didn't mention my new business venture to any of my friends. I had, after all, lost money on my first day of business since I had to invest in bus and train tickets. Losing money is nothing to brag about. That old saying, "Crime doesn't pay," isn't true in the minds of abused-and-neglected teens buying hope with the proceeds of their break-ins. I had to turn a profit to look cool in their eyes.

Lacy greeted me as usual when I got to her house. She looked the same, but I could feel her anticipation, too. She was all in. She never tried to back out, even after having time to think about the night before. Not surprising since she still had the same low self-esteem issues. Maybe even more so now since she had failed to get any guys to so much as pull over for her. She had more to prove now. Many of the girls I trafficked, including Lacy, felt their sexuality was all they had to offer. Very few girls go from virgin to trafficked. Life strips them of their self-worth, so they search for it with their bodies. A master manipulator jumps on that.

I spoke to her mom before heading upstairs without feeling any remorse for what I was doing to her daughter. Later, her mom cooked dinner for us before she drank herself to sleep. Lacy slipped on the same outfit and fixed her hair and makeup like the night before. I wore what I had worn to school. I didn't care about the diamond rings and fur coats yet, so it didn't matter to me if I looked the role of a pimp or not. I didn't think of myself as one. I was just a guy who needed enough money to get high. The only thing different about either one of us the second night was we had a little more knowledge about what we needed to do.

"Hey, Young P. You out here again, huh." I might not have thought of myself as a pimp or looked the part, but a couple of the other pimps acknowledged I was one of them now when I walked up to the Sugar Shack. The bar set a block or so from the prostitution track, so they'd made it their home base. I'd played it better than I thought the night before, telling them I had my girl out there getting me some money. I still felt awkward around them, though, like the new kid in class with all the popular kids. I didn't want them to realize I was a novice.

Lacy had peeled off from me after getting off the train. She headed where she knew the other girls would be. I felt confident she knew what she was doing. I had grilled her on the bus and train: "Do you remember what kind of cars to look for?"

"Do you remember what to say when you walk up to the car?"

I quizzed her on the terminology the girls had told her the night before. She had it down, so I told her to be careful and headed to the Sugar Shack. I hung out there for a bit, but I couldn't see the track from the bar, so I decided to check on her. Despite my lack of guilt, I still had a sliver of a heart, a small amount of humanity, crammed somewhere deep down inside. I cared more about her than I should have as a trafficker. I should have looked at her as no more than a product. Trafficking is, you see, done with your mind, not your heart. But she was my girlfriend, after all.

I looked for her for about 15 minutes. I didn't see her, so I headed back to the Sugar Shack. Remember, I only had a *smidgen* of a heart left. Not enough to occupy too much of my concern.

A car pulled up in front of the bar a few minutes later. I didn't notice Lacy until she jumped out of the car with a big smile on her face, walked proudly over to me, and handed me a wad of money. Both of us were elated. It was like receiving a Grammy.

"Okay, Baby. What did you do?" A blow job. It was easy, she told me impassively. The night before, we worked the track for hours and got nothing. An hour the second night, and we had 25 bucks. Mission accomplished. We'd earned enough money for me to purchase sorely needed dope.

I walked her back down the block, and we celebrated for a brief moment.

"We did it," I cheered her on. "You know what to do now. This is good. Go see if you can get another."

She said, "Okay," and took off. I headed back to the bar.

The other pimps were waiting for me. These guys were cool, I thought – excited to congratulate a newcomer. That was the last thing on their mind. No doubt they knew I was a novice now. In her excitement, Lacy had brought the trick straight to me – the possible heat straight to all of us. Not a good look. Pimps don't have affiliation with their girls out on the street like that because that's how you go to jail. Not only does it pose the risk of arrest, but a girl doesn't want one man to see her taking his money straight to another man. We still had a lot to learn. There was a little more to this pimp game than I had realized.

I'm a fast learner, and they seemed over it, so I brushed it off and headed back to the track to check on her. I didn't see her. She's already scored another trick, I thought gleefully. I wasn't too worried about her now that she had it down. We both were growing a little more comfortable with the routine.

Eventually, I ran into her, and she handed me more money. And then again. I pocketed it both times and told her to get on back out there. I made my way between the track and the bar until around 2:30, when everything started closing. I suddenly felt tired. I had $75 in my pocket, so there was no need to stay any longer anyway. Job well done. She'd made as much money as I would have breaking into a house with a nice TV or yanking a buyer out of his car and running with his money. And all without any risk to me. I silently congratulated myself, "This is going to be alright. Another money-making weapon in my arsenal and one that presents no peril to me." The police had told me to keep moving once, and I kept moving. I didn't have drugs on me, and I wasn't drinking, so it was nothing to worry about. All I had to do was keep my nose clean.

When I found Lacy again, she was ready to go, too. She handed me another stack of bills, and we grabbed a cab. We basked in a shared sense of accomplishment. I counted the money in the back of the cab. We made more than $125. Not a bad night's work.

"Here. This is for you, Baby." I handed her $25. She deserved it. I had more than enough money to get my dope in the morning, and she was my girlfriend, helping me out. We were in this together *since I hadn't grown a pimp mentality yet*. It was a big score to me, and she had done the heavy lifting, so it made sense to give her a little reward for her effort. I was a generous sort of guy.

I don't think she considered it work that night. It was easy, she assured me. I asked her what all she had done. She only had sex with one guy; the others wanted blow jobs. I asked her if she was all right. "Yeah. Not that bad," she nodded. We didn't talk about emotions besides that. She appeared to have put her fears to rest, so I didn't want to stir up anything by saying the wrong thing.

I didn't bother to get out when we got to her house. I told her I'd call her after school. I counted the money again on the way home. I had enough for dope, a bag of weed, and a pack of cigarettes. I was way ahead of the game.

In the moment, I was ecstatic about the wild success we'd achieved in only two nights. No bad experiences. No trouble. Great profit margin. We put into practice what we learned the night before, and I had the result in my hands. Looking back, I wish the second night had not been so profitable. I might have only been doing it for the drugs, but it planted a seed that this could be a long-term venture. Once I realized I could do this and not give the dope man all my money, it messed me up in the head.

I didn't regret pimping my girlfriend, but it troubled me that the dope man pimped me.

## Analysis With Dr. Deena Graves:
### Stage of Teen Brain Development

Not only do I wish the second night had not been so profitable, but I also wish my mom would have seen me pull up in that taxi. Or that my aunt or uncle or someone would have driven by downtown at midnight, seen me, and gone running straight to my mom. I didn't wish that at the time, of course. You know what they say about hindsight.

When I stepped out of the cab with my pockets flush with cash, I didn't care what people thought about me or who saw me. I didn't care if word got back to Gabrielle that I went downtown with Lacy and how she handed me money every hour or so. My only fear in life at that age besides not getting my dope fix was my mom's wrath. Suddenly, though, I found myself unconcerned with what she would think of me. Heroin doesn't give your mom a pass. However, I didn't want her asking questions I didn't have answers for. I knew what that would mean. If she went sniffing around and found out what I was up to, she would slam the brakes on my new, highly profitable hustle.

I wish my mom would have taken a different approach with me before I stumbled into that hustle. She used threats and physical violence, hers and my stepdad's, to keep me under control, which only made me spin more *out of control*. Their harsh punishment didn't correct me as she desired. It made me, like most teens, dig my heels in deeper and hunt for ways to rebel.

I wish adults in general, even one adult, had taken a different tact with me. Explosive anger serves only to leave more fragments and debris in an already shattered life. It can never put those pieces back together again.

I needed someone to help me see the long-term consequences of what I was doing to Lacy and myself. Getting back to that maturity thing might shed some light on what I mean. Again, I'm not trying to make excuses for what I did. I'm trying to help you keep other kids from becoming the vicious predator I grew into. Science has proven beyond a shadow of a doubt that the teenage brain's frontal lobe, which hones critical thinking skills, is not developed enough for them to logically think through cause-and-effect.

Their emotional control panel, meanwhile, is on full throttle simply because they are teenagers.[46] Their emotions drive choices when they are pressured, especially by something tempting. I'm living proof. Dope tempted me, and the violent sickness pressured me. My emotions drove my choice to pimp Lacy. When she proudly handed over that money, solving all my problems, my emotions shifted into high gear. I fell completely in love. Not with her. With what she could do for me.

There you have it. A scientific portrait of my teen years. Lacy's, too. It was in our DNA. Or at least our brain matter.

It's in all teenager brain matter: Their bad choices are rooted in science, and they need us to put on the brakes from time to time. We have to point out the speed bumps and road hazards and help them understand if they hit them at full speed, it will cause extensive damage. "The healthy move to adulthood is toward interdependence, ***not complete 'do-it-yourself isolation***."[47] How they learn to maneuver through their teen years influences their entire adult life. Living proof again.

So, science backs me – and every teenager out there today – when we say yelling, physical force, or a "parent" voice can't compete with the thrill of the moment. The dopamine rush is just too invincible at that age. All that power surged through me like an electrical storm on the cab ride home that night. It supercharged me. They don't call dopamine the "feel good" hormone for nothing. I felt good about myself, my future dope supply, and how easy it would be to stay out of jail with Lacy shouldering all the risk. When a kid's in the thrill of the moment and we come in yelling and threatening, it backs them into do-it-yourself isolation.

If an adult I trusted had talked to me about what was happening inside Lacy, or for that matter me, I might not have done even worse to more than 150 other girls and women. I cared about Lacy. I had enough humanity left to care more about her than dope if someone would have helped me break my addiction. If an adult had explained the trail of destruction I would leave behind and could never change, I might have chosen a different career path. Perhaps if someone had dismantled the movie version of a pimp, the lure might not have been so overwhelming. A hopeless teen doesn't understand what a pimp's life is like when they park the expensive car and take off the fur coat and diamond rings. It looks like hope through the lens of a kid from the hood. That viewpoint doesn't capture the remorse, emptiness, and grief that never truly leaves you when you wake up to what you've done.

Surely, at least one adult caught a glimpse in the difference in me and in Lacy – but no one ever acted upon it. We cannot let that continue. The cost is too high for our children and our society. A change in demeanor, falling grades, missing school, falling asleep in class, changes in appearance. Keep your eye out for these and other red flags listed in *Appendix E*.

We also must help them think through the cause-and-effect consequences. We open teens' eyes to the stark realities through M³ Transformations' interactive, evidence-based *The Traps of a Trafficker©* youth program.[48] Not only have countless trafficking victims been prevented, but teens have been diverted off the path of becoming a trafficker. Thousands of youth also have disclosed trafficking through *The Traps*, resulting in multiple felony arrests and convictions of child sex traffickers. Why has this program been so wildly successful? A lot of reasons. We engage with them as individuals before we ever start talking about this topic. We take an interest in what they're interested in. We make it fun despite the subject matter. We lay out the facts in a way they can relate to. But above all, we are authentic. *That's* how you get and hold a teen's attention, helping them to not only think through real-life cause-and-effect but act accordingly. They crave authenticity.

They also crave kindness and compassion. I can't stress enough how many teens I trapped through a single act of kindness. You might be the only compassion they've ever had. Here's an example of how the smallest thing can make a huge difference. At the end of *The Traps*, we ask them to draw or write whatever they want to based on what they just heard. At the end of one of our *Traps* programs in a juvenile detention center, a boy drew a picture of Skittles and wrote, "Thank you. No one has ever given me anything like this before."

Sometimes something as simple as a bag of Skittles can give a teen hope.

## Two-Minute Introspection

What other ways can we help youth logically think through the cause-and-effect consequences of their actions before it is too late?

# 12 The Silence is Deafening

Lacy and I had a whirlwind romance with pimping and prostitution the following two weeks. We *thought* we were having fun. Keep in mind, I adored the heroin pimping afforded me, and she cherished the attention sex provided her. I kind of savored the acceptance of the older pimps myself. We'd have a little fun at the buyers' expense sometimes on the way home, too. We'd joke about the ones who smelled funny or had weird requests. You have to understand – our lives lacked adventure before that.

We went downtown nine or ten more times during those two weeks. We made money every time we went. A little more. A little less. Always good. That kept me inspired. Her haul in one night paid for my dope for a couple of days with pocket money left over. A stolen TV or snatched purse didn't stretch that far. Lacy stayed enthusiastic, too. I made sure of it. I always gave her a few bucks from what she made me so that she could buy a drink and chips on the way to school or a bag of weed for her and her girl-friends. That made her feel important.

When we didn't head downtown, we did what we always did. Went to school. Hung out at the bowling alley or the park. I'd spend time with Gabrielle and then head to Lacy's house. We'd smoke weed and have sex. Sometimes we'd go to the movies or grab fast food since we had a little petty cash at our disposal. We'd wonder who might be out that night on the track or at the bar. We'd talk about what they might be doing and how we missed interacting with them.

We never went shopping since that wasn't something we usually did. It didn't come naturally since we hadn't had much opportunity to shop for no reason. If you're not used to buying clothes and jewelry, the mall doesn't pop into your head when you get $100. If you're used to buying weed and having sex with your girlfriend or boyfriend, that's what you do. I didn't realize yet part of a pimp's job is buying his girls the right outfits. Lacy mixed up her look a little with what she had in her closet but kept her makeup and the wig the same. I kept wearing what I'd worn to school or the pool hall.

One night toward the end of our first two weeks, Lacy put on one of her usual outfits, and we jumped on the bus downtown. We did our regular thing there, too. She turned off to the track. I hung out at the bar, shooting the breeze with the more experienced pimps, and walked the track, keeping tabs on Lacy.

I went looking for her when it started getting late, as I normally did. I couldn't find her, so I headed back to the bar. I knew she'd work her way there when she got done.

The bar closed, and still no Lacy.

I didn't get nervous because she was a pro now. Some dude must have paid her for extra time, or maybe she'd landed a last-minute date. I waited around, anticipating how much money she'd adoringly slip into my hand. I didn't pay much attention when a green Cadillac Seville with Ohio plates pulled up. I recognized it. It belonged to Fly. I liked him. He was older, somewhere in his late 20s, and well-established. Fly and a couple of the other guys had taken me under their wings and taught me a few rules of the game. Fly had three girls, and they gave Lacy tips, too.

Fly hopped out. At least I'd have someone to talk to until Lacy showed up.

"Yo, Young P."

"Yo, Fly."

Then I saw her. Lacy. In the back seat between two of his girls. She wouldn't so much as look at me.

"Your girl chose, Young P," he stated as if it were the most natural thing in the world. "You understand this is how the game goes."

As a matter of fact, I didn't. I was too green. I guess that was insinuated in the "Young P" nickname you gave me, I thought. I wondered if he knew that was my girlfriend sitting in his backseat, avoiding my eye.

"I don't have to do this, but I'm going to give you a couple of dollars so that you can get on your way. I like you and know you're out here struggling."

Fly handed me a few bills, got back in the car without another word, and drove away. My girlfriend didn't bother to look back.

I stood there dazed a while before I headed to the taxi stand like an odds-on favorite football team stumbling off the field after losing the Super

Bowl in the final seconds. Somehow, victory had been snatched right out from underneath me.

Betrayal, abandonment, and confusion washed over me. They weren't new to me, but they always managed to catch me by surprise. That wasn't a prostitute sitting in his car. It was a girl who told me all the time how much she loved me and constantly wanted to have sex with me, even after a long night of sex with other men. How could she turn our adventure into a joy ride with some pimp she didn't know?

It seemed my friendship with the older pimps wasn't all I thought it was. "Young P" was more than a nod of acceptance. It was code for "we have your number." Their help ended up working against me. They were watching us without us having a clue. We had no idea we stood out, our inexperience dangling out there for all to see like a price tag you forget to remove. I might have been a pimp in my mind, young or not, but the older pimps were thinking, "She's coming down here getting money for this kid who doesn't know what he's doing."

We probably should have gone shopping, after all. I mimicked their be-havior, but I didn't mirror their appearance. It didn't slip past them that I wasn't showing up with new clothes and jewelry. We rode to the track on the train. Lacy wore the same old thing over and over on the track. They knew she pulled in the money, though, because they saw her jumping in and out of cars. So, one of them got her to jump in his. Grace period was over. Someone had to teach both of us the rules of the game. One lesson I needed to learn was how to take care of my girls.

I tried to call Lacy the next day, but she wouldn't take my calls. I left mes-sages with her mom. Each time, her mom reminded me that she knew I'd called.

The betrayal hung over me like a storm cloud. Why wouldn't she call me back? Had she forgotten so quickly that she loved me? Did it slip her mind she was my girlfriend? How could she leave me for some other pimp who she had never even met? It was our adventure. Not theirs.

On the bright side, I wasn't stressed about money. I had enough to keep me in dope for a few days. I beat myself up for getting too comfortable and not making her give me her money after every trick. I'd fallen into the habit of collecting it all at the end of the night. A rookie mistake. A costly one, for sure. He not only got my girl, but he also got all my money. I later learned it's called breaking a girl when a pimp collects money at intervals throughout the night. It's insurance to make sure nothing happens to his money like happened to mine. They could lose it, get robbed, choose another pimp as I'd so harshly learned, all kinds of scenarios not worth risking.

Oh, well. I still had crime to fall back on. After using up what I had left, I snatched a few more purses and broke into a house or two to support my habit.

Finally, Lacy called me. She'd been home all this time, she told me. She'd left the game – permanently.

She soothed my hurt pride as she explained what had happened. She didn't betray me. Unbeknownst to me, his girls had done more than give her a little advice here and there. They intentionally befriended her. They'd gained enough of her trust to talk her into hopping in his car. When the door closed behind her, he filled her in on another rule of the game we were clueless about: Girls don't talk to or look at another pimp. Not even a glance. They certainly didn't get in their car with them.

Tricked, plain and simple. Bamboozled. Both of us.

Fly took her to their hotel after they left me dejected in the bar parking lot. The next day, he bought her a new outfit. I guess he wanted to establish from the get-go how real pimps treat their girls. He pulled out all the finest pimp moves. They went out to eat. She hung out with his girls. They didn't let her out of their sight. He'd come by their room and check on them. At least he didn't have sex with her.

They got ready for work that evening, as usual. It was going to be her last night on the track, he informed Lacy. They were leaving town the next morning and taking her with them.

Lacy wasn't having any of that. She wasn't in this thing for it to be her life. She was just helping me out because she loved me, having a little fun in the process.

She caught one date and then caught a cab home with the money he paid her. Luckily, she had never told Fly's girls where she lived.

Relief flooded me as her story unfolded. She didn't betray me for him. I was so happy about that and so glad she called me that I didn't care when she told me through her tears she was done. Love or no love, she was not selling herself anymore for me or anyone else.

I respected her feelings. I got it. The experience had been way too traumatic for her. It taught her we didn't know what we were doing. The game turned out to be way bigger than us and not quite as fun as we thought. There were things out of our control, and she wasn't going to risk it.

For a split second, I didn't worry about my dope sickness. I momentarily forgot I didn't know how to experience emotions as gratitude washed over me that she had been smart enough to get away. I didn't cry or anything, but I was happy she decided not to go with him in pursuit of more adventure. I might not have loved Lacy, but I cared about her as much as a dope fiend could care about another human being. I sure wouldn't have done for her what she did for me, so I was thankful nothing happened to her because of it. I was proud of her, actually. He outsmarted me, but she outsmarted him. He only thought we were novices. My girl showed him.

The thought crossed my mind that I probably shouldn't have put her in a position to have to fend for herself against a skilled pimp twice her age. I felt a little remorse and managed a weak apology through my embarrassment.

My mortification at losing her and failure at being a pimp didn't have to keep us from having a boyfriend-girlfriend relationship, though. Sure, she was hurt and upset that I'd put her in danger, but she didn't blame me entirely … at that time. She took some of the responsibility. She figured we both made a dumb choice even if all the risk was on her.

The next time I saw her, we smoked a joint, had sex, and talked a little more about what happened that night. I knew she probably would've kept working for me if that hadn't happened, so any lingering emotions about betrayal and abandonment faded away.

I was bummed, though. Such easy, risk-free money, and it only lasted two weeks. I was the one at risk for jail now that I had fallen back into my breaking-and-entering ways.

The only person I could talk to about this unexpected turn of events was my Uncle Danny, my mom's brother. He owned a unisex beauty and barbershop. He cut the hair of a lot of pimps and their girls. When I first started pimping Lacy, I had to have someone to boast to, or I would have exploded on the inside. I had to hide it from regular people – one more thing to add to my unworthiness – but I knew he would understand since he liked the people from the life who frequented his shop. He wouldn't rat me out to my mom, either. I had swept his floor and ran errands for him when I was a kid, so we were tight.

I walked into his shop deflated and shared what had happened. He kind of chuckled since I had been in there a couple of times, bragging and boasting about how I was a big pimp seeing how I got my girlfriend to do tricks a few times.

I hung my head.

He chuckled again. This chuckle was different somehow. It wasn't a mocking chuckle. It was more like a knowing chuckle.

"Go get another one," he advised, shrugging off my defeatist attitude.

"What?"

"That's what you do when you're a pimp," he explained. Another rule I didn't know about. There sure were a lot of them.

"Yeah, you need to find someone you don't care about," he encouraged me.

I still didn't get what he was saying.

"That pimp didn't betray you at all," he went on patiently since he had a lot more insight into the game than me. "That's just how the game goes. If you care about someone, you don't put her on the street to have sex with other guys for money. How much could you really care? If you're going to have a girlfriend, you can't be a pimp. It's as simple as that. To have a girlfriend, you must involve your feelings. To be a pimp, you must have mind over heart. In that pimp's mind, she was a ho, not a girlfriend. You took her down there to jump in and out of cars and hand the money over to you, so she was open game for any pimp. The one who just happened to get her first was actually pretty cool for showing you some of the basics," he sided with him.

Not to mention giving me a few dollars to make sure I could get home. I felt pretty sure that wasn't part of the pimp rulebook.

"Besides, one of those tricks could have taken her somewhere and killed her, so how much could you really care?"

What? Was this another hidden rule? I didn't know tricks were allowed to be violent. I was just trying to feed my heroin addiction, not take on all this extra stuff.

"Look, Derek, it's like I said. That's just how the game goes. If you're going to pimp, you go get another one. One you don't care about. Every time you send a girl out there, she might not come back, so you can't have feelings."

Wow. There was a lot more to this than I realized. That must be one thick rulebook. I'd never thought about the bad, the ugly. I wasn't overconfident. I just had no idea. It was like riding a bike. You get on and peddle. You don't think about falling off.

It sunk in just how much danger I had put Lacy in. She could have woken up the next morning in Florida or Delaware. One of those buyers we ridiculed could have raped her or murdered her. It would have devastated me if something worse than getting in another pimp's car had happened to her.

No. I couldn't take that risk ever again. It wasn't worth it.

Uncle Danny was right. I had to find someone I didn't care about.

## Analysis With Dr. Deena Graves:
### Teens Prone To Putting Self In Danger

My uncle gave me the green light to pimp and didn't sugarcoat what it took. I had a choice to make. I either put myself or someone else in danger to support my habit. Drug addiction revolves around two core tenets: Feeding your selfishness and lack of empathy. Those tenets made someone else a better choice. My uncle's blessing gave me the okay to turn my heart off and take on the mind of a pimp.

It was time for me to get all the pimp rules down if I was going to turn what had been an adventure with my girlfriend into an ongoing means of supporting my addiction. I'd learned a hard lesson. When I send my girl out there with condoms I paid for, she might hand not only them but the money she made using them to some other pimp. Why would I put my feelings on the line for that kind of lack of loyalty? That doesn't deserve my emotions, I concluded. No. Even Lacy had shown a lack of loyalty in some ways. She betrayed me by getting in Fly's car in the first place. I had to justify such remorseless thinking to keep going down this path.

It's hard to know for sure now, but maybe if Lacy had had a bad date or Fly had driven out of town with her at 2 o'clock in the morning while I stood by and watched helplessly, I might have chosen a different path. I'll never know.

I do know, though, that the realization of what could have happened made Lacy choose a different path. It goes back to what we talked about in the last chapter. Neither of us could understand the long-term consequences of what we were doing because of the stage of our brain development. It was just fun to us. An adventure, like I said. A short-term consequence that thankfully didn't turn into an enduring stat opened Lacy's eyes. I chose to keep my eyes wide shut. The only consequence, short- or long-term, I could see was not being able to stick a needle in my arm every morning.

Despite how hard I had grown in my short 16 years, I believe that if we can help youth understand the harshness and dangers of this life, many will choose a different path, just like Lacy. I'm not just talking about prostitution. I'm talking about pimping, as well. Let us give you a concrete example. As we said in the last chapter, one of the primary goals of *The Traps of a Trafficker©* is to help youth logically think through the probable life-altering consequences of just one decision. How can one decision change their life forever? One fact it helps them understand is that many victims of child sex trafficking try to escape through suicide. Research is suggesting that almost 50 percent of victims attempt suicide because they don't know how else to get out, and they have a 40-percent higher mortality rate than the national average.[49]

During a *Traps* program with boys in a juvenile detention hall, a 14-year-old raised his hand and said he didn't believe that could be true. Deena was the speaker and assured him that suicide is a reality of trafficking. She kept going, and, a few minutes later, he raised his hand again and said, "Ma'am, are you sure? Are you sure they commit suicide?" She told him again, "Sadly, yes." She kept an eye on him for the rest of the program because he was visibly upset. Afterward, he asked if he could talk to her privately. Goal accomplished. Consequences were obviously on his mind. She could see it in his eyes and hear it in his voice.

He told her he had a friend at school who other students bullied. To try to become popular, she had sex with anyone who would have sex with her. The 14-year-old explained that he had been in and out of juvenile hall several times for drugs, but he had friends selling girls, and they had never been to juvie. Like me, he liked the idea of making himself detention-proof, so he went to his friend and told her he had a great idea.

Since she already had sex with multiple boys for free, what if they made a little money off it? He'd do all the work. All she had to do was show up and have sex with people, and they'd split the money.

She was in. They made good money, and all was well. Or, so he thought – just like I did with Lacy.

Right before he went into juvenile detention this time, she posted on social media that she wished she were dead. He worried about his friend and wondered what was wrong with her. He landed back in juvie before he could talk to her, though, so he felt there was nothing he could do.

Until he heard *The Traps*. He had no idea he played a significant role in her thoughts of suicide until someone helped him connect the cause-and-effect dots. Brain not fully developed. Cannot logically think through cause-and-effect – unless we help them understand the possible outcomes.

The good news is we helped him make the connection in time, in time to divert her off the suicide path and him off the path of career trafficker.

Like Lacy and me, this 14-year-old and his friend had never thought about the "what-ifs." When you're a teen, you don't think about things like, "What if that next guy is a serial killer?"

"What if a sadistic maniac decides to tie you up out in the woods naked and leave you to find your way back in the dark?"

Too late.

Neither traffickers nor their victims know anything about the buyers. They're jumping in the car or closing the door to a motel room with a total stranger who most likely has not given his full name – or even his real name. Is a little cash worth the risk? I didn't realize, and I'm sure this 14-year-old didn't understand, the extreme jeopardy we put girls we cared about in. Neither did the girls, and they were the ones who would pay the ultimate price.

Remember I said it was like Lacy and I were on an exciting adventure. Like going to Disney World. Those other two probably felt that way, as well. Adventure and risk-taking are wired into a teen's DNA. Their bio-logical, emotional intensity often leads to "impulsivity, moodiness, and extreme, sometimes unhelpful, reactivity."[50] Thus, they are prone to putting themselves in danger, escalating their chances of dying compared to a child by 200 percent.[51] As I illustrated with me, their emotions take control of their choices when they are pressured, especially by something tempting.[52] That wired-in increased responsiveness is driven by the aforementioned dopamine rush stimulated by rewards, including money, conversations, and adventure.[53] That's what all four of us found in trafficking in a nutshell.

Science says that teens might even understand negative consequences could be lurking in there somewhere, but they are more focused on what they think they will get out of an interaction or relationship, "gravitating toward thrilling experiences and exhilarating sensations." They act without thinking through what the negative consequences could mean.[54] If all four of us were honest with ourselves, I'm sure we'd agree we knew there were negative consequences on the other side of our decisions, but we brushed them off. Think of it as an arm-wrestling match between excitement in an otherwise dreary life and ...

And there's the problem. Their brains don't think through the "and." Think back to when you were a teenager. Did you always think through what came after the "and"?

Thank God for all four of us that it didn't turn from a "could be" to one more heart-wrenching news story that people felt remorse over, only to fade from memory with time. Tragically, that heart-wrenching news story is the reality for thousands of kids today because no one helped them learn how to logically think through the dangers.

I wonder how my story – and more than 150 others – might have been different if someone had helped me understand the far-reaching consequences.

## Two-Minute Introspection

With the teen years putting our kids at a 200-percent greater risk of dying because of unsafe or dangerous behavior, how can we help them understand the realities of playing with fire?

# 13

## The Thrill of the Ride

After I started snatching purses, I was always on the lookout for someone holding theirs a little too loosely. Once my friends taught me the art of breaking and entering, I unfailingly spotted the house easiest to force my way into. Now that I knew how to talk a girl into selling herself for me, I turned my eye to finding my next victim.

Uncle Danny helped me understand it was nothing more than the next hustle. Nothing more. Nothing less. It made sense to me. I had a hustle mentality, not a pimp mentality – thus far. I didn't even know the correct terminology – that I was targeting a girl to "turn out" into her first time in prostitution. I didn't care what they called it. I just wanted a girl to hop in enough cars to supply me with heroin for a few days, hopefully before I got arrested for one of my other hustles. I knew how to support my habit. Why should I risk my freedom, though, when I knew girls would happily risk theirs for me?

Gabrielle and Evelyn flickered across my mind, but I immediately ruled them out since I cared about them as girlfriends like Lacy. Besides, I knew their parents and shot dope with their brothers, so that somehow just didn't seem right. I still had a shred of conscience left, like I keep saying.

I started looking wherever I went. I sized up every girl who came across my path as possible new inventory. It didn't matter if I knew her or not. She was purely a viable replacement product for the one that went out of stock.

I checked out each girl who walked in the bowling alley while I shot pool.

"I wonder if she'll go," I'd cut my eyes up from my cue stick when I'd hear the door open. "Nah," I'd tell myself about each one. Most of them were from the neighborhood, so it could get back to my mom or sisters. The majority genuinely came to bowl at any rate. Those of us who hung out in the poolroom thought of ourselves as cool, but they viewed us as the bad boys. We understood they were the good girls. That made them hard to approach, even in the hopes of making them a girlfriend. I didn't kid myself. It would be practically impossible to convince one to let me take her downtown to sell herself for me. Why waste my time?

I looked at the park. That wasn't a good hunting ground, either. Since we lived across the street, most of the girls who hung out there knew my sisters. It decisively hindered my search living in a neighborhood where everyone not only knew everyone but usually their business, too. I could only pull off three girlfriends because they lived in three different neighborhoods. Evelyn lived in my hood, Mattapan. Gabrielle lived in on the Roxbury line, and Lacy resided in Dorchester.

I looked in the projects when I went to buy drugs. I knew those girls might be willing to try anything because they needed to support their habit as much as I needed to support mine. I mentally crossed them off as quickly as I thought of it. Drugs had taken their toll on most of them. They looked ravaged by their short lives. Besides, they were just as street savvy as me, if not more. They might take my condoms and then make off with the money they made to get high themselves. I shrugged. That's what I would do if I were a girl with a habit, so I couldn't blame them.

I had the same thought about every girl I saw: Could she be the one? It became second nature. Naturally, I'd think to myself that I might want to have sex with her before I took her for others to pay to have sex with her. Traffickers like to know how their product performs.

I looked at school, of course. As luck would have it, I had moved up that year into a new school, a school that had just transitioned from an all-girl school. They mixed in around 200 of us boys with roughly 800 girls. Quite the hunting ground.

The bowling alley wasn't the only place they considered me a bad boy. I proudly wore that label at school, too. Our group hung out in the hall, the principal's office, or in the bathroom, playing cards while the good kids went to class. I went to class just enough to pass. That wasn't too hard since I had transferred from Catholic school to an inner-city public school.

The principal and vice-principal tried to put a dent in our fun by rounding us up and sending us to class. It was like a game of hide-and-seek. They'd find us, and we'd find a new place to hide. The gym. The parking lot. The various boys' bathrooms. Finally, we got smart. Most of the girls went to class, so they didn't bother checking their bathrooms. We started sneaking into the second-floor girls' restroom to smoke weed and drink wine. A few girls skipped class, too, but they didn't mind sharing their space with us. The square girls would come in, do their business, and leave, not giving us the time of day. We were fine with that; we had fun with the girls who liked having us crammed in there with them.

One of my friends, Mona, hung out in the bathroom during classes, so we'd say a few words to each other. Her friend, Karen, followed closely behind her. She didn't talk too much, but I caught her staring at me *a lot*. In fact, she couldn't take her eyes off me. I noticed she laughed at all my overly loud, overly boisterous jokes, too. Yeah, she obviously liked me. I zeroed in, making it a point to toss a smile her direction and say little things to her.

Luck struck again. We ended up in a class together. I smiled at her more intimately, like old friends, as I grabbed the desk next to her. That's what hunters do. They circle their prey at every opportunity.

She smiled back. I knew the trap was loaded and set. Now it was time to spring it. I intensified my attack. I passed her little notes about questions in class.

"You know the answer?"

"No."

"Here you go," I slipped answers to her. Another benefit of Catholic school versus public school. I had the academic edge over most of my classmates. I could have excelled if I had wanted to. I'd lost my love for school, though. I think it drained out of me when the life did back at 10.

I talked to her more in the bathroom. She talked back. She smiled my way even more.

But never a full smile. She only let me see half her smile. She hid the side of her face covered in scars that looked like they'd been caused by a burn. She kept that side of her face covered with her hair or turned away when she talked to anyone besides her closest friends.

Low self-esteem. I might not have a pimp mentality yet, but even a novice knows that's a plus.

I built up enough relationship to ask her to meet me at the train station one day after school. I couldn't talk to her too much at school for fear people would warn her I was a bad boy. She already knew, and she hung out in the bathroom with kids who stayed in trouble, but I had made too much progress to take chances. I had to get her away from all other influences. I had to get her off by myself to lay on my full charm and find out what I needed to know. I didn't know what her family life was like, if she had a boyfriend, or was sexually active. Too many unknowns to keep investing time if it were a dead end. Later on, I started calling that the interview.

I still might not know the right words or rules, but I instinctively thought like a trafficker without realizing I was thinking like a trafficker. My father, the streets, taught me that much.

We grabbed a drink at a place near the train station and then headed to the projects to buy marijuana. That was an intentional move on my part, as well. A test, if you will. If she freaked out buying a little weed in the hood, she certainly wouldn't be able to handle the Combat Zone.

I learned enough on the walk to know I most likely had a product in the making. She freely told me she had a boyfriend she was sexually active with. No problem betraying him by meeting me behind his back, I noted. The fact he went to our school made that little tidbit even more insightful. If I had gone to the same school as one of my girlfriends, I knew without a doubt she'd be waiting for me after school. I asked Karen who her boyfriend was. I didn't want to keep going if he happened to be one of my friends. Thankfully not.

She also confirmed what I already knew. Always nice to stroke your over-inflated ego, though. She thought I was cute, funny, and liked me.

I didn't tell her anything about me. Instead, I kept her talking about herself as I walked her back to my house to have sex. Another trafficker trick that came naturally to me. Deflect attention from yourself while learning all you can about them.

I walked her to catch the bus home before my mom or sisters returned. I didn't have to dip into my money to buy her a bus ticket. She got an allowance, enough to buy a bus ticket and her lunch at school. She didn't need the money. I could tell she liked the attention, though.

Not bad for a couple hours of work.

I smiled on the way home; she liked me. I liked her, too. How could I not? She was pretty, fun, and easy to talk to. I enjoyed sex with her a lot. I smiled to myself again.

Wait. What was I thinking? Uncle Danny's words came rushing back. I have bad intentions for her, I reminded myself. I can't *like* her. But I did like her. I had a choice to make. This was a fork-in-the-road moment. My decision would take my life in one of two directions. One, I could run with those warm feelings washing over me a couple of minutes before. Two, I could rein them in so I could send her out there without worrying about what happened to her. I knew the average teen boy would jump on her as a girlfriend. We'd been looking at each other for a couple of weeks. I'd finally made my move. She didn't shoot me down. We had a good time. I scored. My thoughts bounced back and forth. I wouldn't mind her as a girlfriend.

But I wasn't an average teen boy, I reminded myself. I was a wannabe pimp. Young P. A full-fledged trafficker in the making just like she was a product in the making.

Still, I really liked her. Then my first love flashed across my mind – Heroin. That put an end to my mental acrobats. The desire to make her a girlfriend didn't hold a chance against the pull to make her a supporter of my habit.

With my path settled, I called her to let her know I had fun and would see her at school the next day. It all was part of the game. Only I didn't know what game I was playing yet. I knew I wanted to keep that slight rift I had created between her and her boyfriend growing, though. Every step was intentional. After all, I'd been out of product for about a month and a half now. It was time to restock.

I hung up and headed to Lacy's.

Karen and I didn't speak about our time together in front of people at school the next day. We talked casually in the bathroom and class. We met up again after school for sex.

I told her a little about me this time. Not much. Just enough to make her think I cared. And I definitely cared, especially after what she told me that day. Her stepfather had sexually abused her. The shame stoked her shyness. He didn't live with them anymore but would come by and fondle her or sexually abuse her from time to time. I guess her mom didn't know what he was doing to her because she cared about her. She'd check out her report card, kept Karen on a strict curfew, and didn't let her freely roam the streets, so I knew she cared.

I learned that the abuse killed any real emotions Karen had connected to sex. Her stepdad drained that out of her the first time he climbed on top of her. All her self-esteem oozed out with it. She believed the only reason any guy looked at her was for sex, so she did it to please them. It made her feel wanted, like she had a *little* value at least.

It was like a birthday present wrapped up in a beautiful package with a big, shiny bow. The perfect opening to build up to asking her to sell herself for me.

"I understand how abuse feels, Baby," I comforted her. "I abuse myself." I made my addiction sound equivalent to what her stepdad forced on her.

"Wow. I never would have thought that." I could hear her heart breaking for me.

"Yeah. The clown you see is the same as how you get shy. It's me covering up how I really feel about myself." I went straight in for the kill. Her sympathy landed in my hands, and I clasped my fists around it.

I didn't hand her any of my sympathy. None. If I allowed myself to feel sorry for her, I would have to worry about her well-being, I reminded myself. How could I ask her to flag down cars if I let that happen? I made that mistake with Lacy. I wouldn't do that again. No, it affected me too much when I saw her pull up in Fly's car. The whole reason I hunted Karen down was so she could climb in tricks' cars instead of me climbing through people's windows.

I pried any lingering empathy, sympathy, and feelings off my heart for a final time and packed them away for the next 32 years.

I kept practicing my embryonic pimping skills on her by intentionally investing in *her* emotions. I spent time with her over the next five or six days, talking, getting high, and plying her with sex – the things she would expect from a boyfriend who cared about her. The things a manipulator who didn't care about her would do.

After a few days of building relationship, I opened up to her about Lacy. No, not that Lacy was my girlfriend. She didn't need to know that. Just that I had a friend who was a girl who went downtown with me for a couple of weeks to help me out with that abusive habit.

"Wow. Really? Did y'all make money?" I could see the intrigue on her face.

"Oh yeah, Baby," I assured her. "We made a lot of money. Being addicted to heroin is expensive. I get sick without it, so I have to find ways to come up with good money. Those days you don't see me in school, it's because I'm so sick. I have to go out and do crime to get more. I can't be sitting in class with you because I'd be throwing up everywhere. I don't want you to have to see that." I poured it on thick.

She bought it: "Aww. Really? I noticed you don't come to school a lot, but you always know the answers and make good grades. I can't believe you can do that when you're high." She was genuinely impressed when she realized I had passed her all those answer-filled notes jacked up on heroin.

I had her just where I wanted her. Well, maybe. One more test. I told her what had happened with Lacy and Fly. I sure didn't want to go to all the trouble and expense of taking Karen downtown with my condoms and instructions just to have her come back in some other pimp's car.

Her heart went out for me a little further. Sometimes I surprised myself at what a masterful manipulator I was.

I had her reeled in enough now that I felt sure I could take it to the next level. I'd timed everything perfectly. I hadn't wanted to run her off by just throwing my question out there too soon: "Hey, this is what I do. Are you down or not?" No. That would scare her off. Honestly, I might be masterful in my mind, but I wasn't that savvy yet. I stumbled all over my words and drug the conversation about Lacy out over three days because I was such an amateur, not to mention nervous. Lacy had a reason – the unwritten code – to do it for me. Karen had no such distorted "obligation."

The more details I dribbled out there, the more curiosity and fascination took over her face. I felt confident when I finally threw the idea out: "You should come down with me sometime, and I'll show you what I'm talking about." I dangled it out there like a carrot in front of a horse.

Like a horse chasing a carrot, she agreed. "Okay."

Almost too easy. But I have to admit, my charm alone didn't convince her. All the movies and songs and stuff made it enticing: Might as well see how it works. People use me for sex anyway, so how bad could it be? Who knows? Maybe I'll make enough that I won't ever have to worry about someone hurting me again. That's a typical thought pattern when predators have stripped you of all your self-worth. The scars on her face didn't hurt my case, either.

We made plans to go the next night. We had to work out a few more details than I did with Lacy since Karen's mom wasn't always sleeping off a bender. We decided she should go straight home after school to do homework rather than coming to my house for sex. She'd sneak out when her mom fell asleep.

She caught the bus and met me at the train station right on time. I never felt any hesitation from her, just like I didn't from Lacy. A few jitters like Lacy, but who wouldn't have a few butterflies their first time?

We took the train downtown, smoking a little weed on the way.

I could see her excitement building as we walked around. She'd never seen downtown Boston by night. She'd been shopping in the daytime with her mom and to see movies with her friends on the weekend, but she had no idea what it transformed into at night. It mutated from a relatively family-friendly area, as much as you could find in the inner city, into the Combat Zone with flashing neon signs lulling guys into strip clubs and bars, drug dealers making deals on the streets, and prostitution as the most prominent tourist attraction. It was like pulling back the curtain and seeing the Wizard of Oz for the first time. A sense of shock and awe all at once.

"Yep. Huh-uh." I fed her astonishment at every opportunity, showing her everything I could think of that I'd learned from Lacy and the knowledgeable pimps.

Speaking of the experienced pimps, I walked her past the Sugar Shack to stroke my ego a little more.

"What's up, man?" I yelled to the pimps hanging out in their usual spot.

"Hey, Young, P." Check. I could tell she was impressed they knew me.

I pointed out the girls standing in doorways and jumping in and out of cars: "See, they're working."

"Wow. That was fast," she noticed when one girl came back 15 minutes after driving away.

"Yeah, she probably just did a quick blow job and pulled in 25 bucks." I acted like I was sure of what I was talking about.

"Wow," she repeated.

"Why are they running?" she asked about a group of girls moving down the street quickly. I pointed out the undercover cop car. "He's going to make them move or harass them, so they move before he can get to them."

We walked to King of Pizza across from the train station after a couple of hours. We sat in there and talked and watched for another hour. She asked lots of questions. I could tell she was even more interested in trying it out than I was in her trying it out. So, I threw it out there. Nothing to lose except my time and the cost of the train tickets, a couple of slices of pizza, and two drinks.

"That's what I did with that other girl I told you about," I tilted my head out toward the Combat Zone. "You want to try it? We get money," I added as an extra incentive. I might be wrong, but I don't think she knew what I was up to until I said the words.

Either way, she jumped right on it. "Sure." Not even a slight lull. She didn't pause before asking more questions. That didn't surprise me since, just like Lacy, she didn't think too much of herself. They didn't think too much of people taking sex from them, either. They just didn't realize everything else they took with it.

"What about the other girl? How'd she do it?" she was ready to take mental notes.

"The same thing you saw. Someone stops. You ask them what they want. Get the money. Always make sure you get the money first (I wanted her to be clear on that). Get in the car. Go do it. Come back. Easy as that."

It was like she was looking down my throat for the next words to come out. I had done an outstanding job of selling it. As we established, she didn't need the money like I did, or Lacy did. She wasn't rich, but she wasn't deprived like us. At least for money. Nothing in her life gave her purpose, though. This looked and sounded like fun. When you have no excitement, sometimes even running down the street from police can seem like an adventure. You explain it just right, and it fuels their intrigue. I knew how to stoke the intrigue.

We laughed and joked and kept strategizing on the train ride back. Just wear something cute, I explained. I didn't need to tell her what to do with her hair or makeup. She had good hair and knew how to fix herself up.

"Where do I take him if I get in the car with one?" she asked. I had no idea. I'd never thought to ask Lacy that. "Don't worry. He'll know where to take you," I faked it. All I knew to tell her was to make sure she kept her door unlocked in case she needed to jump out quickly. That didn't scare her. She was from the hood, after all.

It's funny. I was a little scared, even if she wasn't. Maybe nervous is a better word. More nervous than I was with Lacy. I didn't care about her, but I did care about me. I didn't know for sure if it was a good thing or bad thing that she was so willing. I hadn't known her long. How much did I actually know about her? Lacy was my girlfriend. She loved me. That meant she'd be loyal if anything happened. I didn't have a clue what Karen would do if the police grabbed her or a trick did something to her. Would she rat me out to law enforcement or give a trick my name?

Her family had a little more, too, so she wasn't quite as street smart as Lacy. Could she figure out how to get away like Lacy did? If someone said, "What you doing, Little Girl?" would she start screaming, "He made me do it"? Those kinds of thoughts danced around my head. None did about her well-being.

I was kind of putting myself out there a little bit, I worried.

I shook off the nerves and thought about how I could protect myself. "Don't make friends with the other girls," I warned her as if that could be dangerous for her. I didn't want to risk losing more condoms or money after Fly and his girls outwitted us. I might have been gullible but not stupid.

I made sure she knew not to walk with the crowd if someone saw police coming. "Walk the other direction," I emphasized.

I gave her a few more rules to minimize my risk before we made it back to the train station.

She jumped on a bus home, and I started walking to my house. I felt the excitement overtaking any lingering nervousness. I could hear my uncle saying, "Go get someone you don't care about." Indeed, he'd be proud of me. If she didn't come back from a trick, I thought, I'd just go to school the next day like nothing. I'd give it a couple of days and find someone else like I found her. This was all about the money. With Lacy, it was an "us" thing. With Karen, it was a "me" thing.

I nodded in approval: I'm finally living up to the name "Young P."

## Analysis With Dr. Deena Graves:
### Sex Buyer Violence

Looking at Karen's face as we walked around the Combat Zone that night was like watching someone thinking about riding a roller coaster for the first time as they peered up at its towering drops and sharp turns. They might be scared, but they want to try it, even if it's just once. The thrill of the ride outweighs the mechanics of it all. Traffickers prey upon that. All those other people are getting off the roller coaster okay. Some of them even run right back and hop in line again. Can't be too bad. All those girls look okay when they step out of one car and go straight to the next. "See, Baby. It's nothing at all. A few minutes for a lot of money."

They don't stop to think about what happens if the roller coaster gets stuck at the top and they have to crawl down the side, or the safety bar flies up as they race down a curvy hill and they fly out. It's all an adventure until that happens. For many hopeless teens, trafficking can look as exciting as a roller coaster when they've never ridden one – adventure, fast money, clothes, travel. They don't think about the operator, or the trafficker, getting them halfway up or halfway across the country and then leaving them on the track alone. They have to figure out how to rescue themselves while he moves on to the next ride. Or the car flies off, and they land in juvie. He fixes up the car, fills it with more girls, and never looks back.

Many hopeless kids look at trafficking as a grand adventure, like following the Yellow Brick Road and meeting all the interesting characters along the way. They don't know that, like the Tin Man, most traffickers and buyers don't have a heart. You'll see what a trafficker is capable of as my story unfolds. Let's talk now about buyers. They can be just as maniacal, if not more, as traffickers.

Research studies have found many sex buyers are inhumane and hostile to those they pay to have sex with. They often could care less if the person, including children, clearly does not want to perform a sex act. One buyer compared it to a delicatessen where you order up what you want. Let us translate. Think of it like going into a deli and picking out your bread, meat, cheese, and veggies. You don't think about whether the person making the sandwich likes those things or not. Doesn't matter. You're just there to fill your craving. The manager, or the pimp, decides what's on the menu and how much to charge.

Buyers routinely view people in prostitution *fundamentally* differently, with significantly less empathy for them. They justify their actions and desire for domination by shoving them into a lower class of humans – or non-humans – based on the fact they are in prostitution. Consider how they bragged in the research studies. The following quotes are exactly as they wrote them.

- "I treat them like they're just another dog in my backyard. It's fun to watch."
- "You know that prostitution thing. It's like a cup of coffee. When you're done with it, you just toss it out."
- "Even us normal guys want to say something and have it done no questions asked."
- "You can find a ho for any type of need, slapping, choking, aggressive sex."
- "Unquestionable obedience. I mean that's powerful. Power is like a drug. The minute you walk in the door you are the lord and master until the minute you walk out the door."
- "I can tell her to shut up. She's just there to serve and that's it."
- "They submit to me. Whatever I want to do, they do. Mentally it makes you superior."[55,56]

That's only a slight taste of what buyers have to say. It's a lot to wrap our mind around the fact people can do that to our children, so we'll unpack it slowly. For now, just consider that all Karen saw and heard was what I wanted her to. I showed her the thrill of the ride without any of the "malfunctions." If someone had shown her one of those quotes, perhaps she wouldn't have gone along for the ride with me.

Of course, I didn't understand all the "malfunctions," either at that point. Perhaps, despite my heavy dope addiction, if someone had helped me understand right then and there, I wouldn't have taken so many girls on a ride. I'll repeat it one more time: I still had a sliver of a conscience. But it was evaporating quickly.

## Two-Minute Introspection

We often hesitate to expose youth to the truth of what something such as trafficking can truly entail despite how it's glamorized. How do we balance the reality of what teens face at the hands of a savvy predator with protecting them from the trauma of hearing about it?

# 14 Occupational Hazard

Karen and I played it cool at school again the next day. We didn't say a word to each other about the night before. We could tell in each other's eyes, though. We had bonded over the underworld I exposed her too, just like I bonded with the "role models" who showed me the ways of the streets. We both thought we'd found someone to make the pain go away.

I didn't tell Karen, but the anticipation of selling her far eclipsed the high hopes I'd felt with Lacy. She had qualities, a look, that set her apart. She obviously had enough money for a little nicer clothes, and I could tell a shop did her hair.

She savored the idea of trying it out, while Lacy did it out of that sense of obligation for the guy she loved. I could hear the raw anticipation in Karen's voice the night before. It sounded almost like, "I'm finally going to get something out of what people have done to me." Lacy chose who she slept with. Karen's stepdad robbed her of that choice.

Plus, I had more of a joint venture with Lacy. I established myself with Karen as a sole proprietorship. Sure, I'd give her a few dollars like I did Lacy. I did that with all my hustles. Like when I stole the typewriters with Robert. We split the proceeds. Well, I guess this hustle was different from anything I'd done before. I sure wasn't giving her half. She wasn't my partner in crime like Robert. She simply made money for me. I was still getting used to a pimp mentality, so I had to wrestle through how every-thing worked.

I quizzed her as I had Lacy on the train ride downtown. Except I tested Lacy on what she had taught me. I acted like I was the source with Karen. She didn't need to know where I got my information from.

"Are you nervous?" I needed to know what to expect when we stepped off the train.

"A little bit." Understandable. She'd had multiple sex partners, including unwanted ones, but she'd never had sex with a stranger. Or for money. I went over the safety precautions again. I emphasized watching where they took her.

"If they try to jump on the highway, you jump out. They'll take you to back alleys, parking lots, motels. That's okay. Don't let them take you too far, though. Not the highway."

I reminded her that she needed to maintain as much control as possible. She'd lose that on the highway. I pointed out that she could always hop out at a red light if she ever felt unsafe. No need to worry her with the reality she didn't really have much control of where he drove to.

"I'm good." She wanted to reassure me.

I'd done my job well: It escaped her that it wasn't her I worried about. It was the money she'd owe me for getting in that car. I held my head higher. Fly could take my girl, but he couldn't take my game. It hadn't taken me long to recover from his scheme. Here I was on the train, taking another girl down there to get me some money.

And this time, I didn't have those pesky emotions in the mix. Sure, it probably would bruise my ego if Karen came back in another pimp's car. I could swallow it a lot better without my feelings sitting inside the car with her, though, especially since I now understood that's how you play the game.

As we walked toward the track, I reminded her how much to charge for a blow job or sex in the car. Motels cost more, I emphasized.

"Be careful. I'll be standing in front of the bar. In a little bit, I'll walk around to see if you're okay. If you get a date, have him drop you off where he picked you up." No more rookie mistakes with my girl stepping out of a trick's car at the bar with all the other pimps watching.

I swatted away the fact I still didn't know what I was doing and walked to the bar to get my ego stroked.

"You back, Young P?"

"You got your girl back." It wasn't a question but an assumption. "I heard you got knocked." Knocked meant your girl chose another pimp. Only a few minutes in, and they punctured my overinflated ego. No need to have it completely deflated. They didn't need to know Lacy was my girlfriend, or Fly tricked us both. That'd be two more strikes.

"Yeah. He had her for a day, but she left him," I puffed up my chest. "She's not down anymore. I got me some new work." That's like a stripe, a trophy, if you will. Two, actually. Lacy left Fly. Stripe one. I got right back in with "fresh work." Stripe two. Not bad for a rookie.

I kicked it with them for about 45 minutes before heading to the track to check on Karen. Checking on her so early in the night *was* a rookie thing. Some of the experienced pimps *never* went to the track. Others waited several hours in. Mostly they'd drink in the bar, walk outside to smoke some weed, maybe do a few cocaine deals.

But I wasn't an experienced pimp. I wasn't even a real pimp in my way of thinking. I was a junkie eager to find out if I had money for the next morning. I spotted Karen standing around with some of the other girls. I walked past her.

"Come here," I motioned in my most resounding pimp voice.

She walked over. "You all right?" I feigned concern for her.

"Yeah, I made $25! You were right; he knew where to go." She handed me the money proudly, enthusiastically. I could see the sense of achievement in her eyes.

"Did you remember to use a rubber?" It was only a blow job, but it cost them more to forgo a condom.

"Yep."

I could tell she was anxious to get back out there, so I walked away non-chalantly but secretly elated. Wow. An hour in, and she'd already broke luck (had her first date of the night). I patted myself on the back for choosing her. If she didn't do anything else that night, it had been a successful adventure – for both of us.

The rest of her short night proved uneventful but productive. She racked up multiple dates, pulling in as much money as Lacy did on her first successful night in half the time. We didn't want to push it by staying there too long. Karen's mom wasn't out cold drunk. She could wake up and notice Karen's empty bed. We left in time to catch the train home, so I saved taxi money. What a night. I had a natural on my hands.

She chattered the whole way home about going back the next night. Her enthusiasm far overshadowed the sense of adventure that kept Lacy going back for those two weeks. She driveled on about the men who had bought her, what'd she'd do differently, what she'd wear back. Instead of a regular top with her miniskirt, she'd wear a halter top, she told me eagerly. I was exhausted and thinking about my dope run in the morning but acted like I cared.

We worked the Combat Zone around 10 times over the next couple of weeks, just like Lacy and I did. We also went to the movies, had sex ourselves, and ventured downtown one night to have pizza without working.

I made sure to take her shopping for an outfit, too. I didn't want to make that beginner mistake again. I had to do what pimps do to keep my girl from hopping in another pimp's car. They take their hos to buy an outfit and get something nice for themselves, too. I proudly bought myself a pair of new jeans and shoes. It was the first time I put any of the money I got from the game back into the game outside of condoms and transportation costs. Yeah. This is what pimps do. I smiled haughtily. I'm big pimping now. I'm also a successful businessman, I concluded, reinvesting my profits into the organization. I celebrated my new level of success.

The other pimps didn't seem to understand how far I'd come in such a short time. My new jeans and kicks didn't impress them. Honestly, they didn't even notice them.

No matter. Everything was going smoothly, so I undoubtedly was successful. Smooth and success equated heroin, so I didn't care too much what they thought anyway. I just liked the attention. My girl stayed loyal to me, too. She heeded my warning not to get too friendly with the other girls. I didn't realize that would draw more attention from other pimps. It came too naturally to her; she looked like a pro in their eyes. They'd speak to her when they walked or drove by in a fruitless effort to get her to choose. She ignored them and walked on by. I understood the pimp motto now: "They come to pay, not come to stay," so it wouldn't have fazed me too much if she had chosen. It would slow me down for a few days, but I knew now I could smooth talk another girl into it. Despite my mind already thinking about my next victim, I still didn't see myself as a career pimp.

After all, I shared my profits with her. I gave Karen about the same amount of money that I gave Lacy. I also bore the expense of our weed for school. I'd slip her a bag to share with her friends. We kept chill at school, though, not talking too much. I didn't want to draw attention to our relationship. She still had her boyfriend, and I had a reputation I didn't want to tarnish. I might of been a bad boy, but people liked me at school and around the neighborhood. They called me "Little Derek" and laughed at my jokes. It might have been the hood, but, even there, people looked down on pimps and junkies. I had a lot to hide.

I needed to share my latest conquest with someone, so I headed back to Uncle Danny's shop.

"How are things going? I haven't seen you in a while," he greeted me when I strutted in.

"Yeah, I got another one. Got one from school." I might as well of been talking about a notepad or pencil for how routine it sounded.

He let out his usual chuckle. It wasn't necessarily that he approved of what I was doing. It's just what teen boys do in the inner city. Why fight a losing battle? I don't think he saw me as a career pimp. Just his young nephew trying to be something he wasn't. He looked at it as a phase I was going through, trying to emulate what I'd heard in movies and songs.

"She's not my girlfriend," I threw in for his approval. "She has a boyfriend." That'd wow him.

He laughed again.

He wouldn't have found all this so amusing if he had known it wasn't a phase. It was a life-threatening, no-mercy, hardcore drug addiction. And, I wasn't its only victim.

Lacy loved me. Karen loved the thought of helping me out with the sickness brought on by my addiction. Neither they nor I thought about the cost to them. We had fun together, so we thought, while we raked in the money.

No one else noticed the cost to any of us, either. Alcohol made Lacy's mom clueless. Karen's boyfriend and mom missed all the signs. Other than Uncle Danny, my family stayed too busy to worry about what I was up to. I'm not sure what made the other adults in our lives fail to notice. Pimping and prostitution, not to mention heroin, change you. Markedly. I'll say it again. Someone should have picked up on all the red flags in our lives, especially our spiraling demeanors.

But no one did. The adults in our lives missed it day after day, so I put Karen's life at risk night after night. She had plenty of opportunity to get hurt, too. I had created a consumer favorite. Every time we went downtown, she broke luck by the time I'd hit the track the first time to check on her. She had to look ravaged by the physical, psychological, and emotional consequences of a string of faceless men. I guess she was faceless, too.

One night, she handed me a fist full of money, as usual, the first time I ran into her on the track. The next time I went to check on her, I couldn't find her. I walked back to the Sugar Shack to wait for her date to end so that I could collect her latest earnings. I didn't have to go looking for her, though. Before long, she came running up to me crying. I hurried her away from the other pimps before asking if she was okay.

"Yeah. No. Not really," she got out between sobs.

"What's going on, Baby?" I wasn't sure what else to say. I had no idea what was going on. This had never happened before with her or Lacy.

Her story came tumbling out. A date paid her $100 for sex in his car. He acted fine during the sex, but, when they finished, he demanded his money back. She refused to hand it over and started to jump out. He grabbed her, slapped her around, and snatched the cash before he shoved her out and sped away.

I didn't understand all the implications, but I knew he raped her and smacked her. He damaged my product; I hoped he didn't bruise her. That'd be a hard sell.

She was distraught, but I still had no idea what to do.

"Okay. Let's get out of here," I finally mustered. I got a closer look once we hopped on the train. No bruises. That was good.

"My face hurts. It's burning."

"Where?" I still didn't know what to say or do, especially since I couldn't see anything resembling a burn.

"He slapped me right here," she pointed out the redness.

I saw a little swelling but breathed a sigh of relief. It wasn't enough for her mom to notice. I could tell she was more traumatized and afraid than hurt.

She never apologized for losing the money, but she was upset, so I let it slide. I apologized to her, not just to keep her going, though. I felt a prick from that ever-shrinking morsel of conscience. It still popped up occasion-ally but just for a second. Like one of those Whac-A-Moles. It was gone as fast as it appeared. Besides, I still didn't know what to say. I knew Uncle Danny had said a buyer could hurt them, but I didn't believe it would really happen to me. Therefore, I never thought about what I would do in this situation. I didn't know what to make of it. Things had been going too well.

As I consoled her, she kept repeating, "I'm never going back down there again. I'm never going back down there again. I'm never going back down there again." Her words sounded robotic, catatonic even.

"Okay. This might be over with for her." I seethed at the unknown buyer who had messed up another girl for me.

"Maybe not, though," I consoled myself. "There's still hope once she calms down."

Her tears dried up by the time we got off the train, and I put her on the bus home. Sure, she was shaken, visibly so, but we were in our territory now. In the inner city, you do what you need to do. She needed to get on the bus by herself and get home. I'd shown her a little pity, and she wasn't the only one traumatized by that trick.

"Wow. I'm probably feeling just as bad as her," I told myself.

I gave the feelings trying to well up in me the cold shoulder. Fly hadn't derailed my game, and neither would some nameless, underhanded trick. I merely had to figure out what had just happened. I knew I'd go back down there again. Maybe with Karen. Maybe with someone different. Heroin depended on me.

We didn't talk about it at school the next day except for her assuring me she was fine. She was not only okay, but she was also very friendly. Like normal. She didn't blame me. It wasn't like I put her in that situation in her mind. The fruit of a master manipulator.

Nevertheless, she didn't change her mind about not going back downtown. We had sex a couple more times. I wasn't looking for a girlfriend, though, and since she didn't want to be a ho, our relationship fizzled out as quickly as it started.

I felt like an utter failure. As much as I thought about what went wrong, I couldn't figure out what I could have done differently to protect my investment. I needed expert advice. Not my uncle this time. This was too big for him. He only had second-hand information. I needed a true expert to help me navigate something I didn't know how to get control over. How could I be responsible for what tricks did once they pulled away with the product I sold them? That'd be like trying to control what someone did with a piece of meat they bought at the butcher shop. They decide if they tenderize it or char it.

I needed to go straight to the source.

I headed to the Combat Zone to talk to the experienced pimps. I grabbed a slice of pizza when I got off the train. Comfort food. Surely this had to have happened to at least one of them at some point. Maybe not. Maybe I was just so green that people saw they could take advantage of me. Hopefully, they could give me at least a few pointers.

"Yo. What's up, Young P?"

"This is what happened to my girl. Now she won't come back down."

They didn't seem troubled by my story, to my surprise.

"What? Bad date? That's nothing more than an occupational hazard. They're jumping in and out of strangers' cars. It's going to happen."

Occupational hazard. I would never have thought of that.

I was too busy being a hazard to the occupation.

"Yo, Young P. You can't be taking her home. She's never gonna come back down now. You make that bitch wash her face, dry her eyes, and get back to work."

Another infantile pimp mistake. I could see it clearly once they said it. It's like riding that bike we talked about. You fall off; you get right back on. I should have picked Karen up, dusted her off, and put her back on the bike – or in a trick's car. Now she'd never ride a bike again. Another costly amateur blunder. Would I ever get this all down?

They had a little fun at my expense, but they taught me a lot about the business side of pimping that night. Say a cop offers your girl an exchange: Sex for not going to jail, for example.

"Your girl just has to do it and get back to work."

"You look at it like you saved yourself some money," they enlightened me.

"She puts out a blow job that costs you nothing but a little lost time. But you keep the cost of bailing her out of jail in your pocket." I understood the math.

If she gets beaten up, you help her understand she's happy that's all he did to her. She walked away with her life.

Yeah, that made sense, too. Occupational hazard. That's it. Whatever happens to them is no different from me cutting my hand climbing through a broken window to steal a TV.

That must have been what it felt like when the Grinch's heart shrunk a few more sizes.

## Analysis With Dr. Deena Graves:
### Sex Buyer Reviews

Let us caution you. The quotes from buyers in the last chapter, as hard to read as they were, are nothing compared to what you will read in this section. They will help you process the pimps shrugging off what happened to Karen. That was gentle compared to some of the things buyers do. Words such as "prostitution," "john," "trick," "date," or even "child sex trafficking" and "Commercial Sexual Exploitation of Children" glaze over the torment our children live in the arms of traffickers and buyers.

Prepare yourself before you continue and take care of yourself after you do. Take a break after reading it. Go on a walk, journal your feelings, process it with someone. It is hard to wrap your head around what they intentionally do to our children. But they do. We need to understand the depths of what our children truly live if we want to help them. Without understanding it, it's like trying to fix a car without any clue about what makes it run.

Once "hobbyists," or frequent buyers, finish with one of their victims, they often write a review similar to reviewing a product on Yelp or Amazon Prime. Only instead of rating them on a scale of one to five with stars, they rate them with things like bananas. The next consumer knows what he'll get based on the review. Let's say a man on a business trip to Boston wants to buy a 13-year-old who performs fetishes. He reads through the reviews to find precisely how good the child is at what he's looking for.

Just like a Yelp review, buyers can also add open-ended comments to detail their experiences – or, in this case, their conquest and the torment they inflicted. Here are a few examples of how buyers talk about our children and their other victims. Again, these quotes are exactly as written.

- *"Very young."*
- *"I was almost 50 years older than her."*
- *"One of a kind young lady who almost reminds me of a young sister who provides pleasure in a fun way."*
- *"Deep and fast with gagging and DT (deep throat)."*
- *"She started out surprisingly firm for her size. Had to slow down a bit because she got sensitive."*
- *"... took everything I threw at her."*
- *"... I took her to my back room and tried her out on my newly built sex pedestal."*
- *"She assumed the submissive position on her knees."*
- *"Little, easy to toss around...and enjoys every minute."*
- *"A thick soft lil' body made for tossing about and punishing from behind her best quality I'd say were her lifeless eyes."*
- *"Until my whole fist was in her. Man she loved that."*

We spend a lot of time talking about traffickers in child sex trafficking trainings and awareness programs, as we should. However, we neglect to talk about the buyers too much. When people toss our children around, punish them from behind, or intentionally ram their entire fist inside them and then brag about how much they loved it, the conversation becomes urgent. This is Dr. Graves, and I don't know about you, but I don't know any child who wants that kind of diabolical abuse, no matter how much a buyer wants to try to convince himself.

It's no wonder all the life drains out of their eyes. That pay-per-rapist gleefully described that as her best quality. They have about as much remorse as the cold-hearted traffickers. I'd say they deserve at least as much training time devoted to them.

Derek interacted with thousands of buyers. Here's his take on the difference between traffickers and buyers: Let me be perfectly clear with you from the perspective of a former 32-year trafficker, a ruthless one. I didn't care **anything at all** about the girls who followed in the footsteps of Lacy and Karen. The men who paid me to rape them cared **even less**.

Go back to the buyer's quote in the last chapter before you challenge me: *"You know that prostitution thing. It's like a cup of coffee. When you're done with it, you just toss it out."*

A buyer views someone in prostitution as a ***disposable*** product. A trafficker sees them as a ***reusable*** commodity. Get the picture? A trafficker treats them a little better because they have an investment in them. Think about how you treat your car versus a rental car, for instance. You keep it tuned up, change the oil, avoid all the potholes. Compare that to a rental car. Are you quite as careful when you spot a hole in the road? Do you pick your gas station as cautiously, or is the watered-down gas plenty good enough?

The buyer hands over what he considers hard-earned money for 15, 20 minutes, maybe an hour. He probably won't ever see her again unless she's a favorite. If he rips her open or leaves a few choke marks around her throat, it's someone else's problem to deal with. The person selling her is responsible for the maintenance and upkeep at the end of the day – or the long, destructive night.

## Two-Minute Introspection

What root issue, if solved, could make the most difference in ending the demand for sex with our children?

# 15 Creature of a (Drug) Habit

Karen spoiled me to life as I knew it before her. Not really Karen. The money she raked in night after night. I blew through what she made as if there were no end to it. Why would I think there would be? Why save when she enjoyed the game so much, and we had such fun together? I didn't give a thought to my source of income drying up.

Quite the opposite. I started thinking like a pimp thinks: The sole purpose of the money she worked all night for was to make my life one of ease. For instance, I shouldn't trouble myself walking to the projects to buy dope when I could catch a cab. I splurged on me, her, my girlfriends. I became accustomed to a whole new way of life in the span of two weeks.

It all came grinding to a halt with one cheap date. A little frustrating that his selfishness ended her final night early, shortly after it began to be exact. His greed not only drove her out of the game, but it also left me with limited funds to finance my new, comfortable lifestyle. It also left me scrambling to feed a much bigger heroin lust than I had the first night I took her down there. With cash freely flowing in, I hadn't seen the need to let my high fade away as the day wore on, so I'd give it a bump or two. At long last, I could afford to shoot dope at will and still have money left over for other pleasures.

Who am I kidding? Heroin **was** my pleasure. I had somehow escalated from one bag a day to three bags in my short two and a half months trafficking girls. That's not to say I became a hardcore addict in those couple of months. I had already long since hit that point of no return. Somewhere in the last year, I had gone from shooting dope because I wanted to, to shooting it because I had to. Nevertheless, my hunger grew with other people paying to feed it.

The realization of how far gone I was had come as a shock. I woke up one morning a few months in and decided not to get high that day. No sweat, I thought. I skipped a day or two of marijuana and wine all the time. I could go three, four days without them when I wanted to. I had no reason to believe heroin would be any different. I did a little weed and downed half a bottle of wine before I went to school that morning to give me a little buzz.

I could feel the sickness rising from the pit of my stomach shortly after I got to school. It spread in every direction. I dashed to the boys' bathroom before stuff started coming out both ends. Cramps clamped around my stomach and squeezed the breath out of me. I broke out in cold chills at the same time sweat drenched my body. The shakes joined in.

I had to get out of there. I bolted through the school and out the doors. It wasn't that I cared if anyone saw me leave. My body, submerged in the throes of dope sickness, needed me to get it to the projects as quickly as possible. My trembling hands injected a needle into my thirsty veins right there in the hallway where I bought it. The hot rush of the dope instantly snuffed out the attack ravaging every molecule in me.

"Wow. I have to have it." The thought tried to alert me to the severity of my addiction, but I shoved it aside and went about my business. Nothing I could do about it right then, and I felt fine now.

The following day, I decided I needed to know if my body's betrayal was an isolated incident or if I had a problem on my hands. I couldn't risk getting caught in that state at school again, so I jumped the train downtown to find out how my body would handle hustling. By 9:30, 10 o'clock, I felt the cold chills and sweat clamoring against each other for space on my skin. My stomach started churning. I hurried back on a train to the projects.

"Wow. Habit." The bombshell revelation refused to be ignored this time. It unquestionably petrified me as it sunk in that heroin now controlled my existence.

It left me with no choice. I had to find another girl. I couldn't do this on my own, and I didn't have time to waste. I clearly could no longer buy heroin when I got a few extra dollars like I did weed and alcohol. I went on the hunt for another girl in the same way I had for Karen, only more frantically. I was desperate to find someone to get the cash flowing again, so I could keep the heroin flowing.

However, my approach to the hunt changed without me realizing it as I fell headfirst into a deeper pimp mentality. Desperation takes you places you don't want to go. I found Karen through trial-and-error, an inexperienced kid trying my hand at talking a random girl into supporting my habit. A habit I had yet to comprehend commanded my days.

This time, I knew my habit didn't merely control my days; it dictated everything about my life. That left me with only one option. Burglary no longer would cut it. I couldn't split stolen TV money with a buddy and have enough to score the amount of dope it took to fill my screaming veins. Robbery fell short, too. Snatching a purse likely wouldn't yield enough to buy the number of bags I needed, let alone leave me with pocket money like in the good old days.

Neither would being Mr. Nice Guy with potential new products. My patience for wooing them with my boyish charm and clown act wore off faster than my heroin-induced euphoria. I didn't care about them anyway, so why waste time on sensitivity or even subtlety? The only reason I talked to them was for them to get me money for dope, so I didn't want to invest even a second on feelings. My only concern was if they had a little street, a little hustle, in them. My attitude became, "You're nothing more than a means to an end. If you're not getting me to that end, I'm not wasting my time or condoms on you."

Despite my lack of humanity, it's crucial to keep in mind that I still hadn't mutated into a full-blown pimp mentality. I wasn't acting out of that mindset, which would soon take me to increasingly darker places. The only thing on my mind still revolved around avoiding dope sickness. I didn't have time for niceties. She wasn't going to be sick. I was.

I didn't have time to protect my reputation anymore, either. Everyone and everywhere became fair game. I didn't care if a girl walked in the bowling alley with her little brother or sister. I didn't care who caught on in the neighborhood or at school. I lost all concern about it getting back to my sisters. If my mom spotted me out our window at the park, it was her issue, not mine. None of that was going to help me in my hand-to-hand combat with the creature that woke up every morning in my bed. My body had heroin on its side. Even my mom wasn't scarier than that.

I targeted girls everywhere I went without thinking about it.

"Hey, Girl, what's going on with you? What you doing?"

"Nothing. Just hanging out."

"What you do for fun?"

"I smoke weed."

"Hey, I got a little weed."

We'd have sex after sharing the weed. I made it plain I wasn't interested in an emotional connection. This was purely a business arrangement, and I was the boss.

"What you do for money?"

I usually knew the answer to that question before I asked. Most didn't have a way to get money. Full-time employment for a boss who shared weed and sex sounded pretty good to girls longing for a sense of belonging, a reason for being.

"I have a hustle we can do together," I slid a little hope within the reach of girls who had never had that.

I shot straight to save time. I told them right off I did hard drugs. Like I explained, dope called the shots, not me. When I opened my mouth, it decided what came out.

It didn't try to sugarcoat its motives: "I need support for my habit." Somehow, it knew how to elicit compassion from girls despite its rashness.

I went through 15-20 girls as fast as I went through a bag of heroin. I was young, so they were all young, too, a mixture of underage and 18, 19, 20. They'd last a day, two days, a week or so. I'd also go weeks without a girl, bouncing back and forth between pimping and other crime when that was my only option. Funny, though. I didn't think of what I did to them as crime. I knew I violated people's homes and businesses when I broke in. Didn't question it at all. No need to because I didn't care. Somehow, it never crossed my mind that I violated the bodies, the self-worth, the identities of the girls I sold. They didn't particularly cross my mind at all – except as a source for my next injection.

It's not that I disliked them or wanted to see anything bad happen to them. I took a few to the movies or to grab a bite to eat. Gave a few a little money. No different than when I stole a television and made sure not to drop it. I handled my merchandise with care so that I could get a good return on my investment.

That's all the girls were to me. They weren't worth investing the time in product development as I did with Karen, let alone Lacy. If they didn't immediately entice the dates with what they were selling, I'd cut my ties, even as they walked the track. I'd leave them dumbfounded right there by themselves to do what they wanted. It didn't matter if I met them there or took them there; they could find their way home. Think of it like pouring out a stale pot of coffee if you run a restaurant. You're not going to keep your customers with an unappetizing product. I might still be an inexperienced entrepreneur, but even I knew that.

"I can't stay down here with you until 1 or 2 in the morning, and you not getting any money." I didn't care about hurt feelings or the dangers I left them in. "I'm going to wake up sick in the morning. You're not doing your job, so I'm going to have to get up at 7 to go snatch something." It's hard to find good employees sometimes.

I didn't bother hanging out at the Sugar Shack, chatting it up with the other pimps, either. I'd acknowledge them with a "Hey, what's going on?" as I walked by, but I didn't need their advice anymore. I admitted I was inexperienced a minute ago, but I wasn't a novice now. I knew enough to get by after all I'd been through with Lacy and Karen. Lose one? Get another. The string of girls coming and going proved that. Quicker than getting a job at a fast-food place or the movie theater. Besides, their employment interview with me included sex and weed. Where else would they get that?

I might not be trying to be one of the pimps in front of the bar any longer, but I was becoming more like them with each passing day … and each passing girl. They all taught me something new, and I soaked every detail in.

This is what this date did.

This is what that cop did.

This trick told me to say this when the cop walked up.

Some of the girls taught me a hard lesson – I wasn't the only one willing to throw someone out like garbage when they weren't living up to expectations. Those girls who only hung around a day or two didn't see me as living up to a pimp's job requirements. How was I to know pimping came with a job description? I thought I was the big man slipping them a few dollars here and there, buying them something to eat occasionally. They saw me as a wannabe pimp – nothing more than a teenage boy from the hood using them like everyone else. I wasn't doing the stuff a pimp was supposed to do for his girls. Experienced pimps, I found out after enough ditched me, take care of their girls. They make sure they have a place to sleep, the right kind of clothes to wear, get their hair and nails done. All I knew and cared about was what they were supposed to do for me. Girls who had been with a capable pimp weren't good with that for long. I didn't fulfill my responsibilities in their eyes, so *they'd* leave me standing on the track.

They call a pimp's group of girls a stable for a reason. If you have a stable full of horses, you take care of them because they provide you profit or pleasure. You feed them, run them, brush them out, make sure they have a place to sleep, stroke their noses. I'd never been around horses, so I probably wouldn't have treated them well, either. Probably better than I treated the girls, though. Most pimps would.

Despite the setbacks, I kept feeling my way along for a few months and finally gained enough confidence to add something new to my pimp resume: Targeting other pimp's girls like Fly targeted Lacy. Pimps call it "campaigning."

Instead of silently walking the track to check up on my girls, I started doing what pimps do. I'd strut by girls and work my magic. It failed to work on a lot of them. The track was like my neighborhood in a way. People knew each other's business; word had probably gotten around that I didn't treat my girls well. Possibly that I was a wannabe pimp, too.

I didn't let that faze me. I was no stranger to rejection, after all. One night while campaigning, a group of girls ignored the words I threw their way, as usual. I caught one looking my direction for the briefest second, though. I'd seen that look before. Like when Lacy caught my eye at Gabrielle's or Karen smiled at me in the girls' restroom. Only on the track, it's called "reckless eyeballing." It comes with a consequence. I hadn't learned the entire pimp rulebook yet, however, so I missed the opportunity to "charge" her or take her money.

"Hey, why you looking at me?" should have been my response.

Her money would be mine either way. If she didn't answer me, it didn't matter because I'd already busted her. If she said she wasn't, I could claim her for answering me. Most pimp rules are like that. They work to his advantage no matter what.

Except when you're too unversed in the rules of the game to know you have the advantage. I kept walking, my shoulders slumping a tad in defeat and as a defense against the frigid weather.

I'd been saying little things to her for a week now, and she'd never acknowledged me in the slightest. I had no reason to think I had any chance with her. Maybe she'd just looked my way out of annoyance. I decided to protect myself from more brush-offs and the cold, so I made my way to a diner near the Sugar Shack to get coffee and warm up.

I sat there dejected, thinking about how to get the money I needed for my next bag of Snow. I was lost in thought when the door opened. I looked up as she walked in. I knew she hadn't followed me. I'd been there too long. Be that as it might, she kept glancing my way while she talked to the person behind the counter. She'd also look over her shoulder toward the door.

I finally decided, "Why not?" and motioned her over.

"What's up with you, Girl?"

"Nothing." I could tell she was timid. She was younger than the other girls out there and conspicuously inexperienced.

"I notice you been looking at me."

"You don't seem like everyone else. You don't seem like you're abusive."

"Let your next move be your best move," I said in my most convincing pimp voice.

I didn't have to work that hard for it. Her pimp, Slick, ruled with an iron hand, and it was heavy. She was looking for an escape. I looked like an escape route.

"I don't have much money."

Every dollar got me that much closer to my next bag of heroin, so I didn't care how much money she had. Why was she telling me that anyway? One date, and I'd be on my way to my next high.

She'd only been in the game a few weeks, but, as it happened, she already knew something I didn't. When girls go with a new pimp, they pay him a "choosing fee."

I went along with it.

"How much you have?"

She pushed around $70-$80 across the table to me. I scooped it up.

Her story started spilling out with the money. Slick, a New York pimp, picked her up there when she ran away. She thought he cared about her. She quickly learned, though, that she wasn't just one of his girls. She was the least of them.

On top of that, he got angry when he felt she didn't carry her weight. I mentally shrugged. No doubt she should be pulling in good money because she was fresh, young, and attractive. She knew he'd lose it on her anytime now because she'd seen him beat some of his other girls for less.

She'd already handed me almost $100, so what did I have to lose? I asked for his name and description and told her to head back to work while I found him. I rehearsed something in my head along the lines of what Fly said to me – except for the "here's-a-few-dollars-to-get-home" part.

Slick ran into her before I found him. She told him she didn't have any money, and he flew into a rage. He let her know if she didn't get him money quickly, they would have serious problems. She didn't mention me. The girl never tells. It's always the new pimp who breaks the news. She doesn't want him to knock her teeth out. Her new pimp doesn't want him to knock her teeth out, either, because that'd hurt his wallet.

I saw her again shortly after he left her. She told me what had happened as she handed me more money. She's serious about making this move, I realized. My first time for a girl to choose me. I felt a mixture of excitement and nerves, a little apprehension. I had to "serve" him now, showing him the courtesy of letting him know his girl chose me.

I knew it was part of the game, but I also knew a few of the established pimps still snickered at me, looking at me like, "Who is this little boy?"

They had good reason to snicker. I hadn't known what to say to his girl; what would come out when I approached him?

I stumbled across him at one of the other bars on the track.

"Hey, Slick. What's happening? Yo, man. Candy chose me." I should have stopped there.

"She gave me the money, too. She's really afraid." I regretted letting that last statement come tumbling out since I knew he had a violent side. I didn't know if he'd play by the rules of the game. He might laugh me off or, worse, take his anger out on me. Who was I, a kid so green I didn't bother telling him my name?

Would he respect me as a fellow pimp? I obviously didn't know how to serve him properly and still didn't have the finesse of a serious player. Here I was in my jeans and tennis shoes telling a an older, polished, New York pimp I'd taken his girl away from him. He wouldn't care that I wasn't going to divert any of my drug money for sharp clothes or jewelry.

He was about 10 years older than me and had the flair of the stereotypical pimp look down.

"Yeah, man. She wants to be with me now." Words kept spilling out. I couldn't stop them. It'd been a while since Fly schooled me. In the heat of the moment, I couldn't remember how much he'd said to me. I did stop short of handing him money to get home. He had a car.

And experience. Enough experience to know he got the better end of the deal. I'm sure he thought the two of us deserved each other.

"Alright, Young P. Do your thing."

"Yo, Young P. You know she's a turnout, right?" He was letting me know she didn't know what she was doing – either.

He gave me the respect of the game, though, letting me walk away with her as my girl. Relief. Probably for both of us.

I didn't know it (surprise), but he knew the next move if he wanted her back. According to the pimp rules, he could approach her on the track and try to get her to choose him. Happens a lot. It's like a game of chess. I've captured your queen. You can come to my side of the board (the track) and try to get her back or play the rest of the game without her because you're still the king. He never came after my new queen. Probably glad to get rid of her drag on the rest of his pawns. One less headache for him.

A headache was a much better option than dope sickness, so I headed back to the track to find Candy after my brief exchange with Slick. It's always a quick exchange when you serve another pimp.

I warned Candy to stay away from him and his other girls.

"Just stay out of his way. Treat his girls like you do him. Don't look at them. Don't talk to them because they'll come at you."

I wasn't worried he'd hurt her. I was worried one of his girls might say something to spark her interest again. I didn't want her talking to someone who was her wife-in-law an hour ago. They could be friends for all I knew. Talking to them could make her miss them despite his anger-management issues. They might smooth it over and tell her, "Oh, girl. He was just mad at you." It's called a "mad move" when a girl leaves upset.

Thanks to the girls who had taught me that girls have expectations of pimps, I knew to put Candy up in a hotel. I'd go to school during the day, and she'd sleep. I lived up to the job description this time, giving her money to get drinks out of the vending machine and eat lunch. You don't have to tell me twice. Not if dope is on the line.

I always checked on her right after school. That was my job, too. We'd go eat, watch a movie, get her nails done, go shopping, have sex. I'd stay an hour or two and then do my thing. I wasn't her babysitter, and I didn't want her in my face all the time. I was a boss supervising his employee.

I'd touch base with her between seeing girlfriends and getting dope or from the bowling alley.

"Hey, Baby. What you doing? I'm shooting pool with the fellows."

I'd head back down around 10, and we'd get ready for work.

I headed to her hotel after school as usual about two weeks in. She wasn't there. I checked the hotel restaurant. No sign of her. I went back to the room. Her clothes were gone, and the room key was on the nightstand.

Two weeks never seemed to be a good marker for me.

I figured she'd probably chosen, so I walked the track that night looking for her. No sign of her anywhere. I went back a couple of more nights, walking around waiting for someone to serve me. I'd seen Slick and his girls at the same hotel, so maybe he came back for her. No one ever served me, though, and I never saw her again. To this day, I don't know what happened to her. I thought she was happy. Maybe she heard me talking to one of my girlfriends from her room phone one night and didn't like that she was selling her body for me to take other girls out. Why am I working and they're not? Maybe she got homesick, stashed a little money, and made her way home. That's what I hope happened now.

Back then, I didn't care that much what had happened. I ran around the hotel and the track looking for my money, not for her. She simply happened to be the conduit to the money. I always experienced some emotion when a girl left, right up to the end. Not because of them. I made sure to keep my feelings detached from every one of them after Lacy, as Uncle Danny warned me. With that said, it's like if you're playing sports. You hate losing any game, but you know it's part of it.

## Analysis With Dr. Deena Graves:
### Pimp Street Lingo

As I've alluded to, pimps have built an underground world around their criminal enterprise, complete with its own rules, language, and hierarchy of authority that their victims must live by. They've dubbed the world of prostitution, as you might have guessed by now, "the game." They also refer to it as "the life."

We've covered other terminology they use, such as "choosing," "campaigning," and "stable." These terms, as well as many others, span the game no matter where you operate. Other pimp slang depends on the region, the city, the trafficker, and other factors. It changes with time like any other jargon. However, developing an understanding of *the way* they think can help you prevent and identify victims, as well as help them heal. The terms and types of words they use provide insight into their mindset.

Let me give you an example. You might have noticed I tossed the endearment "Baby" around a lot as a rookie. Later in the game, I'd walk in and say, "Hey, Bitch." Or, "Hey, Maggot." They responded with a chorus of, "Yes, Daddy?" They all answered – without hesitation. Who acknowledges that kind of terminology? Someone who others have pummeled the humanity out of, one layer at a time. Traffickers methodically strip their self-respect, self-worth, and identity away to dehumanize them. Then, they intentionally keep their identity rooted in those types of degrading words, so they don't believe they have any value outside of their body parts. Keep in mind, many of them land in trafficking because others have already convinced them of that, which plays to the pimp's favor.

Those words become etched in their minds, hearts, and spirits. It becomes so much of who they are that the girls eventually call each other that.

They can't fully heal unless we help them understand their value and worth, unless we help them establish their identity. We must reassure and reinforce that they are none of those things, and they should not use it in reference to themselves or respond to it.

Speaking of responding to it, if you hear these types of words, they are red flags a youth is already a trafficker's victim or on the path to becoming one. Intervene immediately. The longer those identity-stealing character-izations have to take root in their hearts and minds, the more difficult it becomes to get them out of the game and keep them out.

Please see *Appendix C* for a comprehensive list of terminology used in the game.

## Two-Minute Introspection

Close your eyes and imagine someone you love routinely addressing you as "Bitch" or "Maggot." How would it impact your self-esteem and identity? Based on that, how should we adjust our treatment plans to build their self-worth and identity?

# 16

## Worth the Price of Admission

Money wasn't the only thing I had difficulty coming by to feed my habit. Miss Ronnell, the older, diabetic lady in the projects who peddled her hypodermic needles to dope fiends, suddenly cut us off without warning. I wore my only needle out in no time flat, dulling the tip with incessant jabs. Worn-out tips still give you the coveted rush but leave behind the telltale track marks and abscesses. I had finally acknowledged I was a junkie and went through drug-induced stretches where I didn't care who knew. In reality, though, I didn't want anyone else to figure it out, especially my family. But new works weren't to be found. I guess Miss Ronnell left a lot of people hurting.

I didn't give up. I searched as hard for the next needle as I did for the next girl.

"Yeah, man. No one has any, but I'm getting ready to go up there to the shooting gallery if you wanna go." A guy I met on the dope run nodded at a nearby Section 8 apartment complex.

Of course, I did – even though I had no idea what that entailed. I followed him up to 4A, where a medium-built man sitting on a stool at the door like a bar bouncer collected our $3 entry fee. He didn't come across like a bouncer. Just a guy doing what he had to do to keep his habit up. He was friendly. He had every reason to be. The shooting gallery owner fed him a little dope to act as her cashier. He took the job seriously; the benefits were too good not to. He didn't worry about health insurance. He had better insurance in his mind: A dope rush always readily available a few feet away. He knew he'd never be sick. And, he didn't have to pull off regular hustles like me to keep a needle in his arm.

The shooting gallery owner, known as the house lady, was far more calloused than her doorman. She was bigger than him, sported healed abscesses on her arms, no makeup on her face, and an occasional wig when she didn't feel like fixing her hair. She was pleasant enough but no-nonsense.

I could smell something simmering on the stove while I waited for one of the stools around the dining room table to open up. She kept the table bare except for spoons, bottle caps, hypodermic needles, lighters, a cup of clean water, and a cup of murky water. When someone pulled the needle out of their arm, the house lady "cleaned it" in the murky cup of water, so the next person in line could handle their business.

I knew "clean" was a relative term. I doubted the house lady or her cashier used the works she rented to us, although I had no doubt they were dope fiends like the rest of us in that apartment. All that's trivial when you need a hit. This was the circle I traveled in now. It came with a dose of blind trust. Seemed like poetic justice since I became a dope fiend by blindly trusting people I knew.

The needle might not be the cleanest, but she made sure it didn't have a bent tip or "tit" that would leave the dead-giveaway eruption on your arm. I appreciated that more anyway.

As I got closer to the table, the smell of body odor snuffed out whatever was cooking on her stove. I lost any appetite I might have had as I saw oozing abscesses for the first time. Some hadn't washed their face or brushed their teeth. Their greasy hair clumped around their face. I could tell some of them had undoubtedly slept in the hallway right outside her apartment, eager to get going as soon as she unlocked her door.

One of those fleeting thoughts of regret flickered across my mind – heroin couldn't possibly love me as much as I loved it. Look what it had driven me to. I'm about to share unsanitary needles with probable disease-ridden people.

Yeah, but you won't be sick, my veins shot back. Argument settled. Shooting up after some guy who wreaked of a month's worth of sleeping under a bridge and who barely missed an oozing sore as he jabbed the needle in took a backseat to sickness. The same as stealing or selling a girl did. The consequences fly out the window.

I'd never sat at a table and shot dope with a group of strangers. It reminded me of the abandoned building where James and Robert first introduced my body to heroin. Despair hung over the room. Not a lot of conversation. No time for that. I no more than got up from the stool, and someone else grabbed my spot. No one lingers in a shooting gallery. They don't share life or laughter, only sorrow and despondency.

The house lady sucked some of the joy out of the high, too. She rushed people along, not allowing them to milk their dope rush, drawing the heroin and their blood in and out of the plunger. They could do that in the comfort of their own home, not her needle factory. You plunge in the needle and get the hell out. She had a business to run. The shooting gallery was her hustle. If people couldn't pay cash, they left a smidgen of dope residue in their spoon. Either way, she won. I broke into a house or took a girl downtown. She trafficked in syringes and bottle caps. From the looks of it, she probably did better than me. People lined up in the hallway, waiting for the next open needle. She ran a tight ship; you didn't want to upset her by loitering if you didn't have anywhere else to get your works.

You're sitting in a room full of heroin addicts day in and day out, to boot. You don't want to hang around waiting for the cops.

As fast as she herded her clientele through, the only thing running through my mind each time I went was, "I wish they'd hurry up." On occasion, someone overdosed, slowing down the assembly line. The house lady shot salt in their veins to revive them or threw them in the tub filled with cold water and ice.

One day, salt and ice failed to work. I'd never seen someone OD and not come out of it. He shot his dope like everyone else, relishing in the euphoria for a second before falling into a nod. He never came out of that nod. When the gallery owner had a couple of guys drag him out, I had a momentary jolt of empathy. Or maybe it was fear. Then I wondered if I could have his chair. Like I said. Momentary. We all wondered where he copped his dope because it must have been a good batch, nice and potent. Too bad he couldn't handle it, we all secretly thought.

I didn't have time to give it more thought because his stool was mine.

When I finished doing my thing, I walked down the four flights of stairs and out the back door. There he lay between the two buildings, out cold, oblivious to the world. Another "Whoa" danced through my mind. "Damn. They just dropped him right there." I'd never seen anything like that, either.

I walked around him, pushed his image and what it meant aside, and got outta there. That wasn't a good look. Someone would report that quickly. Hopefully.

I forgot about it and went about my day from there. Out of sight, out of mind. Just a day in the life of a junkie.

I never learned if he lived or died.

That didn't slow me down, though. I was faithful to my true love. 'Til death do us part.

## Analysis With Dr. Deena Graves:
### Drug Harm Reduction

Shooting galleries made my addiction easier and more convenient. Think of them as a convenience store. You're in and out in no time, and they have just what you need in a hurry.

Then an even easier and more convenient source of works came into my life. Only I didn't have to make my way to it like I did a shooting gallery. Think of it like a musical ice cream truck rolling through your neighborhood passing out free treats. The government rolled into my hood and asked if I'd like free works. Of course, I did. By all means. Now instead of shelling out money to people like Miss Ronnell or the house lady in 4A, I handed the extra cash to the drug dealer and shot it straight into my arm with the government-supplied needles.

They called it harm reduction. I call it throwing a match on gasoline. They might as well have handed me a heroin-loaded syringe. And I could shoot up anywhere now because the works came with a free pass. Before, I feared arrest if I had been caught with works. Not only was it easier, but it was also faster.

More time on my hands. Less money out of my pocket.

The effect was like a snowball rolling downhill. It picked up speed and mass, upping my chances of an overdose and other psychological and physical aftermaths.

The thing about snowballs is the bigger and faster they get, the greater the chance they will cause damage *to things in their path*.

My heroin snowball did a lot of damage to things in my path. To me, the words "harm reduction" are an oxymoron. Free government works not only caused me significantly more harm, but the bigger my dope demon grew, the more harm *I did to other people* – and the more violent it became. It didn't matter who I stole from or who I hurt. I didn't care if it violated someone's home or violated someone's body. And I'm not just talking about prostituting people. I'm talking about armed robbery, as well. As we've established, heroin strips you of compassion and empathy.

It's hard to care about other people when you feel no one cares about you. I believed the government didn't care what happened to me or anyone else, or they wouldn't have paid for something that laid waste to so many lives. I'm not blaming my choice to traffick or rob people on the government. I deliberately tormented other people so heroin could torment me. I still expected other people to pay for the dope I used the government-supplied works for. I own that. However, I do blame the government for fueling the addiction that drove my actions. Please hear me out.

The government says harm reduction principles:

- Aim to reduce the negative personal and public health impacts of behavior associated with substance abuse.
- Put the responsibility of setting goals on the addicted person.
- Meet drug addicts "where they are on their own terms."
- May serve as a pathway to additional prevention, treatment, and recovery services.[57]

Said another way, the goal is to "reduce the negative effects of health behaviors without necessarily extinguishing the problematic health behaviors completely or permanently" by "offer(ing) an alternative to abstinence as a singular goal."[58,59]

The debate rages about the benefits of harm reduction. I'm simply giving you my perspective as someone whose life was destroyed by heroin and who went on to destroy more than 150 other lives because of it. That qualifies me as an expert. Let me apply my expert opinion to those principles:

- It did not in any form reduce the negative consequences for me or public health. And, correct, it did not extinguish the problematic health behaviors completely or permanently – as stated, it tragically worsened them.
- Between trauma and addiction, I did not have the mental or emotional capacity to set healthy goals. I believe it is impossible for any addict to set goals safe for ***anyone's well-being***. Getting high and staying high takes over every inch of mental space.
- Meeting me where I was on my terms. My terms were to force girls into prostitution so I could stave off both dope sickness and jail time.
- Free works did serve as a pathway – but not to prevention, treat-

ment, or recovery services. I never turned down government kits, even if I had some. The more syringes I could fill, the bigger my addiction became. The bigger my addiction became, the more girls I needed to sell to feed it. That drove me deeper down the *path of trafficking*.

The game has what we call "facilitators." A facilitator, for example, can be hotel managers who take money under the counter to turn their heads while pimps and buyers ransack kids. As a former 32-year sex trafficker and 12-year heroin addict, I propose it also can be the government funding drug use that keeps addicts strung out and desperate for money to satiate their lust. Desperation gives birth to a lot of other crimes.

Please allow me, Dr. Graves, to add some footnotes to Derek's perspective in the form of research, which has raised red flags about the success of harm-reduction principles applied to youth.[60]

Consider, for example, the case of a young girl in prostitution who almost died in ICU despite nearly a year of harm-reduction programming. She started injecting heroin at 16. Notice the intersection of hard drugs and prostitution again? We can assume she turned to dope and selling herself, like many others, to relieve her mental and emotional anguish. The government offered harm reduction as the antidote.

"It is difficult to see how the health and interests of youthful users with rehabilitation potential are served by a harm reduction system that supports them in their self-destructive habits for extended periods."[61]

Likewise, Vancouver, touted as a global forerunner in drug harm reduction, sees its "street-involved young people who use drugs continue to be vulnerable to overdose, death, Hepatitis C (HCV) infection, and high rates of syringe sharing."[62] Further, instead of reducing the risk and harm in an Australian harm-reduction drug program for youth, it appeared to escalate it.[63]

Research in the U.S. suggests that the harm-reduction approach with electronic cigarettes leads youth to view smoking as acceptable, fueling their addiction to nicotine and exposing them to additional dangers with actual cigarettes.[64] And researchers have not found a meaningful change in teen gambling after harm-reduction intervention.[65]

I, Derek, relate to all those studies. One research study is literally like looking straight into my soul as a 16-year-old addict: Teens try to control risk in their own ways, based on survival skills developed in their "entrenched poverty."[66]

If someone had pulled me aside early on and told me they cared about what I was doing, there's a consequential chance I might have listened. I ran smack into heroin and pimping in my desperate pursuit of someone to care about me. I found people who cared alright. They gladly took me under their wing. The problem was they were burglars, robbers, junkies, pimps, and other criminals. I suspect the 16-year-old who almost died in ICU shares a similar story.

Twelve years after I fell into heroin addiction, I found someone with wings like an angel who helped me escape it. She didn't come at me with a syringe, cooker, and bleach bottle. She came at me with the ***belief in me*** I needed to hear.

I'll tell you about her when we get to that part of my story. For now, let's focus on the epidemic of teen addicts today. Instead of helping them fan the flames of their addiction by handing them the tools to inject, I strongly urge us to instead extinguish the fire in their minds and emotions. We shouldn't settle for not "necessarily extinguishing" it when it comes to our children. We can completely extinguish it if we approach their addiction differently.

In the aftermath of physical withdrawal from heroin, mental and emotional addictions rise out of the ashes like Frankenstein coming back to life. It doesn't matter how much your body heaves, how relentlessly the cramps squeeze your insides out, or how panicked you are that you might not make it through the withdrawal. The memory of the euphoria creeps back in like a long-lost love who unexpectedly shows up at your door. You know the person is toxic for you, but the temptation is more than you can resist.

Most programs address only the physical addiction and provide camaraderie. Instead of sitting around the table in a shooting gallery doing damage with a group of other people, you sit around a table *talking* about the damage you did with a group of other people. People get hooked on the meetings like they got hooked on the dope. They're still going to meetings 25-30 years later. That's not healing. It's coping, substituting one thing to soothe the loss of another.

It's very similar to breaking up with that first love. You mourn the breakup with heroin like you do a person. You have a flashback or something stressful happens, and your first thought isn't, "I wish my ex were here to help me get through this." It's, "I wish heroin were here to get me through this." It dulls the pain and helps you cope just like the loved one would.

And just like a true love, I would have done anything for my dope. It is the only thing I have ever been willing to die – or kill – for. No, I never killed anyone, but other addicts have. Like a spurned lover, that kind of commitment doesn't go away with physical withdrawal.

## Two-Minute Introspection

How can we help teens break their mental and emotional addiction to heroin?

# PART 2. AFTER GRADUATION

# 17 College or (Pimping) Career?

I'd slowly slipped so far down into the underworld of heroin addiction that the poolroom, the park, and my girlfriends didn't see too much of me. Neither did the track downtown. I became too busy working the tracks in my arm. I didn't have time to find girls and do all the things a pimp had to do to keep them around because I woke up violently sick every morning. I couldn't afford to put my well-being in their needy hands. I'd stuck with pimping as long as I had because I didn't want to risk jail. Now even the fear of jail wasn't as powerful as the sheer panic when I thought of dope sickness.

I also lost easy access to girls at school. Racial tensions escalated with forced bussing, and all hell broke out at my school. A kid slammed a hammer into the back of the head of a kid bussed to our school from my neighborhood. That hit close to home. Students launched bricks at each other's buses like hand grenades, resulting in police escorts. The school board installed metal detectors. I wasn't about to put my life in any of their hands, so I started carrying a knife to school.

It didn't take long for a metal detector to bust me. My mom tried to discipline me, but I refused to go to school without a weapon. She realized I truly feared for my life and moved me to the Massachusetts Experimental School System, which turned out to be a mess. Not for me. For them. The acronym spelled MESS. They quickly changed it to the Experimental School System, and the experiment worked great for me. I excelled in the program. They had me at, "You can graduate in three years instead of four."

I welcomed the freedom the program gave me. No more principal and vice-principal breathing down my neck. No more teachers guarding the hallways like hawks. I didn't have to worry about someone sneaking up behind me with a hammer or other weapon. All I had to do was check in with the counselor at my primary or "headquarters" campus, located in a converted supermarket, make it to my classes on time, and turn my work in.

We took some of our classes at Harvard University and the Massachusetts Institute of Technology. I loved mixing with first-year college students. If I thought I had independence riding the bus from campus to campus without supervision, they lived on campus, far away from the prying eyes of parents and other nosy adults. Naturally, I especially noticed the unsupervised girls. No parental supervision at all. Zero. That resurrected my trafficking ambitions.

"I wonder if she'd do it."

"I'll bet you she'd do it."

"Absolutely not," I jerked my mind back from the daydream of easy money.

This new way of doing school was too much fun to risk getting kicked out of the program. I had to buckle down anyway to keep my grades up if I wanted to graduate early. Shooting dope and hustling to support it ate up too much of my time to add in hunting for and managing girls. My desire to finish school early was way more important to me than luring one of them to the track. Why risk it when she may not prove profitable. It carried the added risk of them reporting me since they could afford to go to a college like Harvard or MIT.

Besides, the college campuses had revived another dream, a displaced one. That long-forgotten childhood fantasy of becoming a lawyer stirred deep down inside me again. The college students always took an interest in us, asking about our program, talking to us in class or the library, eating lunch with us sometimes. We'd laugh and joke. Periodically, I'd run into one who aspired to become an attorney, too. It inspired me to see them pursuing my, I mean their, dream. I admired them for knowing how to go after their dream. I sure didn't have a clue how to do that.

It didn't matter anyway because the streets and heroin chased me down every day, relentlessly beating the hope and dreams out of me.

And while my accelerated, experimental school program equipped me with a more superior education than I would have obtained in my public high school, it also gave me more opportunity to give in to heroin's pursuit. I had plenty of time between reporting in with my counselor and my first class to sneak off to the projects to buy dope. Since no one monitored us, they had no idea if we went to the library to do homework as instructed. A lot of students flunked out because of that leniency. They didn't thrive in an environment that required motivation and self-discipline, but, as I said, I had liked school when I was younger. I still loved learning. It made me feel a sense of accomplishment to make good grades. Somehow, I managed to do that despite my ongoing romance with heroin addiction. I'd shoot four bags and head to class. The more I shot, the deeper I fell in love with it, but I kept school like a girlfriend on the side. Remember your first infatuation, how you couldn't get that person off your mind? I'd never felt that way about a girl, but I did about my Snow.

You'd think someone would notice a high school student with a three- and four-bag-a-day habit, but no one ever did. At least they never said anything if they did. My counselor or teachers didn't spot it despite interacting with me day in and day out. I sat in classes totally strung out. I felt invincible and invisible at the same time. My father, aunt, or grandmother didn't pick up on it. Neither did my mom's side of the family. My sisters were too busy with their own lives to notice me, and I did an excellent job of avoiding my mom when it was noticeable. Then again, we've already established that no one ever noticed.

Until graduation. They held graduation in the evening, so I had plenty of time to hustle beforehand. I shot four bags to celebrate. The speakers droned on and on, and, with my last name starting with a "W," I had a long, monotonous wait for my diploma. I fell into a deep heroin nod. The girl next to me shook me when it was my time to go. For the first time, my mom realized I was wasted. It tore her apart that my grandmother, her mom, saw it, but she didn't say much. She had no idea heroin was my drug of choice, and she was proud of me for graduating a year early. She didn't want to ruin my day, so she silently took my cap and gown while I headed off with friends. I could see it in her face, though. That's a hard look to get out of your mind. Even in the midst of a dope high, it's painful to realize you disappointed your mom.

I was surprised she never mentioned it later, but I guess she encouraged herself with my occasional talk about going to college. She was happy, too, that I landed a good job for the summer, working as a groundskeeper for the Massachusetts State Hospital. It couldn't be too much to worry about because I'd never gotten into serious trouble. She didn't need to know that police had chased me more than once, catching other people I was with. Pure luck I got away.

Ironic that my luck finally ran out right after she finally caught on.

Me, one of my best buddies Scunz, and a few more friends went to an arcade in Boston Garden, where we weren't too welcome as visitors from the hood. A group of White kids swiftly reminded us of that. They chased us back to the train station, intent on making us sorry for invading their territory. With no train in sight, we had two options: Get beaten or jump off the platform to the tracks about three feet below. That wouldn't have been too bad, but I could see the sidewalk through the gaps in the track – the track suspended about 40 feet above the sidewalk.

I glanced over my shoulder and went floundering through the air when I saw one of them racing toward me. We regained our footing and took off running down the tracks. Naturally, a train raced toward us, ruining our clean getaway. The Massachusetts Bay Transit Authority Police stopped the train and grabbed us off the tracks.

They herded us back the way we came. As we walked down the stairs of the train depot, we saw him lying in a pool of blood, unconscious. Scunz' fear of heights convinced him outrunning them was a safer option. He only made it to the stairwell before they jumped him. They beat him near death, bashing his face in and setting his jean jacket on fire with a traffic flare. The officers hurried us past him but not before we saw enough to leave us dazed. A sense of fear we hadn't experienced before swept over us.

One of the officers stayed behind and called it in while the other officer took us for questioning. I think he could tell how deeply in shock we were because he didn't keep us long. I don't think he knew, like us, if Scunz was dead or alive. I believe that softened his heart toward us.

It felt like he kept us forever, though, because I wanted to get out of there so desperately. My mind was back in that stairwell with Scunz. The officer's voice sounded muffled, far away. It didn't matter if his words were loud or not. They couldn't penetrate the thick haze that had settled over my mind. It had a familiar feel to it.

The minute he let us go, we headed straight to the projects to tell Scunz' family. From there, we gathered more friends, along with bats, poles, and sticks. Armed, we set out again for Boston Garden, resolved to avenge Scunz. We ran as fast as we could from the train to the arcade. We bashed machines and people. It didn't matter if they were part of the group who had chased us. We were out for blood – to make up for Scunz' blood – and it didn't matter whose it was. We chased and beat anyone who came across our path just like they did us. One thing ran through our collective minds: Someone had to pay for Scunz. Racial hatred ***never does anyone any good***. It only hurt innocent people when they attacked us, and it only hurt innocent people when we attacked them. Nothing got better for anyone as a result of either.

We took off running when we saw police coming. We raced past where Scunz had fallen, beaten senseless, to the train platform. We had good timing this round. A train pulled in right as we rushed up. We jumped on different cars to blend in. I breathed a sigh of relief. Another near miss.

Then I heard police yelling to hold the train. They did. Officers burst into my car. One snatched a bat out of the hand of a girl with us, shoved it in my face, and told me to take it. I wasn't stupid. I'd dropped the stick I'd been flinging the moment I saw the cops; I wasn't about to take possession of a deadly weapon. I refused, but he arrested me anyway for assault and battery and destruction of property.

Yes, after years of intentional crime and hard drugs, my luck ran out avenging a friend who managed to live through a brutal beating invoked by his skin color.

I dreaded that one call. I was right to.

"You what? You where? You why?"

She was upset I got arrested. She was upset I went back to the arcade. I don't think there was much my mom wasn't upset with. Racial tensions had intensified so dramatically in the last few months that she brought my Uncle Thurman to the jail with her to bail me out. When I told them what had happened, my uncle immediately understood why I had gone back. My mom had zero understanding. She worked at the courthouse. This would not be a good look for her. Luckily for me, the judge ruled it a Continuance Without Finding or CWOF. My first arrest would be nothing more than a bad memory if I stayed out of trouble. That should be easy enough since I had managed to for 17 years.

And I did manage – for about three more weeks. I got into a fight with a co-worker and swung a grass sickle at my supervisor when he tried to break it up. I might have skated by on that one, too, since I didn't hurt him, but being jacked up on dope and anger, probably mixed in with the June heat, made me think it was a good idea to swing it at the police officer who broke that up.

Second arrest within a few weeks, and this time it was assault on a police officer. I managed to get off easy again, though, thanks to all the friends my mom had made at the courthouse. I didn't have to depend on a public defender to plead my case; one of her attorney friends handled it. He didn't have to plead hard since the judge also was a friend. Probation. Only six months – and I didn't have to report. Thankfully, drugs never factored into the conversation. They just assumed I was a kid who used bad judgment in the heat of the moment.

I breathed another sigh of relief and promised to do better. And I did. I worked without any issues, hung out with my friends and girlfriends, shot pool and White Stuff. Same stuff I had shot for years without any run-ins with law enforcement.

That and getting off so incredibly easy two times within three weeks of each other probably caused me to let my guard down. James and I were walking down Center Street fresh from buying dope in the Jamaica Plains Projects. We ran into friends trying to find a place to score. We felt their frustration; it had taken us all morning to find a supply. James took his benevolence too far. The only thing I felt sorry for was myself. I could feel the sickness coming on since it had taken us so long to track down a dealer. I was irritated when he said he'd take them to the dealer.

"Oh, come on," the heroin whispered to me. That was their problem. They should have been with us when we happened upon it. I had no charitableness in the current scenario for anything besides my menacing dope sickness.

I didn't hide my irritation as James handed me our dope bags and told me he'd meet me at the train station. I wrapped the heroin in a $10 bill, shoved it in my pocket, and took off toward the train station. I made it about a block. I froze foot mid-air when a police car pulled up right in front of me as I stepped off the curb. An officer jumped out, stuck his hand in my pocket, and yanked the heroin out. They'd seen James hand it to me and thought I'd bought it from him. Wrapping the $10 bill around it probably didn't help.

He spun me around. "Got anything else on you?" He found a pocketknife, threw it to the curb, and smashed it with his foot before handcuffing me and shoving me in the car. I'd gotten careless.

Possession of a Controlled Substance, Class A Heroin.

No, I did not call Mom. Nope. I didn't even think about calling Helen. I spent the night in jail and went to court on my own the next day. It wouldn't have mattered that much anyway because it wasn't her court-house. The judge ordered me to come back in a week and let me go.

I had to tell her now. She didn't know what heroin was. She asked my uncle if it was like cocaine. "No, heroin is hard stuff," he informed her.

I had to use a court-appointed lawyer this time. The judge saw I had been arrested twice already that summer and asked me if I was addicted. I assured him I was not. He called me up to the side of the bench and told me to stick my arm out. I always went in the same spot, but that spot was pretty worn out, so it wasn't hard for an experienced eye to see.

He continued my case and ordered me back to the Charles Street Jail for two weeks without bail. He wanted to see if I showed any signs of withdrawal.

That's one way to quit. Racking pain. Retching, vomiting, diarrhea, chills, and loss of appetite in a dank, rat-infested, no-privacy jail cell is not pleasant. I could hear the rats scurrying around in the toilet at night, fighting for what I had thrown up in there during the day. Guys up on the tier would throw their food down on the flat, the bottom floor, where I sat in a cell. Everything was nasty and oppressive, including the guards.

Some of the other inmates told me not to ask to go to the nurse. That was the judge's test, they informed me, and I wouldn't get anything to help anyway. I guess that's why the guards didn't report anything.

The judge gave me a two-year suspended sentence. One more strike, and I'd land in prison for two years.

I knew I would strike out. I had no control left, so I walked out of the jailhouse and to the recruiter's office. I saw it as my only option. I'd just been arrested three times in two and half months, battled through the hell of withdrawal, and the only thing on my mind was heroin. Withdrawal might have dulled my physical lust and sickness, but it did nothing for my emotional and mental love affair with dope.

I left the recruiter's office and got high.

My mom didn't know that when she threw me a going-away party. She was ecstatic I had enlisted. Maybe this would straighten me up, give me the positive male influence and guidance I'd never had. My stepfather and a few uncles had served in the military, and we were at peace, so she had hope for me for the first time in a long time.

All three of my girlfriends came to the party. I managed to avoid any issues by staying on the move. The day after the party, I had sex with all three. They all said they'd miss me, told me to be careful, but young Black guys from our neighborhood didn't enlist often, so they were excited for me. I said my goodbyes to Gabrielle and Evelyn and committed to write and call Lacy. We had a special bond I didn't share with the other two. We'd had an exciting adventure together that was like our dirty little secret. It elevated her in my mind to a level above a girlfriend. She had been willing to put her life in jeopardy for me. That was worth a few letters and phone calls.

A group of us recruits left out of Logan International Airport under the supervision of an active member. I think he could tell I'd never flown before and was nervous because he sat with me. I squeezed my eyes shut as we raced down the runway. I snuck a peek and could see the wings shaking.

"Hey, Williams. Look. We're off the ground." I opened my eyes to see the ocean sprawled out below us in magnificent blue-and-white froths. I grabbed my armrests when the plane bounced. I thought we were falling out of the sky.

"That's just air pockets," he reassured me.

I fell in love with flying as I wondered what was waiting for me. I knew what I was leaving, but I didn't have a clue what I was getting into. I felt a mixture of relief, anxiety, and wonder fighting each other for space in my stomach. A little sadness poked its way through, knowing I had left my family and friends behind, but an immense sense of relief that I wasn't going to prison far outweighed any sentimentality. The higher we climbed through the clouds, the more my fear of that file sitting in the courthouse faded away. I settled back in my seat and smiled to myself as the plane carried me farther and farther away from all my troubles.

It only took five days in the Army for them to catch up to me.

## Analysis With Dr. Deena Graves:
### Youth From Poverty and College

After I got arrested, I started saying: I wanted to be a lawyer, and now I need a lawyer. It was a way to try to laugh off my dead dreams, my long-lost hope.

I think I would have made an outstanding attorney. I would have fought hard for people because no one ever fought even easy for me.

Consider, for instance, some of the things I just told you that might not have jumped out on a quick read:

- I **quit trafficking girls** so I could keep my grades up.
- I never targeted girls on the college campuses as potential victims because I did not want to get kicked out of my accelerated program.
- I excelled in the accelerated program.
- I had good enough grades to get into college.
- My dream of becoming an attorney resurrected when I felt a little hope and saw other young people living that dream.
- I thrived under the attention the college kids invested in me.
- The thought of living on a college campus like the students I met excited me.
- I cared briefly about what my mom thought. Her disappointment in me crushed me.

Somewhere in the mix of that list is a kid still searching for hope despite a hardened, tough-guy exterior.

So, what kept me from applying to colleges? The answer is simple.

I didn't know how. If someone had encouraged me, pointed out that I was a good candidate for college, I might have listened. What if someone had said, "You graduated a year early. You proved you can hold your own in college classes while you're still in high school. What an accomplishment. What if you focus yourself like you did in high school?"

If someone had taken me by the hand, shown me how to apply, how to get scholarship money, I might not have trafficked another person. Let me stress that I needed someone to show me. At 17, I didn't have any idea where to start. I didn't have the heart to believe I could get in after all the disappointments and losses. I didn't have the confidence I could do it once I got there. I don't know why my mom didn't help me or have one of her friends at the courthouse. You just don't think about things like that in the hood.

Tragically, things haven't changed that much for at-risk youth all these years later. Like me, their most impenetrable barrier often is a lack of someone to show them how to navigate the convoluted admissions and financial aid process or simply help them believe in themselves enough to try. One research study saw a 12-percent jump in enrollment simply by intentionally reaching out to potential students.[67]

Other barriers block their path out of poverty or additional high-risk situations into college, as well. They don't have the mandatory application fee or deposit, a parent or caregiver to sign, or a way to pay for housing even if they get an academic scholarship.[68]

Let me stress that someone telling me I was college material would not have made a difference. I wouldn't have known how to put that in action no matter how badly I wanted it. Our youth don't need us to tell them what to do. They need us to walk them through it, to do it with them.

## Two-Minute Introspection

What other steps can we take that will make the most difference for college and career opportunities for vulnerable youth?

# 18 You're in the Army Now

In my defense, a boy who'd freely run around the hood, the projects, and the Combat Zone at all hours of the day and night for years couldn't possibly fathom the scrutiny of Army eyes. The hood operates on chaos and rebellion, the polar opposite of discipline and structure. I enlisted spur-of-the-moment to escape jail and heroin. I knew nothing about the military and didn't take the time to learn. I had no idea they'd watch my every move.

I stepped off the plane and into culture shock at the Fort Leonard Wood, Missouri, reception station. They marched us in formation to get shots, our uniforms, see the PX and other essential places on the base, and get a haircut. The Army's idea of a haircut differed dramatically from Uncle Danny's. My last name afforded me considerable time to notice they didn't believe in style. At all. The guys with names starting with A-V walked in sporting long hair. I could tell many of them put a great deal of effort into their style. The Army left the style on the floor in less than five minutes. It reminded me of the shooting gallery – sit down, get the job done, and free up the chair for the next person. No time to do it your way. They shaved the back and side of my short afro, leaving a dab on the top.

Wow. A little intense, I thought. I felt a surge of nerves but no regrets. Nothing could be as unbearable as a jail cell.

We called home, wrote letters, and got to know each other in the dash of free time they gave us after dinner. I made a couple of friends. Just kids like me. We shared more of our stories as we got to know each other over the next few days. You've heard that saying, "It takes one to know one." We likely gravitated toward each other because we all knew our way around a bag of weed. Funny how quickly that comes up in conversation when it's been a way of life.

I thought I could leave all my problems behind but take a piece of the streets with me. The U.S. Army, as it turned out, did not welcome the streets to its base. I considered the marijuana pipe I brought with me a tool to help me get comfortable with this unknown world I signed up for. A little piece of home, if you will. I was there to serve my country, so I believed they'd want me to feel at ease.

My new friends saw the pipe as impressive. One of them thought the permanent party guys, or long-term soldiers, at the PX could help us find something to fill it with. Seemed logical to us, so we headed that way.

We didn't even make it to the PX before the Military Police (MP) spotted us. Our freshly shaved heads flashed "recruit" like a neon sign. Our uniforms screamed "out-of-the-box." The Army hadn't marched us over to the Quartermaster Laundry yet, so they weren't starched and creased and didn't have our names on them.

We might have roamed the streets at will back home, but the Army had a problem with us roaming the base at will. The MP asked us for our unit.

"Reception Station Unit, Sir."

They saw that as an invitation to search us and found the pipe on me. They saw my coping mechanism as a serious infraction. Their reaction reminded me of the judge glaring at my arms. You would've thought they'd caught me with heroin works. They took me to the MP Station and sent my buddies back to our barracks since they didn't have anything on them.

I didn't, either, except for the pipe, but they charged me with Possession of Marijuana. The residue in the pipe might as well of been a full bag.

Five days in, and I faced an Article 15. They found me guilty but took it easy on me. I spent two nights in the stockades until a bed opened up in the holdover unit. I spent the next 14 days pulling extra duty or what civilians would call manual labor. I chopped and stacked wood, raked leaves, and carried out other such mindless tasks. Then they docked my pay, noted the charge in my military records, and sent me to a new unit. I couldn't help but wonder if jail might have been less harsh. I'd gotten lighter sentences for much more than a trace of resin in a weed pipe. If I'd been busted with a pipe on the streets, they most likely would've let me go, maybe handed the pipe back to me, or stomped on it like the officer with my knife.

They weren't playing around. The military and the streets were two different animals. I lived out-of-bounds on the streets; the Army didn't let you step out-of-bounds. It held you accountable. I realized I could no longer get away with whatever I wanted. I had to shape up.

When I say shape up, I don't mean I thought about turning my life around. You might say it slowed me down. I knew I had to be more careful to avoid trouble and the MP. Time to kick in my street smarts.

You'd think I would've learned from the residue incident that street smart doesn't stand a chance against Army grit. It only took as long as the cattle-car ride over to my new unit to land in hot water again. I spit as I jumped off the car. Up to this point, the drill sergeants had yelled when the mood struck them, mostly at the group. Now, they got in your face.

"Did you spit on my rocks, Trainee?"

"Yeah."

"You say, 'Yes, Drill Sergeant."

Just like you see on TV. He was all in my face, barking orders, smelling like coffee and tobacco.

"Pick it up."

"Pick what up, Drill Sergeant?" I was sincerely confused. I spat on gravel.

"Pick up your spit, Trainee."

"How, Drill Sergeant?"

"Pick up every rock that's wet and put it in your pocket."

He glared at me for a second: "Where you from, Trainee?"

"Boston, Massachusetts, Drill Sergeant."

He turned to the other drill sergeant. "Look what we have here, Bill. A Black, damn Yankee." The other sergeant snickered. Our Black drill sergeant, the lowest in seniority, remained stoic. Even when you held rank, you didn't rock the boat in those times.

I came from a racially intense city, so it didn't shock me. It did sting, though.

I sucked it up and started basic training. I didn't regret enlisting. During those 14 days of extra duty, I'd thought about it frequently and had come to that conclusion. The military might be rigid, but it was nothing compared to what I was looking at with prison. Reflecting on rat-infested, cold, steel toilets helps you appreciate the Army. I'd be fine once I learned how to navigate their ironclad rules. I'd made it through Catholic school, after all.

I put my head down and excelled in basic training. I earned Excellent Marksman with rifles and hand grenades. I shined at the physical training. I did so well that I made squad leader, Squad Leader 3.

I also made it almost to the end of basic training without another incident. Almost. One day as we waited after lunch to head to the rifle range, Squad Leader 1 turned and asked Squad Leader 2 to move out of the way. He stepped aside, unaware of what was about to happen. Squad Leader 1 didn't say a word. He hocked from deep down in his throat and spat on my boot. My reaction was immediate. I flashed back to the arcade where the White boys beat Scunz to a pulp for nothing more than being. I kicked him with the boot he spat on, and my fists started flailing. I landed a punch everywhere I could.

One of our drill sergeants ran out. This is it, I thought. Prison, here I come. You can't punch a White boy. He pulled me off and blew up in my face. Out of the corner of my eye, I saw our other drill sergeant, the one who called me a Black, damn Yankee, run out. As if things could get any worse. He ran into the middle of us. I held my breath, waiting for his wrath to explode on me. At least I'd managed a couple more months of freedom.

He pulled the other drill sergeant back. I cringed because I knew this would be worse. He wanted to take me down all by himself.

"He spit on his boot." Yelling came naturally to him.

I did a double-take. I must have heard wrong despite how loud he said it. I heard right. He stood up for me, to my amazement. He'd seen the whole thing, and he did what the Army does. They boot racism out as quickly as they did my pipe. There's no room for racial tension on a battlefield. Black, White, Hispanic. In a fox hole, skin color doesn't matter. They stripped the squad leader who spat on my boot of his leadership position and assigned him extra duty. He got hell from the rest of the Black guys and a lot of the White guys for the rest of basic training.

The one "Black, damn Yankee" comment and snicker were the only racial slurs or innuendos from my sergeants during basic training, as well. I heard several people mutter, "Damn Yankee," while there. It was part of the culture in that part of the country in that era. He added in the "Black" because he saw skin color rather than simply a recruit when he looked at me.

Once again, our one Black drill sergeant stayed silent. I'm sure he didn't want to make waves for himself.

The rest of basic training proved uneventful. I flew home for Christmas after graduation since my family couldn't afford the travel to watch this milestone in my life. I stepped off the train in my neighborhood as someone who grew up many things: An abused child, a hopeless kid, a heroin addict, a trafficker, a thief, a robber, an assailant. This time, I stepped off in full dress uniform. A sense of pride and accomplishment walked with me through the neighborhood. My mom didn't comment on the uniform, but I could see the pride on her face. That made me feel good. My three girlfriends wanted to see my fatigues, too, so I wore them and my combat boots around one day. That's not a sight you often see in the hood, so I didn't see any point telling anyone about the trouble I had gotten into. Especially my mom.

I didn't think once about heroin during basic training. They owned my thoughts. They told me when I would eat, what I would eat, when I could shower, when I could go to the bathroom. They marched me around wherever they wanted me to go. They controlled almost every minute of my day. They commanded my every movement. Who knew the military would give me so much insight for my future trafficking?

I didn't mess with heroin while I was on leave, either. I did smoke a little weed. I had to get a new pipe, though.

I flew directly from leave to Fort Dix in New Jersey for Advanced Individual Training. I looked forward to the rest of my three-year enlistment after surviving my bumpy start. I had done some radio broadcasting in a high school class, so I chose Communications when the Army instructed me to pick a Military Occupational Specialty. As aforementioned, I love learning and was excited about expanding my knowledge of radio communications.

I approached my military career choice like I did my early days of trafficking. I didn't take time to learn about what I was getting into. It sounded good, so I went with my gut. My gut still led me astray. Radio broadcasting for high school students works differently than in the Army. Had I known anything about the military, I would've known the word "tactical" in my job description alluded to the fighting force. The fighting force spends most of its time in the field, not a studio.

I let my trafficking victims change their minds; the Army doesn't let you do an about-face. They outfitted me with a pair of gaffs – iron bars with two-inch spikes on the bottom that strapped to my legs. I never knew I was terrified of heights until they pointed me up my first telephone pole. You don't have many opportunities in the hood to find out you're afraid of heights. It looked easy enough when the drill sergeants did it, and they didn't have much patience for people who fell off. They did warn us not to grab the pole if we felt ourselves falling. I got why when one kid grabbed the pole on his way down and ended up with a six-inch splinter a quarter-inch deep in his cheek.

The strap that fastened my waist to the pole gave me a little comfort, but just a little knowing it couldn't go with me if war broke out. I overcame my fears, though. By the end of training, I could make a circle around the pole at the halfway-up point; circle back around; finish climbing to the top; put my hand on top; shout my name, rank, and serial number triumphantly; and make it down in a qualifying time. I took pride in my accomplishment.

As I conquered the job requirements, I got used to it and surprised myself as I realized I enjoyed the Army. I liked the adventure, excitement, and discipline. I loved learning new skills and new things about myself, especially that I could overcome my fears when I stuck with it. I liked meeting new people and seeing new places. This purposeful life was nothing like the hood, and I was nothing like I was there – where I had no purpose. I didn't mess with drugs. I didn't think about pimping girls. I didn't steal. Instead, I concentrated on excelling. I resolved to become a man.

It's a good thing because they expected you to be a man after completing advanced training. They shipped me to Fort Riley, Kansas, where the Army handed me my life back while still expecting discipline and order. I'd never done that by myself. Everything they taught me in basic and advanced training, they now held me accountable for putting into practice.

I liked the responsibility, and I loved the new living arrangements. The wooden barracks packed with soldiers were behind me. I shared a room in a brick dorm-style building with a White guy around my age. We called him "Cowboy" because he was from Texas and wore jeans, cowboy boots, and a cowboy hat anytime he could shed his uniform. He was a nice kid, and we were friendly, but we didn't hang out outside the barracks. Segregation set boundaries even with roommates.

I worked hard and continued to excel, spending most of my time in the field as part of the Infantry Brigade. I cherished my promotions and pay raises. Outside of doing odd jobs for Uncle Danny and my summer job, it was the first time I'd had the benefit of an income without the threat of jail.

I settled in and got comfortable, so settled that I entertained thoughts of making the Army a career. So comfortable, I spent my off-duty hours with buddies at the bars on base or in town. That's where the girls were, so that's where we were. My uniform gave me no-questions-asked access despite my age. Yes, a military career had its benefits.

In town, I'd have to walk through the waft of marijuana smoke from the people hanging around outside the bar. Worse, I could smell it around the barracks. It smelled like an invitation to see a long-lost friend. Honestly, the only reason I quit smoking was the Army's watchful eyes and lack of availability. Now, with all the freedom, it was like being back on the streets but with a job. Everybody was getting high. I always was a fol-lower.

I stuck to alcohol and weed, though. I hadn't done heroin since the day I got out of jail. That's not to say I didn't think about it once the Army loos-ened its grip on my thoughts. As I explained, heroin isn't just a physical addiction. It dances seductively with your heart and mind. There's nothing quite like her in your arms. I'm not kidding. You can go months or years without her, and one thought can make you weak in the knees like an old girlfriend.

Some of the guys in my unit fell for other seductions like the brothels when we went to Panama for jungle training. It's kind of ironic that I never paid to have sex since I made plenty of money selling it. I stuck to smok-ing Panama Red. When we went to Alaska for cold-weather training, the locals plied us with alcohol, and I freely partook in that, too. I managed to avoid Big H wherever we went, though.

Until Germany. We deployed there to play war games; that's where, once again, hard drugs played war games with my mind and emotions. The Army trained me well to conquer foreign enemies; foreign substances, on the other hand, could always take me captive once they got in my head. Like any strategic invading force, it knows your weaknesses. Mine was opportunity.

Conrads, or German civilians, visited us frequently in the field to barter.

They'd buy things from us, including C-rations, extra uniforms, T-Shirts. Anything American they could talk us into parting with. One guy even sold them his M-16. He didn't make the trip home with us.

In return, they sold us hash and liquor. One day, though, I noticed a small group from our unit with a demeanor that weed and alcohol didn't have the power to pull off. Even combined.

"Damn. What y'all have?"

"Madris. It's a downer."

"Like heroin?" My mind jumped to attention. I'd never heard of it, but downers speak a common language. I hadn't thought about heroin in a long time, but the mere mention of it made my heart start racing like when you see a first love who dumped you. Like I hadn't thought about weed until I caught a whiff in the barracks and my head jerked toward the smell. That's what drugs do to you. Your first thought is, "Who has it, and where can I get some?"

"Yeah. Very similar to heroin."

One of them motioned me over. They were a little older, like the guys I followed on the streets, so I looked up to them. He broke off a small piece of his pill and wrapped my hand around it, warning me not to take a whole one. I didn't hesitate to pop it in my mouth. Follower. Role models. Hard drugs. An irresistible combination.

"Oh yeah. Just like heroin. Whoa. This is cool." I hadn't felt that euphoria in a long time. Like when that first love smiles at you again. That's probably why I had felt almost jealous when I noticed their altered dispositions.

I didn't worry too much about getting caught. Our sergeants distanced themselves from us, hanging out in their enormous command tent. We kept our business in our two-person tent camp. Besides, some of our superiors bought alcohol and weed, too. We knew to keep our activity on the low, so they wouldn't be forced to write us up.

That one morsel from the edge of his pill wasted me. The next morning, the guy who gave it to me yelled over at me: "Yo, Williams. I didn't see you around again last night."

I walked over. I didn't bother answering his question. I had a more important one. "When are they coming back?"

No one knew. They showed up randomly every few days. They showed up enough for us to pop the little pills throughout our four-week stay and ship a bunch back in our radios packed all together. We snuck in a few bottles of liquor, too. Why not? The chances of getting caught were slim since it wasn't ours but property of the U.S. Army.

They weren't enough for me to get physically addicted. After they were gone, I kept my arm and my nose clean. The opportunity wasn't right in front of me any longer, making it easier to resist. No need to put my freedom in jeopardy if I'd have to hunt down an opportunity. I figured it was kind of like saying goodbye to my girlfriends at the end of leave. I'd see them again next chance I got.

I took pride in how well I was doing despite the occasional bump in the road. Then I ran into a rut in the road. Not any rut. A Second Lieutenant in the motor pool caused this rut. It's like a truck driver carrying too heavy a load. This guy carried a heavy load of know-it-all. He arrived in our unit fresh from a college ROTC program.

I took pride in my work, as I told you. I'd also learned that you do better when you stick to the Army's way of doing things rather than your own.

He told me to do something the wrong way, not the Army way.

"Sir. That is not our standard operating procedure."

He raised his voice: "Do what I told you, Williams."

I had worked hard and conquered fears to learn the Army way of my job.

"Sir, with all due respect, that is not our SOP."

"I'm telling you, PFC, you are going to do it this way," he barked.

I didn't know him, and I didn't respect that he flexed his muscle because of a few bars on his lapel. An ROTC degree didn't give him the right to disregard and disrespect Army procedures, especially since he hadn't been there long enough to know our base.

I turned to find the sergeant.

He grabbed me by my shoulder, hard. If I had left it there, it would have been another bump. He would have gotten in trouble for laying his hands on me. I dug the rut deeper instead.

I swung around and punched him square in the face. He yelled but didn't say a word.

I walked to the barracks, right past my sergeant. I looked back once and saw the guy with the bars on his lapel holding his face.

I knew I was in a lot of trouble this time.

"Who is it?" I yelled when the knock at the door came 20-30 minutes later.

The MP ordered me to put my hands on my footlocker, which stood about two feet high off the floor. They held me by the collar so that I wouldn't fall. I was almost lying down in the air. After they searched me, they cuffed me and took me to the stockade.

Field Grade Article 15. They escalated it from my company commander to the battalion commander. It's like the district court bumping your case to the superior court. A dishonorable discharge loomed over my head.

Somehow, I got off easier than I should have again. Easier in the moment; bad news for the long run. They demoted me two ranks, fined me, and sent me to an eight-week stint in the retraining brigade, which is like basic training on steroids times 10. Most people who go there don't make it. They intentionally try to break you. I thought about quitting many times, but then I'd see my mom's face and a two-year prison sentence. After the little German pills, I knew I'd get in trouble in no time in Boston. I knew where all the opportunities hung out there.

The silver lining was my unit didn't want me back, so I got to pick a new unit. I said good-bye to the misleading Radio Communications stint and hello to the Headquarters Garrison Unit. That's where most of the female soldiers served, plus they didn't go to war if it broke out. They stayed behind to run the base. They operated the PX, the Quartermaster Laundry, uniform distribution, the officers' clubs, recreation services, and other administrative programs. Much easier than out in the field day after day. Less disciplined, too.

I picked the gym because I'd hung out in the rec centers in the hood. I knew I could slide by. Sure enough, for the next one and a half years, I rarely had to don a uniform, and I never went to training again. I opened up the gym, checked equipment in and out, and all the other things that come along with running a workout facility. I didn't care that this job cut down on my opportunities to learn and travel. Everything looks pretty much the same when you're out in the woods with rations. I didn't think about the other options it would open me up to.

My new assignment freed up a lot of my time that had until now been structured. Opportunity. Old habits die hard when they've had a lot of time to take root. I ran the streets – on and off base – hanging out in bars, drinking, smoking weed, and hooking up with girls for sex. I ran across heroin a couple of times and crystal meth once.

The Army no longer was a discipline. Now, it was just a job.

## Analysis With Dr. Deena Graves:
### Racism

I will never forget the drill sergeant's face twisted in mockery or the feeling of his judgmental breath in my face when he called me a "Black, damn Yankee." Here is a man who had never seen me before in his life. His first thoughts when he saw my face and found out where I was from were "Black" and "North."

I can still hear the snarl of the other sergeant's snicker.

Those two gentlemen in leadership positions had the opportunity to shape the life of a 17-year-old boy from the hood who had never had a positive male influence. However, they didn't see a young, impressionable boy who had volunteered to serve his country, to fight for it if war broke out.

The words we say leave a lifetime impression on people that impacts their self-esteem, their self-worth, and their identity. We all are accountable for the choices we make in life, and, as I've stressed, I am not trying to make excuses for what I did or evoke empathy. I *am* trying to prevent our kids from becoming traffickers, dope fiends, or other criminals.

With that in mind, let me pose a question: If you don't feel you have value as a human, how do you see value or worth in other humans? It's virtually impossible. If I'm willing to give it all for my country, and that is still not enough because I was born with a skin color not the same as yours, how can I believe anything will ever be enough?

The way we talk to our youth sends subliminal messages whether we intend them to or not. John F. Kennedy said, "Ask not what your country can do for you – ask what you can do for your country."[69]

I haven't hidden the fact that I asked both questions. I was happy to serve my country and thankful that serving my country helped me escape certain prison time. I took a lot from my country in other ways, too. One of my mottoes became, "Ask not what I can do for you, but what you can do for me." That's a trafficker's mindset. Perhaps my drill sergeants could have influenced me to develop a different character.

I agree with Dr. Martin Luther King, Jr.: "I look to a day when people will not be judged by the color of their skin, but by the content of their character."[70]

As a Black man who grew up during extreme racial tensions and bore the brunt of numerous hateful and hurtful comments and actions, let me stress that the current movement to treat Whites with hatred because of what happened in past generations is not the answer. Many wonderful, kind, giving people exist in every race. Likewise, bad people hide out in every race. Let's look at each person as an individual to change the world together.

Please let us also remember that all teenagers are impressionable. The teen years are tough, no matter who they are or what color their skin is, because of all the changes to their bodies and brains. Guard your words when you talk to them. It doesn't always matter whether our words are true or whether we mean them or not. Three small words echoed through every aspect of my identity for decades. They still reverberate when I let myself think about them.

I wonder if history might have been different if instead of "Black, damn Yankee," he would have said something like, "Do Boston proud, Son."

## Two-Minute Introspection

What words still cut you years later? How do they change your perspective of how we should talk to teens?

# 19 Nice Try

The Army gave up disciplining me, but a woman who worked in a base bar drilled a valuable lesson into me. You might say she was like a mom to me. At least she was old enough to be my mother. I flirted with her despite her age and the fact she dated a sergeant I knew. She flirted back.

"Hey, I'm getting off early today. What are you doing?"

"Nothing." What else would my answer be?

We bumped into her son on the way into her house. He looked at me with disdain. Strange. He had no idea why I was there.

The next morning, she told me I needed to leave and made me hitchhike back to base. I knew rejection well, but rejection from women I slept with was a stranger to me. I had to mean something to her, or she wouldn't have slept with me. Maybe she felt guilty since her son saw us.

I'd go in the bar and sit for hours. She'd ignore me. It took me a couple of weeks, but I finally got the message after watching her flirt with a string of other young soldiers. Now I understood the look on her son's face. I felt so used, like an old washrag – kind of like I'd been prostituted. A woman had never treated me like I treated women. I didn't know what to think. A deep wound punctured my heart. My world started spiraling.

Years later, I saw it as poetic justice. You reap what you sow, after all. At the time, I saw it as a slap in the face.

I partied off base more after that. One day, Lance, one of my buddies from base, tracked me down at a bar in Junction City. Lacy had shown up on base asking for me. Good friend that he was, Lance put her up in a hotel and came to find me alone since he knew I'd probably be with another woman.

"No way. Get outta here."

He described her to a T.

What was she doing here after all this time? Without warning. Despite my shock, I was elated. A little piece of home had magically shown up after almost a year of not seeing anyone. Lacy and I wrote often. I'd tell her I missed her, loved her, wished she were with me. I meant it as much as I had it in me to love anyone, but she must have bought it to travel halfway across the country.

Lance let me borrow his car to take her to dinner, and I spent every minute I could with her. When she got ready to leave at the end of the week, I tried to convince her to stay.

"We can get married. Move into base housing. I can make the military a career."

I knew she'd love the idea. She'd flown more than 1,500 miles to surprise me when I'd never taken her anywhere farther than the track in downtown Boston. She must really miss me.

Many guys in the Army brought their hometown girlfriend to base to get married and settle down. It seemed like the thing to do. I cared about her, so why not? I could keep that little piece of home with me.

She turned down my proposal flat, insisting she had to go back to Boston to finish high school. I didn't expect another rejection fresh on the heels of the older woman, especially not from Lacy after all we'd been through together. I couldn't wrap my mind around it. Why would she come unannounced if she weren't madly in love with me? It didn't add up. When you're from the hood, you don't refuse marriage to a guy who can get you out of there. You don't turn down the opportunity for the government to provide you with real housing. My proposal was a win-win proposition. And she'd sure never turned my propositions down before. She could finish school there with me.

So much rejection in such a short time shattered me. My sense of self-worth had a negative balance before these two women piled on. The deficit grew like maxed out credit cards. I fought harder for Lacy than I did the woman from the bar. I poured my love out in letters and calls.

"You hurt me deeply, Lacy."

"I wish you would've stayed."

I told her all the things we could do together.

She rejected every overture. Her mom needed her, she explained.

She had to finish school, she insisted – although she never did. I didn't escape my attention that she never said she'd come when she graduated.

I thought about selling a couple of girls I'd met hanging out at one of my girlfriend's houses to stroke my wounded ego. I mentioned to one that I'd noticed she had a lot of boyfriends. She told me they weren't her boyfriends. She hung out where the GIs hung out. She'd go with them, she said, but it would cost them. I crossed her off my list. She had her own hustle going; why would she share her earnings with me? The other girl turned out to do pretty much the same thing. I had a steady paycheck and didn't know where a track was in town, so I decided it wasn't worth the effort.

I soothed my hurt pride with alcohol, weed, sex, and the occasional hard drug. I frequently hung out smoking weed on my girlfriend's porch when she was at work. I'd strike up conversations with people who walked by, especially women and girls who caught my eye. One girl in particular, Kiara, not only caught my eye, she held it. She was different from other girls in the neighborhood. She lived in another part of town, but she hung out with school friends who lived there. I noticed she didn't drink or do drugs like them. She didn't sneak into bars with GIs. She had this aura of purity about her that I hadn't encountered in a girl before, especially not one living on the edge of an Army base.

She was sweet, not street. Kind of quiet, too, not blatantly trying to attract my attention like many women and girls. She intrigued me. She became a challenge. I didn't know "good" girls existed, and that was just what I needed to mend the broken pieces of my jilted narcissism.

Soon after I met Kiara, Lance and I moved off base into a trailer. I couldn't believe my eyes when I saw Kiara in the trailer park one day. She was my neighbor! That upped my odds, and, sure enough, it didn't take long to sweet-talk her into becoming my girlfriend. I kept working it, doing things like taking her to eat and schmoozing her until I got her in bed. That's where I learned she was a virgin. Something else I'd never experienced before. That made me like her even more. A new feeling for a girl rose inside me for the first time: Respect.

That was a weird feeling. It made me treat her differently than I did other girls. Like I never took her to a bar until she was 18. Don't get me wrong. I was still me, still a little wild even with her. That was part of what she liked about me. She liked the bad boy; I liked the good girl.

I found myself growing to care about her more than I did Lacy. That was a strange feeling, too. Lacy and I shared that dirty little secret. We shared a deep history. She helped me out in my time of need. She flew four hours to see me.

She hopped back on the plane and went home, though. Kiara couldn't get enough of me. We spent all the time we could together. I loved the sense of goodness and morality she brought into my life. It washed away some of the feelings of unworthiness and immorality that I'd lived with most of my life. I wanted to be better for her, not make her worse for me. It felt like a real relationship for the first time. I was happy now that Lacy decided to get back on that plane.

Kiara's mom wasn't. She would have been happy for anyone to take me away from her daughter. She hated me. A mother's intuition, I'm sure. She could feel her underage daughter slipping away. Her ex-military dad had died, and her mom was overprotective. Sometimes you need to be. They were not "hood," and she did not want her daughter acting as if she were. As hard as I tried to be better for her, I still caused her to be worse for me in ways.

Her mom's hatred didn't slow us down, and I was happy, maybe for the first time. My bliss was short-lived.

Everything went incredibly for about a month. And then Lacy's letter arrived.

She was pregnant.

Immediately, I thought it was a setup. Her surprise visit wasn't about missing me. It was about framing me, I concluded. She showed up unannounced to get me into bed. She'd helped me out in my time of need; now, it was time to pay her back.

My anger flared – I begged you to stay and get married. You left to go to school but never walked through the school's doorway. Yeah, I'm nothing more than your mark. You want your baby to have a father – a father in the Army with a steady paycheck. Derek will take care of us.

What was happening to me? How had I suddenly become the victim of females instead of the other way around?

We argued back and forth through letters until I stopped responding.

I threw myself unconditionally into Kiara. Before long, she came up pregnant. This time I was thrilled.

"Let's get married." That's still what most of the Army guys were doing. Remember, I always was a follower.

Her mom was livid and refused to allow her to get married. That kind of hurt, too. I was trying to do the right thing. Kiara said, "Yes," anyway, and the moment she turned 18, we hurried to the Justice of the Peace.

I hadn't taken leave since basic training, so I took off and headed to Boston to show off my new wife. Kiara was very polite, and my mom liked her, but she wasn't particularly excited. We stayed a week, and I took her around all my old haunts, introduced her to some of my extended family and old friends. I managed to avoid my former girlfriends.

Like several girls before her, she loved the excitement of downtown Boston … during the day. I didn't share the nighttime seduction of the Combat Zone – or my history with it. She already was a little afraid of my inner-city neighborhood with its out-in-the-open crime and the steady high-pitched wail of sirens. She liked the bad boy in me, but I don't think she would have liked the monster in her new husband and father of her baby. She probably wouldn't have been good knowing her husband's track record at the prostitution track. She presumably wouldn't have enjoyed the train ride so much, either, if she had known how many girls I railroaded into a lifetime of trauma on it. Good thing we never ran into Lacy.

We had a great time, but when we got back home, she decided to continue living with her mom. She said she needed to take care of her. Her mom still couldn't stand the sight of me, so I'm sure she played on Kiara's sympathies. We were happy despite being married on paper only. She'd come down to my trailer, and we'd go on dates. I'd even walk her back home at the end of the evening together.

I bought an old Volkswagen as her due date approached. I learned another thing about myself when her water broke. I was the nervous-expectant-father type, flying through red lights getting her to the hospital. The police officer who stopped us escorted us to the hospital. I thought what a nice guy he was when he followed us inside to make sure we were okay. I still appreciated him for getting us there safely after he wrote me a ticket for speeding and failure to stop.

I was elated when our little boy arrived. I was even more ecstatic when she wanted to name him Derek. I couldn't believe I had a wife and son. It was a little hard letting him go home to Kiara's mom's trailer, but I went along with it to make her happy. She had made me incredibly happy and gotten me on the right path, so it was the least I could do.

The date was fast approaching to re-enlist, and Kiara and I talked about making it a career. The Army would provide a good living for my little family, and I liked serving my country. I asked for a deployment to Korea, where buddies had made a lot of money buying and selling stuff while enjoying easy duty. The Army refused and notified me I would go back to the field if I re-enlisted. I had gotten too comfortable to go back into the strict military regimen – wearing a uniform, marching in formation, some-one constantly standing over me – so I decided to get out.

I wasn't sure how I would support a wife and child at only 20 with no education beyond high school. My best opportunity would be in Boston, I decided. I sure didn't want to stay in the small country area where I'd spent the last couple of years. Jobs there were scarce, and I liked the bustle of the city. Kiara and I agreed to make a new start. I'd collect unemploy-ment while I looked for a job, so we didn't have to worry about finances.

When it came time to go, Kiara felt her mom wasn't quite ready for her to leave. She needed to get her settled, she told me. She and Derek would join me after that. Sadness welled up in me as Kiara and our baby waved me off at the bus station, but I knew it was short-term. And I was happy to be going home. I would find a job and get us a place to live, so my family could hurry and join me.

I did look for a job, but not too hard since I had a final check coming with my honorable discharge papers. I hung out in the streets while I waited for the check to arrive. Without Kiara's goodness to guide me, I promptly slipped back into my old routine like a pair of comfortable, old slippers. Unemployment kicked in, and I hadn't fallen into a job yet, so I continued to reconnect with my old life. I'd been gone three years, so I was excited to see all the familiar faces and old hangouts.

Kiara, for her part, kept making excuses about why they couldn't join me. Looking back, I believe she did love me but feared moving to the big city and leaving her mom and everything familiar behind. However, as a young husband and father who had lived a lifetime of rejection, it hit me hard. I wasn't good enough, I reasoned, or she would have put our family first.

**176**

I went on the rebound, doing what many jilted lovers do. I sought out my first love – heroin. I hadn't done hard drugs since I started dating Kiara but picking up my romance with dope dulled the pain of getting kicked in the teeth again. I jumped on the first opportunity I had to mask those feelings when someone at the poolroom invited me to go with him on a dope run.

I felt as if I were frozen in time. Nothing had changed in my hood. I felt as if I had gotten off the merry-go-round and hopped right back on the same horse when it came back around.

Then the carousel lurched suddenly and sent me flying. Lacy dropped by my house unannounced. I didn't know it, but she'd fallen into a bad habit with that. My mom brought her back to my room, where I was hanging out with a couple of friends.

"You're not going to say 'hi' to your son?" Lacy asked innocently.

"I'll say 'hi' to your son."

I was not doing this with her. My wife and real son weren't going to materialize, and here she showed up to yank my chain. He didn't even look like me, I thought, as I sized up the almost 1-year-old resting on her hip and eyeing me.

My mom jumped in: "Don't be like that to her." I also didn't know at the time that my family had accepted the baby as mine. I couldn't believe she was trying to force this baby on me when I had a wife and son I was mourning. I was happy with Kiara. Lacy and our dirty secret were the past.

Anger swelled up in me like lava in a volcano about to erupt as Lacy walked over and sat down beside me on the bed. She had jilted me when I proposed marriage, and now she wanted to snuggle up to me with someone else's son.

She shoved him in my arms. I felt nothing and handed him back over.

She got up and headed toward the door.

"Come on, Derek. Let's go," she smiled at the kid she'd named after me.

This bitch is crazy, I thought.

## Analysis With Dr. Deena Graves:
### Generational Fatherlessness

I was at a loss as a father. I had no idea how a healthy father acted. I had no idea a father stays with his wife and son. Sure, I missed Kiara and Derek, but I had been gone from home for three years. It was more important to me to make myself happy than to stay and fight for my family. I felt disappointed and rejected when Kiara chose not to join me, but the keyword there is "rejected." It always came back to what I felt and what I wanted. Even her goodness couldn't compete with that after two decades of it maturing inside me.

I started having fun and didn't think about missing my son growing up. I had so much fun, in fact, that I threw another baby in the mix without concern for my wife or how my lifestyle would impact any of my children. I met Brianna not long after arriving back in Boston from the Army. She'd yell at me from a second-story window as I walked past on my way to the bowling alley, ducking out of sight when I turned. It took me a couple of months to catch her. When I did, I moved fast. Her shyness made her an easy target. Her good-girl lifestyle intrigued me as it had with Kiara. Not enough, though, to keep me from trying to lure her into the game.

I took her to the movies and to eat in the Combat Zone. I casually mentioned on the way to King of Pizza that it was where I had gone when I had girls working for me. The bright lights and excitement of the Combat Zone had always worked before but fell flat with Brianna.

"That's disgusting." Disgusting for the girls to do it and disgusting for me to sleep with them after they did. Not too repulsive, however, for her to sleep with me after I convinced her I always wore a condom. Also, not too disgusting for her to take money through the years to help raise our son, Tyrone. You heard that right. She wanted to name our son after me. I thought three kids running around with my name would be too many, so she pushed to name him after my father. I hadn't seen my stepfather for years, but he was the only "father" I'd ever lived with and the one I still called "Dad," so I settled on his name to appease her.

I didn't have a father involved in my life, so it didn't affect me not being involved in any form in Derek's life and only slightly in Tyrone's. I'm not alone in that. Fathers who did not have a positive father figure often take a cue from their dads for their own behavior, leading to a greater likelihood of missing out on their children's lives.[71] Men who grew up without a father often don't know how to break the cycle even if they want to.[72] Some research suggests the lack of a father's influence can be more detrimental to parenting skills than poverty and violence.[73]

We need to teach our boys about fatherhood while they are still young. If one of my uncles or a mentor had stepped in and bought me a bike and taught me how to ride it, I probably would have realized what a special thing that would have been to do with my son. If a man had come to watch one of my sporting events, I would have known the thrill of yelling for my son.

We need to teach our young boys what a responsible father is *as they grow up*, not *after* they become a father. We can both teach and model that in existing programs such as boys' clubs, recreation centers, community centers, sports programs, and in school.

We need men of all ages who understand what a father truly is to step in and eradicate the epidemic of fatherlessness, especially in the Black community. Coaches had to know all of us on my teams didn't have positive father figures because we never had a man at a practice or a game. They had to talk to our moms about everything.

Men, let's stay on the lookout for those kinds of situations and step up to the plate for our young boys, their future children, and our society.

## Two-Minute Introspection

What other concrete steps can we take to end generational fatherlessness?

# 20 Trouble in Paradise

I managed to land a job at a nursing home despite my long hours back on the streets. I worked hard and got certified as a nursing aide. A staff doctor must have seen potential in me because he encouraged me to go to school on the GI Bill. I thought briefly about my dream of becoming an attorney. Someone told me how long I'd have to go to college, though, so I put that dream to bed for good. I settled on barber school. Uncle Danny had thrived as a barber. He moved his shop out of the hood into a prestigious downtown area and his family out of the hood into the suburbs. He established himself as one of Boston's most renowned Black hair salons. He never gave up on his dream. He fought hard to defy the odds. I reasoned, then, that it must be a good career choice. I could spend a fraction of the time of law school in barber school and walk out with a guaranteed job.

People came from all over the state to the Massachusetts School of Barbering. They flocked from the most impoverished inner cities and the most affluent neighborhoods. A guy from an affluent area taught me about the "rich man's high." I added freebasing cocaine to the mix of alcohol, weed, and occasional heroin. Unlike heroin, though, the high didn't last hours. I had to chase the euphoria all night. Thus, the "rich man's high" epithet.

I learned something about rich girls, too. Some of them liked the bad boy in me and the excitement of a dirty little secret just as much as the girls from the hood. I sweet-talked a couple of them into walking the track a few times to support my rich-man habit. Seemed fitting. They made me feel like an upper-crust pimp. I'd cruise their fancy cars around the track while they worked instead of hoofing it like in the past.

I slid back into trafficking as effortlessly as I did the streets. Might as well go all in if I was going to do it. I sold a few girls from the hood, a couple of girls I met downtown at the arcade, and a girl who chose me one night on the track. I didn't devote much time to trafficking; I jumped on opportunities as they arose. I'd smoke $50 of cocaine in 45 minutes without satisfaction, so I kept my eye peeled for available resources.

In addition to Brianna, I hooked back up with Gabrielle, Evelyn, and any other girl I could use for sex. I stirred clear of Lacy and her son. I wooed a few girls in barber school into bed, too. They drove us to my boarding room for a quickie during our lunch break. Definitely made barber school more interesting.

I enjoyed them and my freebasing buddy for the nine months we attended barber school together. After we graduated, I said goodbye and started working for Uncle Danny at His and Hers. His addition of hairstylists, ads, and word-of-mouth attracted a more well-to-do clientele, including newscasters, businesspeople, and university students. He'd become so successful that he'd conduct hair shows in swanky hotels. He took me under his wing and let me tag along to the shows. He paid me excellent money whether I helped at a show or in the shop.

His entire lifestyle had changed, and he left the poverty mindset in the hood with his old shop. Not me. I took it wherever I went, including the Army, barber school, and Uncle Danny's shop.

Naturally, then, I gravitated toward his employees who did drugs. One day, I made a drug run to the projects, and that's where more than a poverty mindset followed me. My past, which I thought I had outrun, caught up to me. Police stopped me before I bought anything, but I was still in a known drug area infested with dealers and addicts. They ran my name, and, to my surprise, a warrant popped up for possession of heroin. I couldn't believe it. My two-year suspended sentence was long over. My time in the Army was supposed to run out the clock. Unbeknown to me, however, I had an outstanding warrant for that long-ago arrest.

I served 10 months at the Deer Island House of Correction. I blamed the system, not myself. It didn't matter that I was hunting for drugs when I was arrested, that I had gotten busted in the Army for drugs, or that the original arrest was for heroin. All I cared about was what was happening to me. My stint in the military was supposed to keep me out of jail. I decided I couldn't win against a corrupt system.

My barber career was over before it started. Until one of the corrections officers showed me an act of kindness and met one of my girlfriends to pick up my clippers. I spent my time in jail perfecting my craft and earning money for the commissary.

Uncle Danny welcomed me back once I got out. I'm not sure if it was anger at the system, boredom, or reflex, but I turned back to trafficking as a hobby. I certainly didn't have any thoughts of making it a career. I had a career. I dated a couple of co-workers but didn't attempt to traffic them since they made good money. I didn't think Uncle Danny would appreciate it, either. I did traffick a couple of his customers who stayed loyal to him from the hood. He'd approved of me pimping girls from the hood back in the day, so I figured he wouldn't mind now.

Determined not to go back to prison, I started attending Narcotics Anonymous meetings. They stressed transparency, so I poured my heart out. About my addiction. They wanted to push their way into other areas of my life where they had no business, though. They emphasized changing playmates and playgrounds for genuine change. I wasn't trying to get to the change part. Everything you do, you do better clean. The meetings wouldn't just keep me out of jail; they'd make me a better trafficker. Drugs cloud your thinking, divert your attention to things like not waking up sick. I could concentrate fully on my side job as a pimp with a clear mind. The track made an exciting playground and victims lucrative playmates. Why would I want to give them up?

They also warned us not to get involved with each other, but I brushed that advice off, too. All they needed to be concerned about was keeping a needle out of my arm. Therefore, when an attractive woman told me how much she appreciated my transparency, I started dating her. Why not? She understood what I was going through. We could battle the pull of drugs together. Denise made a great safety net for a couple of months. She was trying for the genuine change part, though. Denise was serious about changing her playmates and playground, so she pressured me about God. I'd never seen God at my playground, so I shut her down, and she shut me out.

I didn't mind. She was one of several. His and Hers sat around the corner from MIT and Northeastern University. I started dating college girls and women who worked downtown. My life changed one day when a law student attending Boston College walked through our doors. I always offered to shampoo clients for hairstylists when I wasn't busy or thought someone was cute. I rushed to shampoo her hair. I noticed she kept her eyes on me while the stylist cut her hair. From there, we'd talk when she came in, and she eventually invited me over for dinner.

Nancy lived alone in a nice house and drove an expensive car. Her father was a doctor and her mother an attorney in New York. We grew close fast. I might have given up on my dream of becoming an attorney, but I didn't mind dating one – or all the benefits that came with it, including her parents' credit cards. I made good money at Danny's, too, so we had a good time.

We ate at expensive restaurants. We took trips to New York for Broadway shows and shopping, Florida for Disney World, and New Hampshire for the ski resorts.

One day, she decided we needed a trip to Hawaii and booked us five days in Oahu. I was down for whatever she wanted to do since she paid for most of it. I knew Uncle Danny would never fire me, so I didn't bother telling him. I did think it might make my pregnant girlfriend, Dominique, mad, so I told her I was running to the liquor store to get cigarettes. I did call her two days later to let her know where I was. I had to. I'd met her through my sister, and I didn't want her mad at me.

Nancy and I had a great time in Hawaii, living it up on room service, bottles of cognac, swimming up to the pool bar, nights out on the town, luaus, and all the other tourist stuff. We had so much fun that Nancy decided five days wasn't enough. I agreed, silently thanking her parents for a lush tropical vacation, not to mention the cognac.

She didn't do drugs, not even weed, so I made friends who did. We rented motorcycles one day to drive around the island. It started to rain, and I hit the back tire of the car in front of me as I changed lanes. My motorcycle and I slid across the road, leaving agonizing road rash down my side. I somehow protected my helmetless head but still needed to go to the hospital for the pain. I managed to ride the motorcycle back to the hotel, and Nancy drove me to the hospital.

I didn't have insurance, so the hospital wouldn't give me anything beyond a pan of water and some gauze. Nancy headed back to the hotel to grab a credit card. That's when we learned her parents had cut her off.

They were none too happy she had run up all their cards and stopped answering their calls. They drove to her house in Boston, where they found a photo of me with Mickey Mouse. They also found one of my business cards and made a beeline to His and Hers.

They showed the picture to Danny: "You know him?"

"Yeah, that's Mickey Mouse." He didn't know who they were, so he protected me despite the number of times I had left him high and dry at the shop.

I wasn't too concerned about how her parents felt and none too happy that she was afraid to call them. I was more worried about how I was feeling.

Our good time had come to a screeching halt, and we had no way to get home. How irresponsible could she be?

"You brought me all the way over here, and now we have no way to get back. You have to do something." I had noticed how busy the blade was on Kuhio Avenue, so I already had a good idea of what that something would be.

I had told her I'd sold girls before. I'd taken an ego trip by showing her the track in Boston.

"See, that's what they're doing. See, they're working."

I hadn't planned to sell her at the time. I was showing off, flexing my bad-boy muscle since she'd been so sheltered. She had been drawn to the bad boy in me, after all.

Now, she was frightened by it. Not of me, of what the bad boy wanted her to do.

"Listen, it's not that hard."

"I can't do it."

"We'll go out there tonight, and you can watch what the girls are doing. You don't have to do anything."

She was surprised at how quickly girls came back after jumping in a car.

I talked pimp lingo to a guy we saw on the blade.

"Yeah, man. I'll have my girl show her around."

She reluctantly agreed to give it a try. She had the right clothes and the right look. She didn't even need a wig. The other pimp's girl showed her the ropes, including how to have drinks with the buyers.

She pulled in $300. We were well on our way to making enough money to get out of there, and she thought it was exciting once she tried it. I didn't care that she was sleeping with other guys. I liked her and enjoyed our relationship, but it often felt like I was pimping myself out to her. She footed most of the bill to have sex with me. Now she could see what that felt like.

We worked the blade four days, making enough money to pay off our hotel bill and the airline ticket change fees with a few hundred dollars left over. For her part, she became another notch in my "dirty-little-secret" trail of victims, relishing in the excitement of the moment.

Her parents refused to reinstate her credit cards when we got back, and she had to drop out of law school. She didn't mind because she was in love and didn't like law school. Her parents had made her choose between law school and medical school. An attorney sounded like the lesser of two evils.

We decided to get a fresh start in Orlando since we'd had so much fun at Disney World. The warm and sunny climate appealed to us, too. She got a job in a restaurant, and I took a few weeks off to recover from our bad experience in Hawaii. She made good tips, so there was no need for me to rush.

We stayed in a hotel the first few days. I'd go to ride Space Mountain every day, and I'd squeeze in sex with a couple of maids before Nancy got back from waitressing.

Things started getting tight about three weeks in, so I got a job frying chicken at a water park. I still found time to sprint over to Disney and ride Space Mountain regularly since Nancy was too exhausted to do much after work.

She didn't have as much fun in Florida this time, and waitressing started wearing thin, thin enough that she started talking to her parents again. They urged her to come home. Space Mountain had lost some of its thrill for me by about six months, so I didn't resist when she was ready to go.

She headed back to New York to finish her law degree, and I walked back into Uncle Danny's like I'd been out sick a couple of days. I brushed off his usual, "I can't run a business like this." I knew how to play upon his empathy as easily as all the girls I conned. I didn't have a role model, and his sister was doing the best she could with what she had to work with. He'd never close his door to me.

Nancy and I stayed in touch for about a year. I visited her in New York a couple of times, and she came to see me a few times.

I don't think she ever realized I had no more feelings for her than any other girl I sold. Only difference was she handed me more money off the track than on the track.

**Analysis With Dr. Deena Graves:**

## Because He Loves Me

Nancy and Lacy weren't alone in thinking I cared about them. Most of the girls did. All I had to do was call them "Baby" and throw in a few, "I love yous."

I painted a picture of pimping and prostitution that sounded as thrilling as riding Space Mountain every day. I didn't bother to tell Nancy or the other girls I lured into my trap about the dangers or what it had done to Lacy and Karen's self-esteem and self-worth, how it stripped them of their identity and gave them a perverted view of their purpose.

I was too wrapped up in myself at the time to care that I stole something from each of them that they'd never get back. I left them with memories they'll never entirely rid themselves of.

Today, I encourage young girls who believe they should do this for their "boyfriends" because they love them to consider my story of using girl after girl in the same way. It was always about my profit and pleasure. I didn't care what happened to them in the process – physically, mentally, or emotionally. The "boyfriend" moves on as I did. All the girls I left in the wreckage never again saw the same person reflecting in the mirror.

I never sold Kiara. That unmasks the lie. You can't share someone with strangers who you see value in. A guy doesn't think highly of anyone he's willing to prostitute. But, you should think highly of yourself, I urge young girls. You are worth more than someone selling your body for their benefit. If you're looking for excitement, keep in mind that the excitement will wear off. He'll spend the money in a short time – most of it on himself. Once they're both gone, I can promise you that you won't feel good about yourself. I've seen it in more than 150 women and girls. The pimp and a string of nondescript buyers decimate an intimate part of who you are. They'll go on to ravage other girls, and you'll carry the fact you've been used for the rest of your life. You're more powerful than that. Don't fall for it.

## Two-Minute Introspection

Think back to a time when someone told you a lie you believed that caused you deep pain. What did you learn from that that you can use to help teens understand they are worth honest relationships?

# PART 3. CAREER PIMP

# 21 Who's the Boss

Most pimps find a bottom to use. A bottom found me to use.

You might say she turned me out.

Another case of poetic justice in my life.

I met Tiny in a bar in the Combat Zone. Ostensibly, Tiny didn't just play me; she played all the pimps in that bar.

I watched her with curiosity. She appeared to be a working girl, but I never saw her with a pimp or other girls. She always came in alone. She'd leave and come back in alone again after a while. Most traffickers don't let their girls go in a bar once, let alone in and out at will. She didn't seem to have a lot of respect for the rules of the game.

I sat in amusement as she shunned pimp after pimp who thought he'd be the one to get her to choose. She'd tell them not to bother her, get up and move, or simply spin her barstool around to give them her back. At not even 5-feet tall, she gained the respect of every pimp in there.

I played it cool but managed to make eye contact with her a couple of times. She didn't look away, I noted. After a couple of successful glances, I decided I'd throw my hat in with the other pimps and give it a try. What did I have to lose?

"Give her one on me, whatever she's drinking," I motioned the bartender.

I waited without any expectations while he made the drink and walked it down to her. I prepared myself to suck up another shot of rejection when she didn't move. She sat there looking at the drink. I waited for her to push it away. Instead, she finally looked down the bar, gave me a slight nod, and said, "Thanks."

I always told my girls to "Follow your money," so I followed the drink I paid for down to her barstool.

"Can I sit here?" She nodded.

"I'm Derek."

"Tiny."

"What's going on?"

"Nothing. Just down here getting my money."

"Your money?"

"Yeah."

Renegade. That answered part of my curiosity. She asked if I had girls.

"Not at the moment."

"You're down here a lot."

"Yeah. You know. I had some girls, but they ran off and stuff."

"Yeah. I had a pimp, but he went to jail."

Her man had gone away for five years, so she decided why not keep coming down to get her own money. She sent him a little now and again out of respect.

I liked her style. I got her number and called her the next day for lunch at Bob the Chef's on the border of downtown Boston and Roxbury, where she lived.

She was cute, and my intention was solely to date her since she seemed pretty set on doing her own thing and plenty capable of pulling it off without anyone's help. She quickly steered the conversation to the game, though.

"So, you trying to knock me?" She didn't waste time getting right to the point. "I wasn't," I thought, "but, hey, if you're offering … "

She spelled it out. She liked me. She thought I was cute, and I didn't "sweat" her – pimp lingo for bother her. She'd watched me out of curiosity, too. She liked that I respected her space and noticed I treated everyone with courtesy.

In that first meeting, she taught me things about the game that I didn't know. Her guy wasn't coming home anytime soon, and that slowed down her game. Working her hometown was one thing, but it would be difficult to work out of state independently. The game doesn't work like that. She didn't want to limit her options, so she wanted a pimp. I didn't know yet that she'd worked out of state with her pimp.

Despite her tough-girl facade, she also felt incomplete without a pimp. It's part of the game, the pimp culture: Pimps and hos go together like peanut butter and jelly or cake and ice cream. Pimps and many of their girls agreed: "Ain't nothing better for a ho than a pimp."

Tiny simply wanted one on her terms, not some guy forcing himself on her.

She also wasn't interested in being another girl in a pimp's stable. She was worth more than that, she believed. Bottom Bitch or top-girl material. Honestly, that was probably another thing that attracted her to me. I spent all my time in the bar, so I couldn't have too much of a game going on. I unmistakably needed her help.

I didn't realize she had decided to up my game. I'm thinking I've got a chance to take this girl to the track when she was getting ready to take me to the track.

While I thought it'd be nice to have a ho again, I still didn't understand her. How could she think she could sit in that bar with all those pimps? She could be selling drugs for all I knew. Maybe I'd just date her.

"You ever been to New York?" she reeled my interest back in.

"Yeah."

"To work?"

Needless to say, she had my full attention now. "Never to work. Been there shopping and partying."

"You should go to New York to work," she stated matter-of-factly.

"Yeah, I should," I scolded myself. Why hadn't I thought of that? I'd be considered international if I worked New York. Yeah, I needed to go to New York.

"What ya doing tonight?" I asked.

"Going to work." She paused. "But I don't have to."

"Wanna meet me at the club?"

We both walked away from lunch still curious, interested, but not fully committed. If nothing else, I'd have sex with her.

She showed up to the bar about 15 minutes late, sending a subliminal message of who was in charge, a message I didn't pick up on. I was too busy kicking it with the other pimps in front of the bar, smoking a joint and showing off my new pimp game. I didn't wear sneakers down there anymore. I dressed more like them since I was frequenting the clubs. I'd gone so far as to put a relaxer in my hair, all to look slicker.

A taxi pulled up, and out she stepped, looking every bit the part of a ho in a mini skirt, halter top, and stilettos. We kept dancing around each other cautiously, leery, though, trying to figure out each other's game. We partied all night before getting a room at the Quincy Bay Inn. We enjoyed a leisurely breakfast the next morning before getting ready to part ways.

"Are you coming downtown tonight?" She used a business tone, not an "I-want-to-see-you-again," girlfriend tone.

"Yeah, if you're going to be there."

She popped in and out of the bar that night so quickly that I would've missed her if I'd gone to the bathroom.

"I'm going to work," she informed me. "You going to be here?"

You bet I was. I wasn't sure what her question meant, but I was certainly going to stick around to find out.

I waited with high hopes.

She walked back in a couple of hours later and sat down.

"You all right?" I asked casually.

"Yeah. I'm good. Can you get me a drink?" She got up and walked toward the restroom.

"Here," she said when she came back. She pushed a wad of bills my direction. I played it cool. Didn't count it; coyly pocketed it.

Just like that, I'm back in the game. Little did I know this was a new game. In video games, they call it "powering up." Yeah, she was about to power me up.

It also felt like when I'd find a game in the arcade someone had walked away from with money still in it. I didn't have to work for this. This game just came to me. I'm hanging out in a bar where pimp after pimp tries to knock her, and she chooses me. I'm recognized as a skilled pimp now, a player.

She went back to work and didn't come back until 2 as the bar was shutting down.

"I'm not finished. You going to wait for me?" It was more of a statement than a question.

She was too good to be true. I walked the track and smoked weed by the pizza parlor. She came back when the final buyers started making their way home.

We worked every night that week and decided to head to New York for the weekend. I was excited to work a track bigger than Boston. I might be able to charge slightly more in a bigger city, I thought.

This was the first time I'd intentionally taken my game on the road. My chest puffed up as we pulled out of Boston on the Greyhound bus. I had an experienced, game-savvy ho, and I was going out of state for the sole purpose of pimping. I patted myself on the back. New York City at that. Not bad for a first road trip.

I asked her where we'd stay as we pulled into New York. I shouldn't have worried. She already had everything planned out. She took us straight to a hotel. Then we grabbed a bite at Sylvia's and shopped on 125th Street. I'd brought pimp clothes but bought some jeans at Dr. Jay's just to buy something for myself. Naturally, I bought her an outfit. She deserved it for enhancing my game. We went back to chill at the hotel until time to get ready.

She filled me in more on the New York track. A lot of renegades worked New York, so I might end up with another girl that night, she informed me.

"That bitch ain't staying in our room," she added.

"Whatever," I was feeling big-time pimpish in New York.

"No. I'm serious." She stared me down. I had no doubt she was.

She didn't make a move at 9:30 when it was time to crawl out of bed.

"Aren't you going to get up and get ready?" I was anxious to get out there.

"Nah. Nothing starts around here until about 12."

She'd gotten us this far, so I rolled over and went back to sleep. She woke me up around 11, and we jumped into a cab to the west side of Manhattan near the Javits Center.

I wasn't prepared for the pimp's paradise that stretched out before me. I'd never seen anything like it. The traffic was like rush hour in the middle of the night. Pimps were everywhere, cruising the track in fancy cars with license plates from a wide array of states. Girls of every shape and size walked the track, tall, short, every ethnicity, every look imaginable. They hung out car windows and stood in doorways, yelling at tricks. They gave blow jobs right out in the open. Pimps chased girls down the track. Tricks circled the block three or four times, window shopping before deciding on a final purchase. It was unquestionably a buyer's market. Police rode through, but they didn't do much. Where would they even start in this free-for-all?

Tiny jumped out and told me where she'd be. I walked the track feeling out of my league. In all my years of trafficking and hustling, I never imagined anything like this existed. This was a different level of pimping. Flashier than Boston pimps. Boston pimps had a conservative slant. These pimps dressed in pink pants and lime green shirts. They wore big rings and hats. They swung pimp sticks around. They drove lime green cars with flashing rims and velvet roofs. They spouted out rhymes to catch the attention of other pimps' girls. They were either highly successful pimps or part of the circus.

My heart started beating faster. I drank it in, absorbing everything I could, especially from the pimps. I intensely watched how the girls reacted. What did they like and not like? I relished a new level of respect as they jumped off the sidewalk when a pimp, including me, walked by. My ego ate that up. They didn't see themselves as even worthy to stand on the same sidewalk with us. That was my kind of ho.

The longer I walked the track, the more comfortable I became. I ran into Tiny a couple of times. She didn't hop off the sidewalk for me. That's how others knew she belonged to me. I liked that people thought this pro answered to me. They didn't need to know she had all the answers.

About two hours in, she told me to meet her in the alley, where she handed me $300. This was going to be a lucrative trip. She stayed out until the sun started coming up. I'd never done that in Boston. We could have stayed out longer because tricks were still rolling, but the police were rolling more now, too. Daytime people were starting to come out, so the cops were tamping down the nighttime activity.

She brought in $700 that night, the most I'd ever made. We stayed three nights. My head was blown up by the end because I was getting pimp respect from girls and pimps. I had a vet girl with me. That demanded even more respect. When I'd tell pimps we were from Boston, they'd say, "Hey, got your girl over here." I never told them that, in reality, she had brought me over here.

She did more than introduce me to a faster-paced, wilder track, though. She made me believe I was good at pimping; she gave me confidence. And she showed me just how lucrative trafficking could be if done right. After all expenses for the weekend, I pocketed more than $2,000 profit. I rode out of New York City not only stacked with cash but flush with an attitude. She'd taken my game to a whole other level, probably two levels. In one weekend, I'd gone from the minor leagues to the majors. I was no longer a guy finding any hustle I could to buy drugs or run from trauma. I was a manipulator who suddenly realized trafficking could be a career, not a hobby. And I owed it all to a renegade who manipulated me.

Life had become mundane. Tiny and New York City infused it with excitement. I had fun watching girls reach in cars and grope a man by the loin to get him to go. I still couldn't believe cops had cruised on by as girls gave tricks blow jobs in doorways. I couldn't wait to tell my pimp friends in Boston they had to get over there. I knew I'd be back, and soon. I was hungry to see what lay beyond New York, too, after noticing license plates from all over the country. This must be what it had felt like when I took all those girls who'd never seen bright lights to downtown Boston.

We worked the Combat Zone a few days that week and hung out when we weren't working. I cared about her as much as anyone except my wife since she had introduced me to an exciting new career opportunity.

The following weekend in New York, she knocked a 17-year-old turnout from Ohio. Tiny found Precious crying on the track right after her pimp punished her. They did a couple of double dates together, and Tiny convinced her to hang out with her the rest of the night. When I ran into them on the track, Tiny motioned me into an alley. Precious followed behind her. Tiny introduced us and told me she was coming home with us as Precious handed over her money.

"You sure this is what you want? Tiny tells me you're from Ohio." I didn't want her making a mad move. It would be too much trouble to serve her pimp if she would go back to him after she got over her hurt feelings. I also didn't want any trouble with police. She was a young White girl from another state; I didn't need that attention unless she was serious. She assured me she was done with Spider.

I served him on the track, and he took it like a pimp is supposed to. He told me she was a turnout who didn't know what she was doing. I'd kind of figured that. Tiny could bring her up to par – like she had me.

Tiny wasn't kidding about another girl staying in our room, so we got Precious her own room. We took her shopping the next day and ran into Spider and his other girls. We spoke in passing. To most, it would be just a point in time. For me, it was a point of no return. Precious came face-to-face with her former pimp and wifeys and gave them the cold-shoulder for me. I'd knocked an experienced pimp who'd trafficked a White girl from Ohio to New York and how many ever cities between. She was going back to Boston with me. My pimp friends there would be impressed. Again, they didn't need to know it was really Tiny who knocked her.

I no longer was a local-yokel pimp, trafficking girlfriends and girls from the hood. Here I was, getting chosen in New York City by a White girl, nonetheless. Two girls followed me around the track now. I didn't share with Tiny that I had no idea what was happening when Precious followed her into that alley. I'd never had a girl bring another girl to me.

Precious followed Tiny around wherever we went. Tiny made sure she felt comfortable. I wasn't the only one who upped my game that weekend. In Tiny's mind, she became my bottom the second she brought Precious to me. She probably thought that from the moment she accepted my drink in the bar.

We hung around the pool, laughed, joked, shopped. But Tiny kept a line drawn. She had a relationship with me. Precious was just another ho, there to work and nothing more. She wasn't to cross Tiny. I had a feeling I wasn't to, either.

Back in Boston, we got Precious a hotel room. Tiny stayed at her house but would hang out with her during the day. I did my own thing until time to go to work, shooting pool, sniffing coke, and kicking it with my friends.

I'd join them on the track. One night, I met a girl named Becky as I walked up. I didn't know if she was working or coming from the movies or some other innocent place. She asked me if I hung out down there a lot. I told her I had two girls. She asked if I would be there the next night, and I told her the bar I'd be in.

When she walked into the bar dressed in shorts and a halter, all the pimps tried to knock her. We talked awhile before I told her to come on, and I'd introduce her to my girls. If she wasn't going to work, she wasn't going to hang out in the bar with me while they were working. I'd told Tiny about my conversation with her the night before. Neither of us thought she'd show up.

We found Tiny alone. Precious was on a date, so Tiny took Becky on a date with her. The trick thought he was getting two for one, but Tiny supervised. Becky was all in after the first date. She was from Cambridge and bored. I liked having two girls from Boston. It cut down on hotel costs.

We settled into a routine of working Boston during the week and New York City on the weekends. I was making a lot of money and gaining a lot of respect. We quit riding the bus to New York and started renting cars to make my life more comfortable. Everything was about me.

I became drunk on the power, feeling more pimpish with every passing day. I had my first genuine stable, and, in my mind, it was all my doing. Tiny had nothing to do with it. As my narcissism puffed up, it shoved aside my attention and respect for Tiny. I treated her as no more important to me than Precious or Becky.

It went from, "Baby, take them shopping, and y'all go get something to eat," to "Bitches, go get something to eat, and I'll get with you later."

From "Tiny, meet me downtown," to "See you hos downtown."

From "Tiny, y'all have condoms for tonight?" to "You hos have condoms for tonight?"

The money. The power. The girls talking directly to me now rather than through Tiny as they got comfortable with me. I'd developed a pimp-ho relationship with all of them. I didn't show Tiny any attention outside of sex and no more priority than I showed the other girls.

The Tiny I first met in the bar reared up and confronted me.

"These bitches going with us everywhere we go."

"They paying to be here just like you," I shot back in my most pimpish attitude.

She wasn't into the pimpish attitude, so I added, "I don't spend the night in their hotel rooms or nothing." That was enough, I reasoned. I didn't want them feeling they had to go through her, that they had two pimps, me and Tiny.

She let me know it wasn't enough for her.

"You can leave," I called her bluff. "You know what I'm saying. You're here to pay." No way she'd leave me. She had it too good with me. We worked well together, I'd never been violent with her, and we had fun.

"Oh really. That's how you feel. You're going to do me like that?"

"Do you like what, Bitch? You know what this is. You know better than I know what this is."

No doubt she knew better than me. She had taught me things I was clueless about. I'm sure she thought I'd fold if she pressured me. I needed her, after all. I'd show the bitch who would fold.

"That's how it is? What you think? I'll call you later."

"Don't bother," she yelled as I slammed the door.

I called her when time for work rolled around. I started in like nothing had happened. I decided to throw in a little of the attention she wanted.

"Hey, Baby. Why don't you call those girls and make sure they get ready to go to work?"

"You call them and make sure they get ready."

"What you talking about, Baby? You not calling them?"

"You told me what this is. If you know what it is, make it happen."

"Look, Baby…" she hung up on me mid-sentence.

No bitch could do me that way. I called her right back.

"Stop calling my phone. Stop calling my house." She hung up again.

She called *my* bluff as surely as she had called the bluff of all the pimps knocking on her at the bar when I first met her. She didn't show up on the track that night. In fact, I didn't see her for about a month on the track, in the bar, or anywhere. She probably thought I'd harass her: "Bitch, why you think you can hang up in my face and then come down here and work?"

Maybe I would have. Maybe she didn't want to see my face. By the time I did see her, I went on about my business. I still had the other two girls handing me money. I didn't want her messing with them or taking their money.

They'd asked me about her. "Oh, the bitch is mad at me." That was the end of it. I hardened up, too. I'd let my guard down again. Gotten a little emotionally attached to Tiny since she significantly increased my profit margin. For a pimp, it's kind of like when your dog dies. You feel something when he dies, though it's not the same as losing a spouse or girlfriend.

I couldn't waste too much time on regrets. I had a new challenge to tackle. I had to become hands-on, taking over the tasks Tiny oversaw. I didn't want to make one of them my bottom. I needed to establish my control.

Despite the extra work, I thought more about making pimping a career. Why go back to manual labor when I had two young, White hos into me? I might have my stable under control, but my vanity was out of control. I started playing more mind games with them like experienced pimps do.

I'd take them shopping, feed them, then stay in the same bed with them. I wouldn't have sex with them, though. "I'm your pimp, and you're my hos," I told them. "I'm staying here because I don't feel like going home, and I'm the one paying for the room. You're not my girlfriends; I feel nothing emotionally." I also wanted to get them used to sleeping with me, so I didn't have to spring for another hotel room or the upgrade for double beds when we were on the road.

I played around with them, though. They'd hang out in Becky's neighborhood, coming back giggly from smoking weed. I'd tease them, "Do your little boyfriends know about me?"

"Come on, D. We don't have boyfriends. You're all we've got."

I acted like I cared. I didn't. All I cared about was playing them. I'd sleep in the middle with one arm around each. I'd wake up to them kissing on me and rubbing me, trying to break me down.

"No. No. No. It ain't that kind of party." I waged psychological warfare against their young, infatuated minds.

I treated them well, though. They didn't give me any headaches, and they took care of my business, so I took care of theirs. I'd get their nails done, hair done, take them on generous shopping trips, to expensive restaurants, the movies. I treated them like they deserved to be treated.

They watched out for each other, too. Becky moved into the hotel room with Precious. They went on double dates as often as they could. They got a little nervous when they heard on the track that a couple of girls had been found dead in the Quincy Quarries. I told them to get the license plate and description of the car when they went on individual dates. That calmed their fears. They were having too much fun to dwell on it too long. I think they somehow thought I could protect them whether I was there or not.

They were bringing in close to a thousand dollars a night, so I was a big-time pimp in my mind, as well as theirs. I would soon learn that was nothing. One thing was sure. I was done with the barbershop. I wasn't about to stand behind a chair and cut hair to make in a month what I made in a few nights.

New York pimps told me to check out a truck stop in Delaware and Route 9 in New Jersey, so we expanded our circuit and our adventures. We'd pick up girls for a day or two in the different cities. It didn't bother me when they'd leave as fast as they came because I knew now there were plenty where they came from. I didn't need them anyway. Precious and Becky made good money. So much, in fact, that I paid cash for a used Oldsmobile 98 to save on rental cars. I played more mind games with the girls before I bought it. I took them to see it and told them, "This is what we're working to get."

Notice the language. This is what "we" are working to get. I made them believe it was our business. That made them work harder.

My pimp game climbed another level with the car. I'd drive around the track screaming out the window at girls like established pimps did. One night, I sweated a White girl several times. I'd drive by her, back the car up, drive back around where she was. She did her best to stay out of earshot of my rhymes.

I finally gave up and went to a 7-Eleven for a drink. A Korean girl who had been with her followed me in.

"Hey, D." I recognized her. I guess she knew my name from me yelling out the window at her friend.

"Can I talk to you?" she asked.

Of course, she could. She followed me to the back of the store, but she didn't want to chance a conversation there. She wanted to meet off the track, so I drove to where she asked me to meet her. She wouldn't get in the car.

"No. No. No. No. You come out here."

We walked into an alley where China Doll told me she liked my style. She was interested in working for me. She questioned me about how many girls I had, what my game was. Usually, the pimp does the questioning, but she'd obviously thought this out, so I went along with it.

China lived in Rhode Island with her pimp, Sly. She'd been with him three years.

"I'll need $500 if you want me to serve him."

"Can I call you later?" I never turned down potential money, so I gave her my phone number.

She handed me $150 in exchange. "I don't want to disrespect you by talking to you even if I don't come," she explained.

That's a real ho, I thought. She knows how to show proper deference without being told.

I didn't hear from her for a few days and then just a quick call to tell me she was still thinking about leaving.

"Just let me know when you're ready."

I wasn't waiting around on her, however. I was impatient to add to my stable, so I kept working the track. I noticed a renegade in Boston who liked to make fast money, and I do mean fast money. She ran everywhere she went. Most girls walked the track; she avoided it. She ran in and out of alleys and jumped in vehicles so fast you barely had time to notice her. She didn't jump out of cars back on the track like other girls, either. She'd mysteriously emerge from an alley or side street.

She managed to stay out of the earshot of pimps, too. They'd try to yell her way, but she'd duck out of sight. I was curious what her game was. She managed to avoid them because they screamed out the window at her, so I parked and walked up behind her one night.

"Get in where you fit in," I advised her.

"Take a look and get hooked," I imitated the rhyming style of New York pimps.

She darted into an alley, and I followed her.

"I was wondering when you were going to say something to me," she stated. "I see you out there chasing those White girls and never saying anything to me."

Shock made me forget all my catchy rhymes for a second. Not at what she said but at realizing who she was now that I was close enough to see past the wig and heavy makeup. It was Denise, the woman I dated briefly from Narcotics Anonymous who wanted me to chase after genuine change with her. I quickly regained my composure. She was clearly chasing after something else now.

We fleetingly acknowledged that we recognized each other and then got back to business.

"You always getting sweated and never give them any action," I pointed out.

"I didn't want to have no man," she answered.

"I have two little White girls, so I was trying to get more White girls."

"I make White-girl money," Denise, aka Sparkle, who is Black, informed me proudly. White girls made more money than Black girls. Hispanic girls usually fall somewhere between them, depending on their skin tone. Asian girls made more money than all of them.

We conducted the interview right there in the alley, and she handed me money. She was like a multipurpose tool, I thought. She helped me stay clean, and now she would help me stay flush with cash.

She lived in the projects, so I didn't have to spring for a hotel. We exchanged numbers, and I told her I'd see her the next day.

I took her shopping and to eat. We briefly touched on our past relationship, but I made it clear this was all business. She agreed and officially went to work for me. I didn't know it yet, but, like Tiny, she was about to blow up my game.

Precious and Becky didn't mind Sparkle … at first. She was a little older than them and a veteran on the track. She gradually worked her way into keeping an eye on them for me.

She let me know I wasn't running my stable effectively. If I genuinely wanted to make pimping a career, instead of a hobby or another hustle, I had to get serious about my game. She assured me I could be extremely good at it if I wanted to be. She pointed out where I was slacking off, like joking with hos, making them giggle, and letting them play around with me.

I'd grown content with where my business stood. I made more money now on even a slow day than I did breaking into houses or picking pockets, so I had lost my hunger. Sparkle shook me out of that. You have to stay hungry, she prodded me. She had a business mind, which I admired. Precious and Becky didn't; it sucked the fun out of the game for them. They started complaining I had become mean to them since Sparkle came. I wasn't fun anymore, they whined.

"This is the game, but it's not a game," I dismissed their complaints just as I had Tiny's.

We worked Delaware and New York the weekend after they confronted me. We only stayed two days because no one did well. I yelled at all three of them on the drive back to Boston. A couple of days after we got back, they disappeared as soon as they hit the track. I thought they had gone on a date, but they never came back. I checked their hotel room at the end of the night. It was cleared out. No one ever served me, and I never learned what happened to them.

Their departure made me realize Sparkle was right. I had to stay hungry.

I coined a couple of new phrases: "Hos come to pay, not to stay." "They come going." It's not that I cared that they ran off without telling me. They left behind a car, expensive jewelry, and a stack of cash. They'd been with me about a year and a half, so I felt a sense of accomplishment, like I was big pimping with two White girls who liked me enough to last that long, especially since one of them didn't come from poverty. If they couldn't take the business seriously, I didn't need them.

Plus, now I had this experienced girl who had my back and knew how to stroke my ego. She gave me my first pimp name. I was no longer just "Derek" or "D." Now, I was their "Daddy."

## Analysis With Dr. Deena Graves:
### The Pimp's Bottom

Tiny and Sparkle worked as my first bottom bitches or bottom girls. Many people misunderstand the meaning of the word "bottom." They think it's derogatory, like she's the bottom of the barrel. The bottom helps the pimp hold everything up – from the bottom up.

If he's not around or is unavailable, she's his go-to person. She works her way into the position by earning his trust. Typically, she's been in his stable the longest.

The bottom girl's most important job is to make the pimp's life easier. She'll take the other girls shopping, feed them, pick up condoms, make sure they're ready when it's time to go to work, and collect the money from the other girls, to name just a few tasks.

To be clear, she is not a business partner, and she does not hold a higher "status" in the pimp's eyes. She's not more special, just more trusted. As such, he rewards her with the added "prestige" for his convenience.

Many times, the bottom recruits for the trafficker, as well, preying upon unsuspecting young girls. Often, the bottom has been a victim of child sex trafficking herself, and she recruits because he forces her to. For example, that was the case in a disclosure obtained through *The Traps of a Trafficker©* of a 14-year-old sold in six states in 30 days.

The 14-year-old posted about a fight with her mom on social media. A 19-year-old woman sent her a private message and asked her what was up with her mom. She gained the 14-year-old's trust by empathizing with her against her mom.

Unbeknown to the 14-year-old, the 19-year-old and her trafficker were already driving to her city, which was about an hour away from them. She offered to take the teen for a smoothie or coffee and talk about how she stopped her mother from treating her the same way. She could even stay with her. The unsuspecting teen gave her her address. When they pulled up, the 19-year-old was now driving, and the trafficker had taken her place communicating with the young girl. The teen got in the car despite seeing him sitting in the backseat.

They both had sex with her and sold her in Texas, Louisiana, New Mexico, Colorado, Kentucky, and Florida. The trafficker got all the money, but his bottom helped set up the dates.

William Bernard Jacobs, the 30-year-old trafficker, received a 20-year plea deal in the case. The judge sentenced his bottom to five years.[74] She had been a victim of child sex trafficking and did not receive healing for her trauma when she was recovered at 12. She ended up back in the game, like many recovered victims do without the proper treatment, and eventually in the arms of Jacobs.

Opinions differ on whether bottoms should be charged in such cases. Are they a criminal, or are they a victim? Or are they both? Law enforcement and courts have taken different positions, but most are charged.

Shamere McKenzie, a former bottom, has challenged the system to stop prosecuting bottoms, stating the "bottom girl is the one who's the most victimized; [that's] why she's even in the position … in the first place." They have no choice, she asserts. Others argue it must be looked at on a case-by-case basis, and treatment should be considered in the mix.[75]

Hi, Denise here. I agree the circumstances should be considered on a case-by-case basis. In my experience, the bottom also is a victim of trauma and the trafficker. Did she get effective treatment for her childhood trauma? Did the trafficker force her to comply under the threat of violence? Many questions must be thoughtfully answered. On the other hand, the bottom knowingly commits criminal activity just as Derek did after years of child-hood trauma. He takes full responsibility, and so do I, for the harm we caused others.

This is a complex subject that needs much more research and discussion. A bottom shouldn't want to involve anyone in what they know is addi-tional trauma and danger. However, their life may very well be on the line if they don't follow the trafficker's instructions. We are unpacking my story in trainings and my forthcoming book to help people understand how a victim becomes a bottom – and what that role does to them psychologically and emotionally. For now, let me stress that a lifetime of trauma led to me meeting Derek in the alley that night and kept me willingly doing his bidding for several years. As both Derek's story and mine underscore, childhood trauma leads people down dark paths. The more consequential conversation, in my opinion, is how we divert all children from their first step down a dark path – whether that step leads to becoming a trafficker, bottom, drug addict or to other behaviors that endanger themselves or others.

## Two-Minute Introspection

What questions do we need to answer about bottoms to balance justice with healing?

# 22 If You Build It, They Will Come

China turned back up in the Combat Zone a few weeks after Precious and Becky took off.

"Haven't seen you out here in a while," I sweated her as I passed her on the track.

She ignored me.

Guess she decided to stay. Fine by me. Sparkle and I were doing just fine, hitting New York and Delaware on the weekends and picking up other girls here and there.

My phone rang a few hours later. China asked if I could meet her where we'd talked the first time.

"I'm ready to leave."

"Okay."

"I have a baby. I'll have to bring my baby."

"Okay. Call me when you get all your stuff together, and you're ready to leave."

We'd figure the baby out once she got there. Asian girls made too much money for that to be a dealbreaker. She handed me another $150. She could take all the time she wanted deciding as long as she kept handing me free money.

Two days later, she called me from the Rhode Island Greyhound Bus Station. She didn't have money to buy a bus ticket. Sparkle drove to pick her and her 6-month-old baby girl up from where they were hiding from Sly.

She made $400 in no time on the track the first night. I'd stacked $700 from her; it was time to serve Sly. China Doll was worried he'd come looking for her and the baby, but he took it like a pimp when I called him.

Still, I extended a common courtesy pimps typically show each other, especially since she had a baby with him.

"Hey, man. She'll be on the track in the Combat Zone tomorrow night."

I didn't want the headache of a baby just for her to head back to him in a few days if she had feelings for him.

He didn't show up despite her fears.

We paid Sparkle's younger sisters to watch China's baby while we worked Boston and went out of town on the weekends. China Doll had a bunch of regulars in New York and pulled in $1,000 a night every time we went. She made $700 a night in Boston. I was fired up; I'd never had a girl hand me that kind of money. I bought a second car, so I didn't have to be bothered driving them around.

About three months into China joining my stable, I got a call from a dude named Playa from Rhode Island. He introduced himself to me as Sly's best friend. Turned out Sly did care. He was flipping out in Rhode Island, Playa informed me.

"Yo, man. Just send China back to him."

That was not normal pimping.

"Are you crazy? Where they do that at? If he wants her back, he better get up here and get at her like I got at her. He got to pimp for her like I did."

I confronted China. "What's this? He's down there crying and all upset? What kind of guy is he? He has someone else call me talking about he's upset and send you home."

China filled me in on a few details she'd neglected to tell me. She wasn't just Sly's ho. She was his girlfriend. They had a committed relationship and decided to have a baby together. Playa *was* his best friend. They talked about everything, she added.

"It's kind of funny to me he'd have him call me and not call himself. What kind of pimp is that?"

"He wouldn't do that," China said.

He wouldn't do it because he wasn't a genuine pimp. She was his only girl. He sold her to support them. She had brought a few girls home from time to time, but he'd forget about them in the hotel, not show them any attention, sleep with them too soon. He didn't know what he was doing, and they never stuck around.

I didn't care if she left. She'd bought me another car, and I'd stacked a lot of her money. She was kind of expensive, anyway, and high maintenance. I had to buy diapers, formula, pay for babysitters. As I said, they come to pay, not to stay. She came with extra overhead.

She decided to stay, though.

I sweated two more underaged girls, Kayla and Dyna(mite), on the track and came up with a new rhyme: Four deep. No sleep. I was always doing something for one of them. A savvy pimp not only spends time with his stable as a group but as individuals. Sparkle spent time with them as my bottom, but they weren't paying Sparkle. They were paying me. They needed to feel I cared even though I didn't. It's a businessperson's investment. You want to know your team players. I'd take them shopping alone, to eat, or on car rides. They wanted to talk one-on-one, to feel they had my full attention, my interest, not only on a professional level but in their personal life. I had to make them feel they weren't just another machine in my operation.

"Hey, what's up with you?"

"Tell me about your background."

I knew how to play the game. I'd get them talking about themselves and learn things that helped me manipulate them. It's part of a pimp's job description. I also wanted to know if they were weak-willed or strong-willed. The pressure would come down at some point, whether it was from a trick or a cop, and I wanted to know who was on my team.

I gave them all a $500 quota per night. If they met the quota, they kept working until time to come in. China Doll didn't get special treatment for bringing in more. She was supposed to. It was a known fact Asian girls made more money. That doesn't give them a right to slack. They don't get to knock off early just because they make more money. Uncle Danny didn't close his shop early if he made a certain amount. The pimps would talk among themselves in the bar about how the night was looking. If it was too hot or too slow, we'd call it a night early. They should be thankful for that.

I'd have Sparkle take the girls to work, and I'd meet them there a couple of hours later. They'd call me to break them if they'd made $300-$400. It was in their best interest to. They didn't want to lose it or get robbed. I didn't want to hear that. If she should have $450 and only had $150 when

I broke her, it wasn't going to go over too well, and they knew that.

We'd all have breakfast together at the end of the night, and I'd send everyone on their way to get a little sleep before spending more time with them. I slowly introduced my family to my career and my girls. I started by taking Precious and Becky to my mom's house and leaving them in the car while I ran in so that she could see them out there. They saw me with different girls all the time, girls dressed like prostitutes no matter the time of day. They couldn't help but notice my cars, my clothes, my diamonds and gold chains, my alligator shoes that took the place of my tennis shoes.

The girls treated my mom with respect. "Yes, Ma'am." "No, Ma'am." We'd go to my mom's for dinner sometimes. Occasionally, they'd stay at my oldest sister's apartment. She'd bail the over-18 girls out for me when they landed in jail. It's like I told my family, "It's better you going to get them out of jail than you going to get me out of jail."

I was very liberal with my money with my family, so they were cool with it. It's not that I think my mom approved. I could see her looks of disgust, but I was almost 30. Too late. That was what I was doing. She knew nothing she could say would stop me. It would've pushed me away. At least this way, we had a relationship, and they would know if anything happened to me. The poverty mindset told them they might as well benefit from it, too.

My mom's side of the family was very close, so a couple of my aunts would ask me sometimes what I was doing with all those girls. "What you think?" They eventually left me alone about it. Uncle Danny had long since quit trying to get me to settle down and work toward my own shop. He'd given it everything he had, but I was too far gone by the time he started having those conversations with me.

I didn't tell my father's side of the family. I'd swing by the liquor store every once in a while to say "hi" to my dad, but I never took a girl. I'd also have dinner occasionally with my aunt and grandmother, but we weren't that close, so I didn't talk about my career path. I wasn't hiding it. It just didn't come up. I didn't try to hide it from anyone now. Just the opposite. I bragged about it. I was too deep in, and it was too lucrative to hide it now.

It stayed lucrative until police upped the heat in Boston. They started harassing the girls on the track. One night by about 1, I could tell it was not going to be a good night. China had figured that out, too, and started complaining about not making enough. I told her to jump in the car and head to New York City.

She did well solo, bringing back a substantial amount of cash.

I paid my mom now to watch China's baby. Sparkle's teen sisters had grown tired of giving up their weekends for her. I didn't want to leave my mom with the baby without popping in to check on them, so I started sending China to New York alone on the weekends while the other girls and I worked the Boston track. She had a friend in New York whose pimp also was from Boston, so they'd share a hotel room to save us money. It pleased me that she looked out for the business like that. I'm sure it did him, too.

They hung around a lot, and we let them do their thing since they kept bringing back the bills.

One weekend, I decided to head to New York to check in. I'd spend a little time with her, let her know I cared. Her friend's pimp had gone to jail, so I thought it would be good to encourage them and let them know someone still had his eye on things.

The other girl went to the bathroom when I arrived, so China and I could spend time alone. She handed me her money. I counted it. Pocketed it. She started telling me what had happened with the other girl's pimp. While she was talking, I got up and walked around the room, listening but stretching my legs from the drive.

I noticed a powdery substance on the dresser. I looked closer and could tell it wasn't baby powder. I stuck my finger in it and tasted it.

"What's up with this? That's coke. Whose is it? Who had it?"

"We did."

I flew into a rage. Here I thought she was trying to save me money on a hotel room, and they'd been sniffing cocaine all along. She knew the rules but was defiant.

"How you think I stay up all these hours and work so hard?"

"I had no idea you do drugs at all, and here you're telling me it's a regular deal?"

"Exactly. You didn't know. It doesn't affect the business. It doesn't affect how much money you get. It doesn't affect anything."

It affected me. It made me worry about her. Her safety was my first concern.

If her safety was in jeopardy, my money was in jeopardy.

## Analysis With Dr. Deena Graves:
### Drugs and Victims of Trafficking

Many pimps do not let their girls do drugs when working because it impairs thinking. They can't use their best judgment if they are high. They might say something to cops they shouldn't say. They might get in the wrong car. Buyers might not want to pay them if they've smoked their weed or sniffed their coke.

Some traffickers let their girls use drugs or force them on them for different purposes. For example, they'll feed them drugs to keep them working longer, more arduous hours like China. One teen who disclosed through *The Traps of a Trafficker*© was sold 37 days in a row into bondage sex and videos by two homeless men who used meth to keep her going with little sleep. See *Appendix D* for her case study.

Either way, drug addiction often accompanies sex trafficking. Youth, like China, turn to drugs as a coping mechanism even if their traffickers do not force them into it. Therefore, treatment plans must consider what types of drugs were used and why. What were the consequences in that child's life? We must go beyond simply breaking addiction to other ramifications if we want them to heal fully.

For example, one trafficker used NyQuil to dull the pain for a 13-year-old he took from her school and sold for 10 days to more men than she could remember. Most treatment plans would not take the NyQuil into consideration. However, it can cause long-term damage. Large doses of NyQuil can cause liver damage, for instance.

Also, what happens the next time she catches the flu and someone unknowingly gives her NyQuil? It can trigger her, sending her into fight-or-flight mode or other harmful coping mechanisms to try to outrun the flashbacks.

As for China, I never felt the same about her again. She had purposely deceived me. She had been with me about a year and a half, and I had come to trust her. So had Sparkle. We both were stunned she could hide it from us so completely.

"Can you believe this bitch is getting high?"

"Yeah, she's good."

What else was she good at hiding? The trust was gone. She also had gone from spending every moment she could with her baby to dumping her on my family. Drugs destroyed her life just like they did mine.

Things were falling apart for her, so she decided to go to Miami with her cousin to work in a spa. She hoped to pull herself together and work her way out of the game. At the time, I was cool with that. Now, my hope is she was able to do that.

## Two-Minute Introspection

What other consequences of drugs should we incorporate into our treatment plans?

# 23 Arrested Development

We met California James at the Delaware truck stop. I would never have thought it possible, but he was flashier than the New York pimps, as California pimps are. Close your eyes and imagine a Hollywood version of a pimp, and that was him.

He wore his hair longer than his girls, permanently relaxed and curled with curlers. He decked himself out in plaids and stripes and reptile shoes. He also drove a Hollywood version of a pimp car, jacked up and tricked out with Trues and Vogues, also known as spoke rims and Vogue tires.

He caught my eye with an enormous diamond pinky ring. He caught my ear with his talk of pimping on Sunset Boulevard.

"Yeah, man. Any girl can turn $1,000 a night on Sunset Boulevard."

Police let the girls work there, for the most part, he said. They harass the pimp more than the girls. Just hang back, let them work, and rake in the money. That's the way to do it, he advised.

He was only a couple of years older than me, but he'd traveled extensively trafficking girls. He had three White girls with him in Delaware; he'd trafficked them across the country.

I hurried us home to Boston, where I instructed Kayla and Dyna on how to run the stable on automatic, or their own, while Sparkle and I flew to Los Angeles to check it out. I gave them my mom and sisters' phone numbers and envelopes with their names and dates to seal their money up in each night. They knew the money had better be in the drop safe when I got back. Girls usually like when their pimp leaves them on automatic because it means he trusts them.

"I don't have to have my pimp standing over me. I know how to take care of my man's business without him." Pimps know how to manipulate anything to their advantage.

Sparkle and I threw our stuff in a hotel on the stroll, as the LA track is called, as soon as we landed. We hopped back in the rental car and drove around to see it in the daytime. A few girls were out working. I wanted to see LA, though, so I decided to take the day off. Kayla and Dyna were making money, anyway.

We strolled along the Hollywood Walk of Fame, marveled at the lifelike figures in the Wax Museum, took photos with the characters on Hollywood Boulevard, and did other touristy things. When we got done, we went to the Swap Meet to buy weed and clothes a little more appropriate for the Sunset stroll per California James's advice. I couldn't have my girl going out there all East Coast conservative. I didn't want to look like an amateur. We settled on "booty shorts."

California James also had warned me to send Sparkle ahead when it came time to go to work, so she caught a cab to Sunset Boulevard and Normandie Avenue. I rode the stroll a little later and was once again riveted by what I saw. LA was vastly different than anything on the East Coast, including New York. Way more ostentatious and provocative, while also more reserved because of all the tourists out with kids. The girls dressed more seductively, some even wearing see-through tops, but the scene wasn't as over the top. They didn't give blow jobs in doorways, stand in the street, or hang out car windows yelling at tricks.

They did try to wave them down, though. They tried to wave down my rental car. I learned later they thought I was a trick because gang bangers and dope boys ride the stroll looking to buy sex. The drug dealers made deals with junkies by day and deals with girls by night. They'd buy for themselves or throw drug parties and pay three girls $500 each, plus tips, to provide the entertainment.

Police rolled through and occasionally told the girls to get outta there, deflecting them away from the tourist families. They'd jump in a cab to the other end of the stroll and get right back to work. Later, cops would push them back the other way with a warning: "If I see you again, I'll arrest you."

Massive groups of girls congregated everywhere. I saw Sparkle in the middle of a group, soaking in what the other girls told her. They filled her in on the local dos and don'ts, how much to charge, where to take them.

I headed to the strip club with a poolroom California James had told me about to get my own lay of the land. I saw Sparkle jump in a car as I drove off. We were off to a good start. A full day of sightseeing and now money already rolling in to cover our expenses.

"What's up, Pimping?" some of the other pimps greeted me when I walked into the poolroom.

"Ten toes down, checking out the town," I informed my instant friends. There's a saying, "Nobody likes pimps but pimps and hos," so you know you always have friends at the local pimp hangout.

Sparkle made about $800 while I shot pool. Not a bad night's haul for the first night scoping out a new stroll. She had to get comfortable in a new city, learn their ways, before she'd be at full capacity. Like in Boston, she knew what kind of car Vice drove. She had to be cautious in LA not to flag down the wrong car. She didn't want me coming down on her for calling a cop car over to her.

The following day, we switched hotels. The other pimps had told me the dope boys stayed at our hotel, so police raided it often. One pimp advised us to move off the stroll in case police watched Sparkle. No need drawing them to me at the hotel. Better for her to jump in a cab and drive unseen to a hotel off the beaten stroll.

Sparkle quickly started turning $1,000-$1,200 a night. That made me want to get back to Boston and move the rest of my stable to LA as fast as possible. Why would I be satisfied making $3,000 a weekend when I'm getting ready to make $3,000 a day?

Sparkle and I both felt good about ourselves as we flew home. I saw the Hollywood sights courtesy of a bunch of male Hollywood tourists and natives and still stacked a good profit. I'd gotten a good temperature of the city, too. I knew how the cops worked, how the girls moved, how to dress my girls, how to dress me, how to sweat girls. I didn't bother sweating this trip. Plenty of time for that when we came back. I just wanted to understand how things went down before I moved my entire business there.

A few pimps did sweat Sparkle. They did their job, and she did hers, ignoring them. I knew I didn't have to worry about her getting out of pocket. She had it too good with me. Why would she give up her position as my bottom to go with someone she didn't know? She'd just traveled across the country alone with her Daddy. She'd be the literal bottom person in a new pimp's group, the least important horse in the stable. She was the thoroughbred in mine.

I stacked money for a couple of weeks when we got back to pay for our trip. At this point, I liked to be flush with cash. The girls thought we were flying, but why pay for airline tickets when they could work our way across the country?

We drove down the East Coast and caught I-10, stopping at a couple of amusement parks and other tourist traps. I was anxious to get back to LA, but I always have liked the tourist thing. We stopped to work a few big cities and made more than enough to cover our trip. We stopped in New Orleans not to work but because I was tired. The girls went down to get food, and a couple of students from the nearby university approached them for dates. They made $100 each. I loved pimping on the road.

We pulled into Los Angeles at night. The glamorous LA lights fascinated Kayla and Dyna, as they had us on our first trip, and they were ready to get to work. The long drive wore me out, though, so I decided to take the night off and get a fresh start in the morning.

We showed them some sights the next day, checked out the stroll, and went back to the Swap Meet to buy weed and clothes. I couldn't wait for nightfall to see how much three girls would pull in. I could already see how high my money would stack.

My phone rang not too long after they left for the stroll.

Sparkle.

All three had been arrested. Kayla and Dyna were 17 now, so they went to adult jail with Sparkle.

"Damn. Stupid bitches," I thought to myself.

"How the hell all y'all get arrested?"

What the hell was I supposed to do in a strange city with three girls in jail? Another lesson learned. I hadn't thought when we were there a couple of weeks before to find out what the procedure was when girls were arrested. I headed to the poolroom to find out. I ran into something else I'd never seen when I walked in. A lot of their girls had been arrested, too. About 25 total. They didn't seem too fazed. Seemed LAPD did that from time to time.

The good news was they could go right back to work and probably not get arrested again that night.

"You gonna be okay?"

"Yeah, what's up?" Why was he worried about me? I'd had girls arrested before. Just not in LA.

"You know the bail is $500 a head?"

What the … it was only $125 in Boston, and I got $100 back. In LA, they didn't give any back.

"You straight, Boston?"

"Yeah, I'm cool." Luckily, my habit of staying flush with cash worked to my advantage.

"Who do I send?" I asked.

"Just go down and post the bond, man. They ain't studding you. They're not thinking about you. They just want the money."

Five hundred dollars. Half a night's wages. I got them back on the stroll as fast as I could. We had lost production time to make up for. No one had broken luck before they got arrested, so we were way behind. But they all picked up tricks quickly after getting back on the stroll. I didn't see many cops now, and it was still early, so we should be good, I reassured myself.

My phone rang again.

Dyna.

Back in the slammer.

"How you get arrested twice in the same night, Bitch? What you doing standing around with a bunch of other bitches again? Don't you know to keep moving?"

"I was moving, Daddy. I was in a car with a date."

Occupational hazard. She flagged down a car similar to ours. The driver was young and wearing a sweatshirt. Looked like a college kid. She took him in the alley for a blow job, but he whipped out a badge instead.

In the end, they pulled the night out. Dyna still walked away with $200 despite losing most of the night and her money to a jail cell. Sparkle netted $1,100, and Kayla made $1,200.

Considering the events of the evening, not a total loss. I got my bail money back. That was the main thing. Plus, we learned a lot about LA.

Don't stick together, I warned them. Spread out but communicate. Know where each other is.

They did a good job laying low and didn't have any more trouble with police during our three-week stay. I, on the other hand, was a different story. Police pulled me over and accused me of being a pimp. I was dressed like a pimp and riding around the stroll in the dead of night, but not me, I assured them.

"I ain't no pimp. What you stopping me for?"

"We'll find something." They'd seen me out on the stroll too many times.

They made me get out and sit on the curb while they searched the car.

"You don't have any reason to stop me."

"We're writing you a ticket for obstruction."

"Obstruction of what?" I demanded. I wasn't obstructing anything. They were obstructing my ability to supervise my girls.

"You have a car freshener hanging from your rearview mirror."

"A what? On Sunset Boulevard on the weekend? All these people driving by us with furry dice, and baby shoes, and statutes on their dashboards, and you're writing me up for an air freshener?"

A $500 ticket. They liked that number in LA.

Things were getting a little hot again, so it was time to head back to Boston.

Kayla had to say goodbye to a trick who had bought her three nights in a row. From his mannerisms and actions, I believe he was part of the Russian Mafia. He was infatuated with her, though, so I didn't care what his occupation was. By the third night, he met her as soon as she hit the stroll. She thought it was funny. I thought it was fantastic. He paid her $1,500 for about four hours that night.

I added his money to the shoebox I'd hidden in my hotel closet. I'd made too much money during our short stay to keep it all on me like was my practice.

I couldn't keep it on me, but I was careful to keep the shoebox stuffed with $18,000 near me as we packed up the car.

## Analysis With Dr. Deena Graves:
### Regional Differences In Trafficking

In California, pimps drove around the track to sweat a girl. They pulled up and yelled their number out the car window. They did that in New York City, too, but they'd also get out of the car and get right up on them, harassing them up close and personal. You couldn't do that in California. Both of you would get arrested, and then you'd have a furious pimp coming at you. You'd hear: "You sweating the bitch? Let the bitch work. She can't even get any money to choose you. You steady on her."

Either way, can you imagine doing your job with the competition constantly yelling at you, coming up so close behind you that you can feel their breath on your neck? Calling you a bitch, a ho, a whore. Close your eyes and imagine it for a moment. We often don't take into consideration the full spectrum of the mental duress they live. Or the emotional.

Or that the type of mental and emotional duress they live varies by region, even by city. It's not just the slang, or the dress, or the way they sweat girls. It can be multiple things, including who is selling them and who is buying them.

For instance, I told you gang bangers and dope fiends drove Sunset Boulevard looking for girls to buy. Gangs buy – and sell – girls across the country. So do drug traffickers, but we encountered it nightly in LA. No trafficker treats a girl well, but some bring a different level of violence and evil to the game. What has a child experienced at the hands of a drug trafficker versus someone like China's pimp who sold her to pay rent? What's the difference between jumping in the car with a gang member who just murdered someone and an inexperienced college kid?

Or think about this. What does it do to their heart and their identity to stand in a doorway on a bustling city street and give a blow job in full view of every passerby?

Children who have been trafficked across the country or in multiple states will have different experiences and traumas than those sold only in their hometowns. Our treatment plans should factor that in.

But they shouldn't stop there. Everything about their trafficking impacts them, starting with their recruitment. Go back to the gangs. A child jumped into a gang to be trafficked has a much different recruitment experience than one sold a dream by a finesse pimp like I was. All traffickers have individual styles and unique temperaments. When you hear the word "pimp" or "trafficker," don't be fooled into thinking they fit into one category. There are just as many styles of pimps as there are styles of shoes. We can put them into categories like "finesse pimp," too, but think about the category "supervisor." Then think about different supervisors you've had. Each one had a distinct personality and expectations.

Don't rush it but listen to their story as it unfolds. Important details will emerge with time that will help you adjust their treatment plan to their unique needs. That's what a savvy trafficker does. That's how he gains her trust, her willingness to stay, and her desire to come back even when she has an out. He listens, he adjusts, he listens some more. I often say we have to learn to think like a trafficker. Right now, their success rate is higher than ours, and there's a reason for it. They learn the details and make them work to their advantage.

Understanding the recruitment method, the type of trafficker, the type of buyers, the living arrangements, the area she was sold in, and other pertinent details will help you effectively tailor your treatment plan.

## Two-Minute Introspection

What would be the difference in outcomes if we customized every child's treatment plan to the details of their unique experience? What difference would it make to their future?

# 24 We Are Family

Like father, like son. The streets became my father, and I became "Daddy" to girls searching for the same thing that eluded me.

Sparkle calling me "Daddy" wasn't unique to me, however. Daddies are a dime a dozen in the game. Astute traffickers instinctively manipulate a child's dysfunctional childhood and agonizing search for a nurturing family. You might be wondering how such a thing could be instinctive. It goes back to that old saying, "It takes one to know one." Most traffickers have an innate sense of what abused-and-neglected kids need because they've needed it themselves. That's what this book is about: When you never find it, you try to recreate it any way you can – even at the expense of others. Few people are strong enough to break out of the aftermath of complex trauma alone. Left alone, they go down the path of victim, victimizer ... or both.

As egotistical as I already was, I became fuller of myself when Sparkle anointed me with that nickname. I had achieved a more prominent and respected status. I had worked my way up through the ranks from wannabe to established pimp, from Derek to Daddy. You know you've arrived when you earn a pimp moniker.

Like any good businessperson, I put my title to work. I maneuvered any situation I could into the facade of family.

For instance, I wanted to take the temperature of as many states and major cities as possible on the drive back for future reference. Kayla wanted to go through Denver to visit cousins she hadn't seen in years. I could have said no since it was out of the way, but it allowed me to check out another city while giving Kayla – and the other two – the illusion I cared about her feelings.

Moreover, I figured sex sells anywhere, and I had a carload of product. I was right about that. The part about sex selling anywhere. I was working to take my brand national, and Denver gave me another distribution center. Nothing urgent was waiting for me in Boston, anyway.

We worked the Denver blade four days. I kept it on my list to pass back through but added it to the bottom. Not that I didn't make good money there. I didn't like the ups and downs and curves of the mountains. Don't forget it was always about what made me happy.

In the meantime, the stop made Kayla happy, too. Happy employees typically produce better results.

I assumed her cousins would drop by the hotel or meet us at a restaurant, but they invited us to their house for dinner. I was down for that. One less meal I had to pay for. Kayla had told them she was on a road trip with her boyfriend and two friends, and we dressed the part. We all wore jeans and T-Shirts. I left my garish pimp jewelry at the hotel, and the girls left their wigs there, too. Sparkle even wore her hair in a ponytail. They kept the makeup light, so we fit the story Kayla fed them.

They were middle-class squares, clueless about what her "boyfriend" did for a living. We had a pleasant evening with them that played right into my hands. More than just a free dinner. ***They*** helped me manipulate her mind and emotions without realizing it. I made it possible for her to see family she missed by taking her on a road trip. What were the chances she'd see them anytime soon if it weren't for me? I wasn't sucking the life out of her in her eyes; I was adding to it.

It worked to my advantage in every way. It bumped up her status in the other girls' eyes when I allowed her to introduce me as her boyfriend. It made them want to work harder to earn such a privilege. Dyna decided I needed to meet her mom when we got back to Boston.

I took the family facade deeper at our next stop, my old stomping grounds, Kansas. Everyone wants to be proud of their daddy, so I gave them a reason to be proud of me.

"Wow. You were in the Army?"

"Yeah, when I was younger. I needed to get out of Boston, and the Army was a good way because they paid for me to leave. No big deal."

I let them in on a little secret, too, one you would only share with those you trusted, like close family members.

"I had a baby in the Army. He's named after me. He lives around here."

"Does he look like you?"

"I don't know. Haven't seen him since I left eight years ago."

I didn't tell them that I also had a wife nearby. Nor that I had no desire to see either one of them. We'd gradually quit talking when she never cared enough to join her husband in Boston. I didn't care to stir up that pain and rejection.

Besides, I'd already gotten what I wanted out of the story: Their awe.

Back in Boston, I rented an apartment for me in a middle-class neighborhood and one for them in the hood. Another family move.

They took pride in elevating the status of their daddy. They wanted their pimp to look better than the other pimps, ride better, dress better. Bragging rights.

"Yeah, we went cross-country and made enough to furnish a brand-new apartment for our man."

That was their mentality and mine. I'm a pimp. You're a ho. You're here to serve me, make my life better. My purpose in life had evolved from pimping for survival to pimping for a life of luxury. I acted out of learned behavior – you get up no matter who you have to step on to get there.

They got to enjoy the fringe benefits, visiting me in my home instead of a hotel room; riding in my vehicles; admiring me sporting fancy jewelry, slick clothes, and fancy shoes.

And whatever they needed in the hood, I took care of. I kept them in a motel for a couple of months after we got back. I was still learning the business side of pimping, so it took me a while to realize I could save money by renting an apartment for them. Hotel bills and eating out add up quickly. I could pay a month's apartment lease for a week's hotel expenses, especially with new girls coming and going, costing me extra hotel rooms.

I drew the family line at them staying with me. I especially didn't want new girls near my new wall safe flush with money. I didn't want to worry about stashing my jewelry and pocket cash while I showered. I didn't want to sleep with a stranger in my apartment. The game is full of criminals, after all. You have to think about those things to protect your business. Consider China's "pimp," for instance. Instead of his friend calling me, Sly could have planted another girl in my operation for the sole purpose of stealing from me since he thought I had stolen from him. I think she's chosen me, but Sly's targeted me.

I eventually let Sparkle move in. She'd proven herself. She had taught me things about the game I didn't know and vice versa. It made business sense to have my righthand person, a senior executive, so to speak, nearby.

We had a close relationship, but the game always took priority. I made sure the other girls understood she was my bottom, not my girlfriend, to keep jealousy at bay. I didn't want that headache. Plus, I wanted them to understand traffickers reward according to performance. New girls must work their way up just like in any other career. They prove they're high performers, and I would reward them, too.

I had no problem sticking new girls with unknown motives in their apartment. It's like in a company when a new employee joins the team. You have to deal with it whether you like the person or not.

Girls came and went through their apartment. Their next long-term roommate, Amazon, chose me in New York City about a month before we hit the road again. She wouldn't budge as I walked toward her on the sidewalk.

"Bitch, don't you know you're supposed to get out of a pimp's way."

"I'm trying to learn a pimp's way," she shot back.

I sized her up. She towered over me. This White bitch must be crazy to confront a pimp, I thought, so I hoped she understood the rules of the game.

"Break yourself, Bitch."

She reached in her bra and gave me her money. Two violations back-to-back; she must be serious. I'd never seen her in the mob of hos working the New York track, but she must have watched me.

"You going to follow your money?"

"That's my intention."

"What's his name, number?" She meant business, so I called Kane right there with her to handle the business. He didn't answer.

"Here. Use my phone."

He answered immediately. Another pimp who didn't know what a pimp was, trying to duck my serve.

"Yo, Kane. This is D from Boston. That other number you wouldn't answer was me. Amazon just chose."

He blew up through the phone line. "How you call me from the bitch's phone?"

Despite his lack of business acumen, I left her on the track for him to get back at her if he so chose. He did. She ignored him.

We went back by New York on our way out to LA a few weeks later to see if Amazon's cousin wanted to choose. Amazon had brought her into the game with Kane and had told her about me behind Kane's back. Snowflake chose that night. I served Kane face-to-face, and he took it like a pimp this time. I gave him a chance to get back at Snowflake, too. He took full advantage and tried to get back at both of them. They both rebuffed his advances, impatient to get on the road to LA.

A pimp friend had suggested I try out Norfolk, Virginia, on the way West, so we swung by to take a quick temperature check. Cops ran the girls off the track but not before an undercover arrested Snowflake. I sent Sparkle and Amazon to her court hearing the following day to pay the fine, so we could get going.

The judge gave her 90 days. I'd never heard of that before – and never have since – especially for a first offense **anywhere**. She had a clean record. She had only been in the game a few months. I told them to put money on her books and get back to the hotel so that we could get the hell out of the heat.

I made sure to keep up the family charade, though. It'd be one thing if Snowflake were just some ho who stumbled across our path. They might resent me sending money they worked for to her phone and canteen account, but she had a blood tie to our family. I'd ask about her when Amazon talked to her, and I had all the girls write her letters. Again, some things they didn't need to know like it was a calculated move to keep Amazon happy and Snowflake from turning on me. The last thing I wanted to do was upset her while she was in jail because I had no idea if they were trying to get her to make a statement. She barely knew me, so why should she be loyal? And I did feel **some** sense of obligation since the undercover arrested her while she was getting my money. It had to have been a little traumatizing for her since he'd gone so far as to take his pants off before cops in the adjoining room burst in. I kept up the pretense to the end, supporting her when, deep into her sentence, she decided to go home when she got out instead of joining us in LA.

All in all, it was a good move on my part. Her harsh sentence devasted everyone; we'd never experienced anything like it. Emotions ran high, and I wanted everyone in a good mood when we pulled into LA. I worked hard to make the trip fun and not all business. When we got to California, there'd be no more fun, just business.

That's not to say I didn't take care of business along the way. The trip needed to pay for itself, so we worked the major cities we passed through. I also wasn't one of those traffickers who limited himself to one market-place. Some pimps stick to one venue, such as the track, online, social media, or strip clubs. I liked to try my hand at anything that added to the bottom line. I enjoyed learning about different aspects of the game. So, when the blade in Houston didn't do much more than cover expenses and other girls in the nail salon told them to try the spas, I thought, "Why not?" I was doing all the driving, so it would give me some time to rest and check out somewhere I'd never been.

The ho house owner, as it is known on the streets, split them up between his two spas when they went for an interview. They didn't have to know how to give massages; all he cared about was their look. He gave them a few pointers, and posters on the wall highlighted pressure points.

We had to split the massage fee with him. Of course, they didn't tell him he was splitting it with a pimp. They got to keep all tips and the fees for any add-ons, such as blow jobs or sex. They sized the men up and set their price. If he looked like he had money, they might say $150 extra for sex. If he said he only had $100, they'd still take it.

None of us liked it too much, especially Sparkle. They could sit for hours without a customer, which made her restless. She pressured me to let her work the blade while they worked the spas. She wasn't happy settling for half the money she could bring in. The other hos in the nail salon had warned them cops were hot out on the blade, though, so I wasn't taking any chances. I'd already lost one girl to jail this trip.

"They might get a case because they don't know how to move around," she pled. "I can move around the blade, go in and out the bars."

"Shut up and do what you're told. This is not about you. It's about me. You make your regular money while they're sitting around, and they're going to start whining, 'Daddy, let me go.' I don't need that. This ain't no democracy. We're going to work these spas while I get some rest." I ended the conversation.

The tourist in me wanted to see the Grand Canyon, so we worked Arizona and took the trip up before heading to LA. I didn't think it was worth the lost income. Big hole in the ground. They thought it was awesome, though, and it made them feel like a family watching all the other families together. I considered it product evolution, so a wise business investment despite my personal disappointment.

Anytime you share so many waking moments with other people, you grow closer. We gelled into our own little crime family on that trip. I played up the family front, with things like asking what was going on back home when they'd talk to someone there and listening to their feelings.

The only true feelings I experienced were frustration and a short fuse at their constant chatter. They'd talk over each other and carry on multiple conversations while I tried to listen to my music in the confinement of the car. It felt as if I were jammed into a sardine can. It took a little getting used to, but I had the advantage of growing up in a house full of women, so I knew the drill. When I couldn't take it anymore, I'd yell at them to shut up or threaten them like my mom used to do us: "Don't make me pull this car over." Daddies do that, too.

It got on my nerves, but all bosses have parts of the job they dislike. I could listen to their chatter and pull down a couple a thousand a night or listen to incessant salon gossip and pull down a couple of thousand every few weeks.

## Analysis With Dr. Deena Graves:
### The Trafficker's Family Facade

If a girl leaves, something happens to her, or she dies, a trafficker indifferently replaces her with another girl. Yet, girls typically do anything for their pimp, including going to prison rather than turning on him. One core reason is that pimps are experts at creating the guise of family, as we've detailed in this chapter.

The family facade gives his victim a sense of belonging and hope, whether she is an adult or underage. However, it is especially effective on teens who have grown up in homes of abuse and neglect. They're incredibly vulnerable because they're in the throes of a broken, tragic childhood. They long for family like anyone would who believes no one cares.

A skilled trafficker knows how to create an atmosphere where they feel they matter, where they're deceived into believing they're loved. I intentionally and methodically convinced my victims I cared about their feelings and emotions, lulling them into a false belief they'd found what they'd always dreamed of having.

It also creates a false sense of security and comfort as they're trafficked from state to state. It blurs the trauma that landed them there and the trauma of hundreds of abusers who are lining the pimp's pockets with thousands of dollars raping them.

The longer I was in the game, the more cunning I became at shaping a family atmosphere, a flamboyant family at that. I'd go all out, doing things like buying them matching outfits, renting a limo, and taking them to top-billed concerts. The return on my investment made it a solid business choice.

I also included them in family memories that many had never had. I'd take them, for instance, to my sister's for Thanksgiving and Mom's for Christmas. I'd let them buy my mom a present, and my family gave them gifts, too. We hung around longer on Christmas, but we couldn't stay too late on Thanksgiving because the track got busy. Guys go out to watch a football game or hunt and then head to the track for a different kind of hunt.

I gave every girl the day off for her birthday. I'd let her pick the restaurant where she and I would celebrate. I'd have the waiter bring her cake. I'd give her a present and would give the other girls $25-$30 each to buy her something, too. After all, that's what family does. That typically worked out in my favor, as well, because they'd usually buy the birthday girl makeup or a wig, which I was going to pay for anyway.

I even took one of my girls, Natasha, on a cruise to celebrate her birthday. I ordinarily wouldn't have done something that extravagant, but it didn't cost me anything and made all the girls work harder for their chance. My cousin and I had planned the five-day cruise to celebrate our birthdays, but he got arrested shortly before our departure date. I didn't want to go by myself and thought she might score enough dates to pay for my travel experiences. I had other girls who had been with me longer, but Natasha had taken care of my business, and we shared a birthday.

"You work real hard. Instead of dinner, I'm going to let you go with me."

We had a good time, but she didn't catch any dates. I guess the men were too worried about getting caught in the close quarters of a cruise ship. I didn't try when we'd disembark since I wanted to see the sights.

This common trafficker tactic of creating family makes our job of keeping them out and helping them heal challenging. We must counter it wisely, or they'll keep going back. They'll return again and again to where they feel they belong, are loved, and get attention. I know because they'd run back to me again and again, even when I willingly let them visit their families or caregivers, spend holidays with them, or told them to go back because they had violated a rule.

One strategic way we can counter this is by supporting the grieving process they go through at the loss of their trafficker, aka their daddy or boyfriend figure, and their wifeys. Think of a time you've lost someone important to you, whether one of you moved away or the person died. You worked through a grieving process. We tend to expect these youth, who've experienced so much other loss, to let those feelings go immediately. We have good intentions. We know the trafficker does not care about them. We have no doubt he's caused them life-threatening damage. We want to protect them from additional danger.

They're not there yet.

One teen we worked with had been the victim of a transnational crime syndicate, the MS-13 gang, for five years. They did horrific things to her beyond trafficking. BUT they became her family at 11 when she ran away from a lifetime of sexual abuse. She didn't know how to survive on her own at that age, and they offered her protection, love, and survival – what many of these kids hit the streets in search of. She eventually became the girlfriend of the gang leader, drawing her deeper into the idea of family.

We met her at 16 in a juvenile detention center where she disclosed trafficking. She came into a residential home for trafficked minors Deena had opened. One night, she had a nightmare about her boyfriend. Everything she had loved about him beckoned to her as he gazed adoringly at her in the nightmare. However, the closer he walked to her bed, the more hideous he became. She woke up terrified, jumped from her bed, grabbed her pen from the nightstand, and ran into the kitchen, where she began carving their gang symbols into the cabinets.

Our response could have been strict punishment for the destruction of our property. However, we knew the nightmare triggered her actions and that she was in deep mourning for and confusion about the life she had lived for five years. Instead of a harsh response, therefore, we talked to her about how we understood they had been her family. We understood the deep bond she felt for them and that it was hard for her to turn her feelings off. We realized she'd been drawing gang symbols for five years – in a lot of places. That did not make it okay, though, to destroy our property. She could draw her gang symbols all she wanted, just not on our property. We gave her a journal to draw them and work through her grieving process. Her writing went from statements such as:

> *"Me and my chicka always break-in necks.*
> *Fighting, stabbing, robbing,*
> *and even killing people was all that we did."*

To:

> *"Now I have somewhere I can run to,*
> *somewhere I can rest and sleep*
> *and somewhere I don't have to be afraid*
> *of the next knock on the door."*

Of course, we couldn't let the cabinets slip by unchecked. We had to establish clear boundaries. We made her sand them down, but we took the edge off by taking photos and having fun restoring them. Why would we make light of it? Because a lifetime of trauma and fear carved those symbols into our cabinets. A highly traumatized, scared child fell into the hands of a notorious gang at 11 because she didn't know where else to find food or a place to sleep. They engraved the gang symbols on her mind, and she had to find a way to get them out to heal. How many walls do you think she defaced during her five years with the gang as her teacher? We have to think through our response based on their lived experiences.

We looked past gang symbols on our kitchen cabinets to a grieving child. We concentrated on healing the root issue rather than getting bogged down in the manifestation of that issue. She laughed and joked with us as she sanded the cabinets. If our response had been anger, her response would have been different, too.

Children and adults alike thrive when they believe a trusted adult has their back and genuinely cares about them. Without that type of relationship, their self-worth and self-efficacy crater.[76]

Let's take the role of trusted adults away from the traffickers.

By the way, when you do, it also has a profound impact on you. That child engraved much more than gang symbols on our kitchen cabinets. She engrained deep respect and admiration into our hearts by how hard she came to fight for her own healing when given a nurturing environment despite the horrific things she had lived through. Her name started with M. So does ours.

## Two-Minute Introspection

What other root issues do we need to address during the healing process?

# 25 The Clock is Ticking

It didn't take the Russian mobster long to spot Kayla back on the Sunset Boulevard stroll. He spun his car around when he saw her. I'd put two girls at each end of the track to keep them from all getting arrested again. I had Dyna with Kayla, and he took her, too. For friends, he said.

He eventually grew frustrated because Kayla wouldn't leave me for him. He didn't want to traffick her; he wanted to put her up as his private play-thing. After a few weeks of rejection, she tried to wave him down when he drove past. He'd ignore her.

Kayla had what most tricks wanted – she was young, cute, White, and down for almost anything. Not surprisingly, then, a drug dealer quickly took the Russian's spot as a regular. He liked her so much he sent her home one night with her fee and weed. She knew better than to take drugs from a trick, especially a professional dealer. Could be laced with angel dust or a hallucinogen. She might think she's about to get a marijuana high and end up with an acid high with all the lights on the track suddenly going psychedelic on her. He might say it's cocaine when it's heroin. It's too late after she sniffs it. She's already impacted my bottom line because she snorted a downer that puts her to sleep.

I threw it away and gave her a verbal reprimand.

"Let something else happen again with him or anyone else, and I'm going to cut your head, Bitch." As pimp rules go, I should've banged her head around right then. I was a finesse pimp, though, controlling my girls with psychological manipulation rather than violence, for the most part. The threat of violence was always there, but I'd only used it once, and it was with her. She liked to push boundaries.

I did yell a lot, and I guess that irritated her. Once back in Boston, as she turned to walk away, she had mumbled under her breath, "He gets on my fucking nerves."

"What you say, Bitch."

"Nothing, Daddy."

"Come here ... oh, I make you sick, huh?" I slapped her hard enough to turn her face, to leave a handprint, but not a bruise. I wanted her face to be hot after the print was gone, but I didn't want a bruise to drive any tricks away that night. That was, after all, why I chose to be a finesse pimp rather than a guerilla pimp. Nobody wants a damaged product. It'd be like buying an expensive horse and finding whip scars all over it when you got it home.

A pimp who cared less about his bottom line and more about his respect would have noticed her flippancy toward the rules was rearing its head again with the weed violation. A pimp who understood his bottom line would have realized letting her impertinence slip would impact future earnings. I didn't catch on to either until a couple of weeks later.

I hadn't seen Kayla for a couple of hours. I drove by and told her where to meet me when she showed back up. I needed to break her because she'd have too much money by now to safely keep on her.

She handed me $100.

"What's this, Bitch? You've been gone too long to think you can give me $100."

She'd been with the drug dealer.

"I spent some time with him. He wanted to talk before I serviced him."

I didn't say anything then since we were in the middle of work, but my blood hit boiling point. I didn't have to say anything for her to know that.

When we got back to the motel at the end of the night, I told her we needed to talk.

"After you take your shower, I'm going to need you to come down to my room."

I'm sure she felt safe doing that since I'd never done more than raise my voice or slap her.

I'd carefully thought all night about the best way to remind her who was boss. As aforementioned, I didn't want to pull my merchandise off the market for any amount of time. I had to balance letting her know I wasn't playing with keeping her physically where the tricks would want to play. I didn't want marks they'd see as they sized her up.

I let her in when she knocked. I left her standing in tortured silence while

I took my time walking over to turn the television up. She had to wonder why I turned it up and not down. She knew I'd want her to clearly hear what I had to say.

"You know what we need to talk about, right?"

"No."

I slapped the smartass bitch.

"Do you know now what we need to talk about?"

She started crying.

Tears don't work on someone without emotions.

"Don't start crying now when you didn't cry coming back with only $100 after an hour with a trick."

"I'm sorry. He just wanted to talk."

"You spent all that time with him for $100?"

"He comes to see me often. He's a regular."

"Do you have a personal relationship with him." It wasn't a question. "He's a trick. I don't care if he comes every night. He gets 15-20 minutes top. What do you and a trick have that much to talk about? You and I don't even talk that long. He's there for one thing. You're there for one thing. He's sending you home with weed, and now you're not charging him time. You could have had two more dates or a $300 date for the free time you gave him."

She needed an undeniable reminder that she had one purpose in life, and that was to bring me tricks' money – and as much of it as possible. Her time equaled my profit margin. She wouldn't have sex or give a blow job for an hour for the amount of money the druggie paid. The price didn't change just because part of the time went to a different use of her mouth. It would be like a store clerk selling a box of steaks for the price of one.

"Take your pants off." She looked at me in bewilderment.

"Take your pants off. You shouldn't be out there talking to him when you should be getting my money. What's going on? You want to be with him, or you just don't want to show me any respect?"

I told her to lay across the bed and started whipping her with my belt. She tried to run, but I grabbed her. She tried to cover herself with her hands, so I made her put her hands under the pillow and lay her head on it. She still fought me, trying to raise her legs to block me and roll away. I held her down and gave her about 10 lashes, enough to make her red and sore but not leave any cuts. She cried uncontrollably.

"Shut up, Bitch, and put your pants back on."

She didn't argue.

"Now, you can go be with that dude if you want, but, if you're staying here, you'll follow the rules. You won't spend more time with him than any other trick. You won't be standing there with him when you should be somewhere with a dick in your mouth. You'll get $300 from any trick you spend that much time with. You understand what I'm saying, right?"

"Yeah, I know, Daddy. I shouldn't have done that. It won't happen again."

She tried to calm me down, but adrenaline pulsed out of control through me now. My hands throbbed from the residual anger.

"Here I am in the hotel after a long night's work having to exert energy, Bitch. I had to earn my money from you tonight. I'm hot and sweaty. Now I need a shower. I shouldn't have to work like that. Why you making me have to go through this? It's not like you're a turnout. You know the rules. You know me. The money is short, and now I had to work by putting my hands on you. I'm feeling disrespected. It's like you don't know me or the game. You think I'm soft, or you got it like that, where you can disappear from the track and come back with whatever. I'm feeling personally disrespected. It's like a slap in my face. I'm going to be gone, come back, and give him whatever."

The words wouldn't stop coming; my rage seethed with the unbelievable lack of honor she had shown me. She tried to interject, but I kept ranting.

"This is your second violation with the same guy. You're getting too comfortable with tricks. You're not out here to have fun. You're out here to make me money. I don't want to hear you talk that much. How does that trick want to? Talk to your wifeys."

I took a breath, and she broke in.

"I understand, Daddy. I'm really sorry. He won't get any more time than what he pays for. He's just a trick." She started repeating back to me what I'd said to her. Whether she was as contrite and apologetic as she acted, she played her role well … finally.

I calmed down. I was still upset, but I had gotten my point across. My job was done. I punished her according to her violation and then made sure she understood that she had gotten too comfortable because she wouldn't have done that six months prior. I reminded her that her job was to tiptoe around me and take care of my business the same way at six months as she had on day one.

"I'm going down to get a soda. You want one?" She nodded. "Come with me then. I'm not walking back to your room."

No need to linger on it. I knew it would stay in her head that I'd treated her like the ho she was. I wasn't her friend. I was her pimp. Her sore butt and wounded feelings would make sure she remembered that. Why let it ruin the rest of my night? She could always go home if she wanted. I could easily find more girls. I couldn't let her disrespect my position, not only for her. I had three other girls watching. I had a business to run. If I let her slide, they'd think I was soft.

No way they'd think I was soft after that. I knew what a good thrashing did to you. I got the idea from my stepdad, after all. His blows didn't just rip into my flesh; they ripped into my pride and my self-worth. His stone-hearted delivery made me a lesser person in my mind. You couldn't beat someone with such a lack of compassion and view them as human. His inhumane treatment of me made it easier to detach myself from Kayla as anything remotely human as I flogged her.

I'm sure she thought, like me, that she could get away with certain things because we had built some level of relationship. Neither of us understood relationship is relative.

I didn't understand my stepfather didn't see me as his son. I came along as my mom's extra baggage, and, therefore, I was open game for his violent outbursts. All those years I thought he was my real dad made it worse. A dad is supposed to love and care about you, not break belt after belt across different parts of your body. That's how I knew to make sure I didn't tear her flesh open if I wanted her to work the next day. I could see through my anger that her slight build couldn't bear the full brunt of my fury like mine couldn't his.

It should have surprised me, alarmed me, that I instinctively knew when she couldn't take anymore, not because I cared about her, but because I cared about my business. One difference between my stepfather and me was he had nothing at stake in my success. According to the rules of the game, Kayla was my property, and I didn't want to damage my investment. I just needed to get the bugs worked out of the end product. It's like any other job. You keep screwing up, and you face penalties.

Therefore, it had to be a make-or-break beating. She'd make it happen my way, or I'd break her.

Not my fault the stupid bitch hadn't figured out that driving cross-country or going to dinner together didn't make her my friend. She didn't grasp that lining my pockets with thousands of dollars didn't make her my business partner. Amazing how easy they fall for the "our business" shade I'd strategically throw their way from time to time.

That mental and physical domination of Kayla accelerated my mutation into a full-fledged monster. I liked the results I saw. All the girls got my message loud and clear, reestablishing my respect and authority. I knew they'd ask her what I said, not what I did, because I hadn't ventured into that magnitude of pimping yet. I didn't realize she'd show them, though.

"You beat her with a belt on her butt, Daddy?" Sparkle came down to inform me of the conversation in their room.

They'd all started questioning her when she walked in. She didn't answer. Instead, she walked to the mirror, pulled her pants down, and assessed the damage. They all jumped up to see. Sparkle said she had welts but no broken skin. Job well-done. I didn't want her face, arms, or legs bruised. If a sadist saw the discoloration and swelling the next night and wanted in on the action, it was her job to make him believe another trick paid her to leave those marks there and get his money for the same.

Like most girls do with guerilla pimps, Kayla stayed. She reverted to the frame of mind she had when she first joined my organization, taking her position and my money seriously. Sparkle agreed it had to be done. It was more a mental game than a physical one – like when my mom would make me get the belt when she would spank me.

The whole episode amped up my already over-inflated ego. It didn't hurt that the other pimps liked what they heard.

"Yeah, that was real pimpish."

"That's real good thinking, Pimping," another agreed.

Apparently not good enough to stay in Kayla's memory long. Next thing I knew, she got out of pocket, talking to D Money on the stroll. He found me a little farther down Sunset Boulevard.

"Hey, D. Your White bitch, Kayla, got out of pocket. She didn't want to make a move, so I broke her."

Unbelievable. Would this bitch never learn? I called her and told her where to meet me. I jumped on the highway.

"What you doing, Bitch? What you making D Money come tell me he took my money for?"

"I was just talking to him. He made me give him my money because I talked to him."

"You been in the game way too long to know you can't be talking to another pimp and him not break you."

"I can talk to whoever I want to."

I went ballistic, slapping her while trying to keep the car on the road.

"Put your hands down, Bitch."

"No. I'm not going to put my hands down, so you can keep slapping me," she screamed.

"Okay, Bitch. Get out of my car." I reached across her, forced the door open, and shoved her out with my foot and hand. The car had slowed to 25-30 miles an hour, and she managed to drop and roll. I didn't stick around to see how that worked out for her.

"Damn, Daddy. You threw her out of the car?" She'd gone straight to Sparkle when she made it back to the stroll.

"Yeah, Bitch. She told me she could talk to who she wants to."

"While you were moving?" Even Sparkle couldn't believe I'd gone that far. "She's scraped up pretty bad. Her clothes are torn and dirty."

"Okay. Take her back to the hotel to clean up and then get her back to work."

"I've never seen you this mad."

"She keeps messing up. Now she's talking to pimps and getting my money taken. I didn't make up the rules to the game. I just abide by them. She's becoming a legend in her own mind. How she think there'd be no repercussions? She's going to tell me no?"

Sparkle ran interference.

"You know the rules of the game, Kayla. If you're going to talk to him, you might as well go with him."

I'm not sure if it was Sparkle's calm, matter-of-fact reasoning or my unhinged eruption, but Kayla took it like a ho and stayed.

Violence came hand-in-hand with my anger now. I'd crossed a line I couldn't go back over. Barbarism worked. Why not use it as needed? I stuck to mind control as much as possible, but I didn't blink twice at inflicting torture after seeing how effectively it worked with Kayla.

After that, for instance, it made it seem like child's play to make a girl sleep in a bathtub when she insisted on causing trouble with other girls in their room, arguing, and fighting.

"You're not staying up here tonight, Bitch. You're staying in my room." She got up with a smirk on her face. She'd shown them.

I initially thought I'd make her sleep on the floor. As we walked down the hall, though, I thought I didn't want to look at this broad every time I rolled over. I decided to make her sleep in the bathroom.

"There's no room, Daddy."

"Lay in the tub." I closed the door.

She started complaining about her sore back the next morning.

"Now you know how to act. Get on back down to your room, and no more problems out of you."

Another girl thought she'd take her anger at her pimp out on me. She chose me on the Boston track in the dead of winter. She gave me money for three or four days, so I took her shopping. She brought in good money at 16, so I went all out. I bought her a new outfit, shoes, makeup, a helmet or wig, the works.

She came up a little short the first time I broke her that night. I didn't say anything, but I was seething after all my generosity.

I didn't see her on the track the rest of the night. She wasn't there when I went to pick them up. They hadn't seen her, either. I dropped them off and headed back to look for her. I hadn't gotten a call from a pimp or police, so I was heated. I should have had a clue when she came up short.

I saw her from behind on the track, so I spun the block to scoop her up. I could smell the cocaine on her. She had all the signs of a tweaker. I couldn't believe I'd missed them.

"What's wrong with you. You been getting high."

"No, I haven't."

I reached over the backseat and slapped her.

"Okay, Daddy. Okay, Daddy. I'm high."

"How much money you got?

"Only what I gave you earlier."

"All that shit I bought you, take it off."

She stripped down to her stockings and panties.

"Take that shit off, too."

I jumped on the highway to give her time to undress, flipped a uey, and headed back to the track.

"Bitch, get out of my car."

"It's raining."

I reached back across the seat and slapped her again.

"Get out of my car, or I'm going to crawl back there with you."

She jumped out and ran naked through the freezing rain to a restaurant awning on the corner.

I hadn't made it home when my phone rang.

"Yo, D. This is Righthand." I knew who he was. He came from the same hood as me. We grew up together. I never respected him as a pimp, though. It's like serious traffickers say: "You call yourself pimping, but you got rocks in your socks." I'm pretty sure he was her dealer before he became her pimp. I saw her here and there after that but never talked to her again.

I couldn't stuff the wolf back inside me once he came out with Kayla, but I knew how to hide him in sheep's clothing until I needed him.

My girls quickly learned they'd see the wolf shed the sheep's clothing if they crossed me.

## Analysis With Dr. Deena Graves:
### Traffickers and Violence

When girls chose me, they didn't realize the bite that came with the smile, a bite that drew blood. I shocked Sparkle, and she'd been in the game for years when I met her. She'd been with me a long time before the monster emerged, as well. I would not have thought about beating them or throwing them out of cars when she first came to me. At that point, I'd rather them leave than mess up my manicure by hitting them.

But I was still a follower. I followed James and Robert to a flame and a bottlecap and other traffickers to guerilla warfare. I constantly heard pimps talk about the high they got from adoring submissiveness. I always chased a good high. The power trip gets to you like a heroin euphoria. Just like I never would've seen myself shooting up in a gallery after junkies with abscesses, I never would have seen myself crushing another person the way I had been crushed. No, not the way my stepdad dehumanized me. I took it to a new level of depravity. Who does what I did to another human being, especially a child? How do you throw someone out of a moving car or make a 16-year-old girl visibly desperate for help get out of your car in the wee hours of the morning in freezing rain?

The answer is simple. Trafficking *is* an addiction, the same as heroin. The progression of the addiction and the need to act upon it intensifies with time. Trafficking controls your mind, your emotions, and your actions like heroin. The same euphoria that pulsates through your body when you stick the needle in your arm pulsates through your ego when another person gives you unquestionable obedience.

You can see in the punishment I chose that it wasn't as much about the violence as it was their absolute degradation. The physical pain eventually fades, but the mental torment is meant to stay in their head. It's a reminder that you just got treated like the ho you are. Kayla exemplified it. When I berated and humiliated her, she immediately apologized and groveled, even repeating back mortifying things about herself. For what? Talking to someone a few minutes. Degradation reinforces their false belief that they're not worth anything and have zero human value.

The *only value* they often see in themselves is in how well they satisfy another person's needs, in this case, the trafficker's. They shoulder all the responsibility for that person's barrage of insults and slurs.[77]

We've stated several times that we must look at each child's unique story. We can't say it enough. The type of violence a pimp uses influences everything from their self-esteem to their self-worth to their identity. It also impacts what it will take for them to get the strength to leave and the strength to heal.

## Two-Minute Introspection

Think back to a time when someone intentionally embarrassed or humiliated you. How did it make you feel in the moment? How does it make you feel now? With that in mind, how do your treatment plans address degradation and humiliation? What additional steps do you take if violence was part of it?

# 26 Name That Tune

I liked everything about California, including the pageantry of the pimps. I sported brighter colors, more expensive shoes, and meticulous manicures. I also experimented with different hairstyles, striving for just the right statement.

My cousin in LA took me to a hair salon known for celebrity styles. The hairstylists and clients had one conversation going on, and my cousin casually tossed in my occupation. Most of the talk centered on weed, though, which was not legal at the time. Rona, one of the older ladies, about 10 years my senior, told her hairdresser she had run out. I kept the girls' weed with me, so they didn't smoke it all at once. I was enjoying the camaraderie, so thought, "Why not?"

Rona walked out to the car with me. I handed her a bag of weed I'd brought with me on the trip. She offered her marijuana connection since we were new to the area. And some say people in LA aren't friendly. She slipped me her number in case I needed anything else. I gave her my number in case she needed anything.

She headed back in the salon to finish her hair. I settled in my seat, listening to them chattering about trivial things. My appointment happened to be with Rona's stylist, so I took her seat after she said her goodbyes.

"You know who that was, right?" Her stylist filled me in. I'd just given free weed to the mom of one of the world's top pop stars. The girls would not be happy if they knew since I rationed it out to them. She could have afforded all the weed she wanted.

I liked the reaction I got when I gave people gifts, so I discarded the thought of their whining. It was mine to give. Rona had been full of gratitude for the quick fix, but I doubted I'd talk to her again. She'd screen my calls, I figured, if she'd even given me her actual number. I was satisfied with meeting part of the Hollywood elite.

I never would've thought the wildly busy mom and co-manager of a renowned singer would be lonely. I learned precisely how lonely when she called me to invite me to her house for dinner – and sex. She wasn't interested in a one-night stand, either. She became more than another sex partner, however. She became a haven. I'd kick it at her house while the girls worked or when I needed a little peace and quiet. I'd escape to Rona's to lounge by the pool, eat a homecooked meal, and recover from the rigors of pimping without one of the girls banging on my hotel room door. I didn't bother telling them about Rona or where I was.

I also didn't bother telling Rona where I was when I wasn't with her. Unlike my girls, though, she wasn't used to being ignored. I didn't notice her when she first drove by me one night on Sunset Boulevard. Not to be deterred, she came back around and blew her horn at me a second time. I motioned her to meet me around the block. I jumped in her car when she pulled up.

"What are you doing out here?" I hoped she could tell I wasn't pleased.

"You haven't returned my calls."

"I'm busy. I'm taking care of my business."

"All you have to do is pick up the phone and say, 'I'm busy.'"

I couldn't believe she'd drop in on me at the track ... at my place of work. She met all the big names, hung out at the celebrity-studded events – and she was jealous of a no-name pimp? She was either into her feelings for me, or the lifestyle intrigued her. Maybe it was a little of both. For me, she was merely something to do, and she had a fun place to do it.

"Look, Rona. I like you, but I gotta take care of business. I can't sit around waiting for your call. The way your son's career is booming, you could be gone at any minute. Where would I be if I let you interfere with my business? If I didn't have these girls, I'd never have met you."

"I'd give you the option of going with me," she reassured me.

She'd already introduced me to some of her celebrity friends and parties, but I resisted the temptation to prostitute myself fully to her.

"This is my life. It's a sure thing. I make good money. Why would I depend on you and have to ask you for money? I'd be dependent on you like these girls are dependent on me. This is who I am." I went into pimp mode, coldly shutting down any counterargument.

We both had something the other wanted, however, so we came to an unspoken agreement. She wouldn't bother me at work, and I wouldn't ignore her calls for more than a day. In return, I gave her the attention she wanted, and she gave me inside access to the inner workings of Hollywood and the music business. She took me to the Black Entertainment Television and Soul Train awards shows. We frequented recording studios, album release parties, and TV sets. She introduced me to people I heard on the radio and saw in the movies. I ate dinner with them at legendary restaurants; I shared Thanksgiving dinner at a record producer's home. She included my mom and daughter when they came to visit me. We became family. Seemed she knew how to create that facade, too.

It was like living a dream for this boy from the hood. I'd gone from scrounging for coins on a pimp's floorboard to living a life most pimps, even California pimps, never get close to. Living a life most people *in general* never get a glimpse of. My arrogance grew with every passing party, but something deeper grew inside of me, as well. Something I'd searched for my entire life – a sense of worth. She made me believe anything was possible. I had to be valuable for the Hollywood elite to mingle with me, to welcome me to their high-profile events. After all, I'd willingly had sex with her multiple times before she introduced me to any of that. She saw something in me besides a kid from the hood who deserved to be abused, who had lived a life invisible to most people.

Rona understood something that also comes intuitively to most child sex traffickers: You sell hopeless people, especially kids, a dream, and they'll do just about anything for you. I just didn't have to pay the price my victims did.

## Analysis With Dr. Deena Graves:
### Selling the Dream

Traffickers deal in dreams. They peddle fantasies to buyers and kids alike. That's their business model. Kids who've never had anyone tell them they matter fantasize about someone to love them. Youth running from the abuse in their homes look for hope in something as basic as food to eat and a warm, dry place to sleep. Some teens desperately seek escape from what they believe is a boring existence. It doesn't matter where you come from. Everyone is looking for a dream to come true.

A savvy pimp sells a potential victim a dream and ***keeps it alive*** once he has the child under his control. His job is to keep her inspired, keep her looking forward to it coming true. If she wakes up and realizes it was all a nightmare, his money walks out the door, so he has a lot of motivation.

Let me give you an example of how I made them believe I'd make their dreams come true.

I smiled at a teen I walked by in the mall. I noted she was absorbed in her music, bouncing her head to the beat. She went into a music store and then made her way to the food court, where she sat alone with her new CDs.

"I see you like music. You've been walking around to it and bought some new tunes, huh?"

"Yeah, I really like music."

"Yeah, I've been watching you. I saw you getting into it."

"I saw you watching me." She had to of been watching me to notice that. I'd made myself noticeable. It's not that hard when you're wooing a younger girl who thinks you're cute. Traffickers smooth-talk them, making sure they don't feel threatened. I talked music with her long enough to gain her trust before asking for her phone number and giving her mine.

"Give me a call. Let's go to lunch."

She didn't need to know the topic of the lunch discussion. In her mind, I wanted to date her because I thought she was cute. Flattery is a powerful weapon in a trafficker's arsenal. So powerful that she called me the next day.

I plied her with more sweet talk at lunch before pivoting the conversation to my sole interest in her.

"Yeah, you know those girls you saw walking with me when you first saw me at the mall? They work for me."

"Really? What do they do?"

I made it sound enticing.

"If you want to try that out, I can set it up."

Let me stress: A monotonous life can make young girls curious about something they've seen glamorized on TV, especially when a sophisticated, older guy sells it to them.

To be clear, Kasey wasn't abused, neglected, or in need of anything – except excitement. She was bored. She felt nobody paid attention to her, including her parents. They didn't understand her desire to pursue music. She was a loner, which I picked up on at our first encounter in the mall. Those kinds of details play to traffickers' advantage, so they pay attention.

She stayed with me for about a year because I not only sold her a dream, but I also kept her dream alive. She always had her music going when she wasn't working. She'd walk around in her own world, humming and bopping her head as she did at the mall. Her preoccupation with music kept her out of the drama between the other girls. I wanted to show her I took note of that while feigning interest in her musical ambitions.

"So, you always wanted to play the guitar?"

"Yeah."

"Let's make that happen. You keep doing what you're doing, you keep getting my money, and we'll see if we can use my resources to get it going."

I let her simmer in that a few weeks before I surprised her with a cheap guitar from a pawn shop. She was like a kid at Christmas. Someone finally understood her passion for music.

A couple more thousand down the road, I bought her a used amp. Now she's thrilled because she has something to plug her guitar into. A few more thousand, and I took her dream to a new level.

"Hey, you willing to lose a couple hours sleep each week?"

"Yeah, why, Daddy?"

"You're doing so good with that guitar that I thought you might like to take private lessons."

She's made me around $10,000, and I'd invested about $500 of it back into keeping her dream – and my cash flow – alive. Not a bad ROI. She was willing to do anything for the person who finally saw music was part of her DNA.

We will be much more successful with the youth we work with if we do the same. Watch the details – there's that word again – in their lives. What motivates them? What gives them a rush of excitement? You notice I didn't do everything at once. I kept dangling it in front of her. I commented on it when I first met her. I talked to her about it as we got to know each other, making her believe I genuinely cared. And I did. I cared because it kept my bottom line healthy. Then, I rewarded her good behavior. I praised her when she played. It was nothing but noise to me, but I was excited when she'd come home with a new chord or a new music term. I was excited because she was excited. Yeah, she's going to work hard tonight.

The difference between a person like I was and a person like we are is that we genuinely care. The difference in her reaction to the two? Eventually, the novelty of what I offered her wore off, and she wanted to go home. Someone could have prevented me from being a novelty to her in the first place. Listen to the youth in your life, whether they are your own or you work with them. Get involved in the fine print of their existence, no matter how subtly they express it. If you don't, there's someone out there who will be all over it.

## Two-Minute Introspection

Recall a time when someone noticed something you were passionate about that no one else paid attention to. How did it make you feel about your passion? How did it make you feel about that person? What insight does that give you about how traffickers keep our kids sold on a dream?

# 27 Yank My Chain

I bought Holly from a pimp on the Sunset Boulevard stroll because I'd loved dogs since I was a kid. I had no idea she'd be another weapon in my arsenal.

I kept my pet snake and iguana in aquariums in my motel room. The caged-up reptiles had never bothered Dyna, but she couldn't stand to see Holly, named for Hollywood, in her kennel for even a second. She'd immediately take her out when she came into my room. The night she chose me, she told me that her previous pimp, Stackz, locked her in a dog kennel. But, I didn't realize how deeply it wounded her until Holly.

It hadn't made business (or pimp) sense to me when she initially told me about the dog crate, so I only half-listened. I got that Stackz was dehumanizing her: You're nothing but a dog. As we discussed, degradation is standard pimp operating procedure. But he took it too far, in my professional opinion. He'd invite the girl from next door over. They'd joke, laugh, have sex, and smoke weed – the weed Dyna sold her body to pay for – all within her earshot. The girl-next-door not only reaped the benefits of Dyna's labor, but she also routinely witnessed her humiliation. She walked past Dyna caged like a dog in the living room on her way to the bedroom. I could read Dyna's mind once I knew the details: I thought I was his girlfriend. Here I am going out to get his money, risking my freedom and my life, and he's going to do me that way.

Don't get me wrong. At that point in my life, I didn't have empathy for her. My only concern was how I could use his ineptness to my advantage. I jumped on it in the beginning to keep her from going back. After all, she might have been making a mad move.

"You shouldn't be treated like that. He didn't even go downtown with you. You going downtown taking care of his business, and he's home in bed with some bitch. That's the thanks he gives you?"

Now that I had more insight into how profoundly it devastated her, I leveraged it to forge a deeper allegiance to me. I also instinctively knew I could get away with more with her now. She had staying power if she was willing to put up with that as long as she had.

I hadn't realized the sheer power of mortification yet. Remember, when I'd made the teen get out of my car naked, she chose before I made it home. Hadn't seemed to work that well. It began to sink in just how effective it was as I listened to Dyna and other girls in LA who told me things like their pimps led them around on dog collars – and they stuck around for months or years.

Some traffickers threw a little trepidation in the mix for good measure. Like the pimp of a 16-year-old who chose me after he terrified her. She jumped out of a cab on Sunset Boulevard and ran over to my car.

"I want to talk to you."

"What's wrong?" She'd caught me by surprise, but I could hear the panic in her voice.

She hopped in my car. "He's crazy. He tried to kill me. I didn't make all the money I was supposed to, and he hung me off the balcony by my ankles. He told me he was going to drop me." He'd dangled her from the third floor to both humiliate and put fear in her. His problem was he put a little too much fright in her.

I figured I already did a suitable job in the fear department, but I needed to step up demoralizing them. I thought about what disgusted me the most. I drew on my childhood again. The dogs would get in our garbage, strewing it across our yard. My mom made me clean it up. The maggots swarming in it repulsed me, so I started regularly referring to them as "maggots."

"You're nothing but a maggot to me. You're less than a fly. You disgust me."

Around the time I downgraded them to maggots, they elevated my pedestal. They were sitting around talking one night about how they'd hear pimps say, "That's D's girl. You know, D from Boston."

"We're getting known, Daddy," one of them stated proudly.

"Yeah, when I was at work, I heard someone yell, 'Yo, D,'" another one chimed in. "I didn't want to look, but I wondered if he was calling my daddy."

A lightbulb went off in Sparkle's mind. The pimps called me "D." They called me "Daddy," but I lacked a distinctive pimp name. She couldn't tolerate that for her man.

"Daddy D. We're going to call you Daddy D."

"Yeah, that's a good name," the other girls jumped on it.

"All the other pimps have names," someone added, as if that mattered to me. In all my years in the game, I'd never cared about a pimp name. "D" generated more than enough income, and I didn't care about impressing other traffickers. I let the girls amuse themselves with it while I kept my attention on impressing all the celebrities I rubbed elbows with now.

I had grown as enamored with the Hollywood lifestyle as Rona had grown captivated with me. I did whatever it took to keep her happy, and I spent as much money as necessary to fit in with her glamourous show-biz friends, right down to buying a luxurious Benz S550. I paid it off with cash in a month, or I should say the girls did.

I liked the status her friends elevated me to. I no longer felt like a grimy pimp from the hood. My overinflated self-importance equated me with the superstars I schmoozed with. The only difference was I didn't have to work as hard for my money. I watched how many takes they had to do to get a song just right for a new release and how many hours they had to rehearse for a concert or TV appearance. They should envy me, I secretly thought.

The girls eventually caught on to my relationship with Rona. Maybe it was the night I rode around the track with an international rapper. Perhaps it was because she'd drop me off at the hotel or leave me gifts. Jealousy reared its head, but I tamped that down quickly.

"You know that concert we went to? She gave me the tickets. You benefit from her, too. A lot. That weed you think is so good? She got that. If you don't like it, you can leave. What I'm doing has no effect on what you're doing."

They liked the perks, so they kept their complaints to themselves. I think they eventually realized what I was doing did have an effect on them, though – a positive one. They could do whatever they wanted when I wasn't around. No one stood over them now, watching their every move. I didn't care what they did as long as they kept the money coming in.

With that in mind, I turned every opportunity into calculated mastery of their emotions. I bought them matching outfits and rented limos when we'd go to concerts. I bought them T-Shirts and posters of their boy-band favorites. I rode the rides with them at Disneyland and Knott's Berry Farm. I'd win them a teddy bear or two on the midways. I wined and dined them at the finest restaurants and treated them with the best weed. I stopped short of including them in my Hollywood life, but I spoiled them with a lavish lifestyle of their own. They raked in $1,500-$2,000 a night, so I considered it a wise business investment.

Why wouldn't I? Happy employees look for ways to build the business. Take concerts, for instance. If a young girl mentioned she liked their outfits, one of them would respond, "You can have one, too." They stayed in recruitment mode, much to my liking.

I did resist the temptation of putting them to work when we were out together. Not that I didn't have lots of opportunities. Men solicited them wherever we went. I played up making them feel special on those occasions, pretending I wanted them all to myself. I showered them with all my charm and attention. All part of my master plan.

"You're not at work. We're here to have fun. Let's enjoy ourselves. This is why we work so hard, so we can play even harder."

Their favorite concerts were Boyz to Men and Jodeci. I sang to them when we listened to their music in the car. I serenaded them individually when we were alone. I'd take her hand and look directly into her eyes. Do you see the mind games? Impressionable teen girls can't resist a good love song, and I was the object of their love. I knew they were all thinking, "That's me and Daddy."

And it was. It was a mutual love affair. They were head over heels for me, and I was head over heels for the money they brought me night after night.

## Analysis With Dr. Deena Graves:
### Trauma Bonds

Contrast my game plan with Stackz' or the trafficker who dangled the 16-year-old over the third-floor balcony. They scared girls out of their organizations. I "loved" girls into staying in mine. I kept them in a constant state of lovesickness, so to speak. I'd shred their self-worth and then build them back up with intentional "acts of love," such as imitating their favorite teen idol. I methodically erased their identity until sex for pay became not only what they did but who they were.

I also strategically used tattoos and branding as an "act of love," reinforcing that they belonged to me with a heart and "Daddy D" banner on their left breast. I made them earn it; not every girl got one. They had to earn the right to wear my name. It played emotional and psychological games with their minds. It gave them a sense of belonging, but it also marked them as my property. It was a constant reminder of who they belonged to – even if they eventually left.

Each deliberate act tightened the trauma bonds clamped around their minds.

While my actions were calculated, I didn't realize, like most traffickers I'd venture to guess, the science behind my manipulation. It came naturally. It's not like it was that hard to do, either. The majority of child sex trafficking victims have a history of trauma, low self-worth, and loss of identity, as many as 90 percent, to be exact.[78] That debilitating history increases their vulnerability to trauma bonds.[79]

The trafficker "nurtures" children desperate for someone to love and care for them. They withhold dehumanizing and violent treatment until they have them right where they want them mentally and emotionally. After they inflict the psychological and physical torture, or both, they bounce back over to love and nurturing. It's the same cat-and-mouse game deployed by domestic violence abusers.

That solidifies an almost impenetrable attachment or trauma bond. The bond blossoms and deepens as the trafficker plays emotional Russian roulette with her heart and mind.[80] Biological and emotional bonds intensify and become harder to break with time, shared experiences, and extreme situations and feelings.[81] I took full advantage of all three of those.

Stackz didn't. You'll recall I said I thought he took it too far with Dyna. Dyna grew weary from the chain that weighed her down psychologically and emotionally and left him. I wrapped my chain around her brain lightly, but more tightly, on the other hand. It felt so lightweight that she never realized I used what he'd done to her as another link in my chain.

We can take a lesson from that in our work with trafficked youth. I'm sure Dyna would not have shared her dog kennel experience with a guerilla pimp, such as the one who suspended the young girl over the balcony. A guerilla pimp would pounce on her story, inflicting more extreme cruelty.

She trusted me with it from the beginning. Throughout the book, you might have noticed that several girls chose me because they'd heard or sensed that I didn't operate like their pimps. There was a reason I operated as a finesse pimp. Consider synonyms for the word "finesse": Manipulate, maneuver, jockey, bluff, pull strings, finagle. I knew how to finagle my way straight into their hearts and minds, and I gained a reputation for it.

Kids hear or sense things about those of us trying to help them, too. It's worth repeating that they'll open up to us more willingly when they believe we care about them as a person rather than another case. Our advice? Take the time to get to know them before diving into your job requirements. It doesn't matter what that job is or how long you will interact with them.

If your role only provides the opportunity to interact with them once, for instance, still take the time to make them feel like a person before getting to the business at hand. Find a way to build a connection based on what you observe. Ask them about their favorite music group, television show, movie, actor, or sports team. Talk to them about what they want to do in life or about your kids. Have you ever stood beside someone who towers over you or who has the power to make decisions about your life? It's somewhat intimidating. We can calm their fears simply by taking an interest in them.

For the longer-term, understand that they can't break old attachments, aka the trauma bond with their traffickers and wifeys, until they form new attachments.[82] This is again where mentors and relationships with other healthy adults and youth become crucial. Animals also are a fantastic sounding board. They don't talk back, and they can't tell your secrets. We're not talking about formal animal therapy, although we highly recommend it. We're talking about something as simple as letting a traumatized kid pick out a rescue dog or cat – a traumatized pet – at the local animal shelter. A rescue animal gives them an outlet to streamline their passion at the injustice done to them – and the animal – into something productive. As the traumatized child and traumatized pet pour into each other, both will begin to heal.

It's hard enough to help someone recover from a harrowing experience or extreme danger, but throw in psychological warfare, and it becomes nearly impossible. Unless we do it strategically. These examples arm you with first steps to sever those chains.

## Two-Minute Introspection

Have you ever moved to a new area and left everything familiar behind? How lonely did you feel? Once you started making new connections, how did it change your feelings about your new city? What insights does that give you about the need to help youth removed from their home or their trafficker's home form positive new attachments?

# 28 Risky Business

Even the glitz and glamour of Hollywood wear thin after a while, especially when you start missing home.

Kayla grew homesick first. Boredom and complacency faded her memory of me shoving her out a moving car. Her attention-seeking antics threw my entire organization into chaos. She ran off new girls and routinely picked fights with her longtime wifeys. She went so far as to mouth off to me a couple of times.

"It's time for you to go." I didn't mean out of my business. She made too much money for that. Just out of my face. I sent her back to Boston to take care of business there.

I soon got wind that she was talking up the benefits of working alone in Boston to Sparkle, and Sparkle hadn't bothered to tell me.

"Maybe you need to go back on the Eastside, too, and take care of the apartment and Kayla."

She didn't argue. She was longing for home, too.

I fought my anger at how blatantly the two of them defied me. They'd been around too long, gotten too comfortable. I had new girls who were as into me as Sparkle and Kayla once were. They thought they could do what they wanted because they helped me build the business, and I was preoccupied with Rona. I'd show them I didn't need them. All I needed was their bodies, and I didn't care what city those bodies operated in.

To my surprise, they didn't care that I didn't need them. They weren't just over their infatuation with Hollywood; they were over their all-out infatuation with me. I didn't fire them or take away any of the profuse perks they'd grown accustomed to in LA, so they were happy to go it alone at home. In Boston, they didn't enjoy freedom a few hours a day while I hung out with Rona. They reveled in around-the-clock independence while still benefiting from the protection of a pimp. Without that, someone would smack them around and take their money. That's a known fact of life for a renegade or outlaw.

I knew they abused their newfound autonomy, stashing money and lying to me about how much they worked and what they did with their free time. I didn't care. They still met their quotas most nights, so I acted like I believed them when they said the track was slow. They took care of the Boston bills and still sent me enough to keep my income from dropping below $1,500 a night. It was a business decision: The bottom line stayed healthy, and I had fewer headaches. That's not to say they didn't give me some headaches.

Think of it like a teenager whose parents go out of town for a few days. The cat's away; the mice are going to play. They're going to push the limits. They naturally bend the rules almost to the breaking point when they're not supervised as usual.

The same is true when a pimp leaves his stable on automatic. Let me give you an example with one of my girls. Kayla, of course.

I got a call in LA from a young, nondescript Boston pimp.

"Yo, man, this is Silk calling to let you know your broad Kayla got out of pocket with me, so I broke her."

"What do you mean she got out of pocket?" Would that bitch never learn? I wasn't really surprised, though.

"Yeah, I don't know where you are, but she's over here in my face. She was talking about she didn't want to make a move, so out of respect, I'm letting you know I broke her."

"I appreciate the notice, Pimping."

I'd have to deal with her when I got home now. She could get away with smoking weed on the job or working fewer hours, but she knew the rules about talking to another pimp. A turnout mistake. Not acceptable for a pro ho like her. He could say whatever he wanted to her. Her job was to keep her mouth shut and get out of his earshot. She probably ignored his initial spitting, so he smarted off to her, and she shot back, thinking he was too young and green to deserve her respect. He didn't have to put up with that.

"Hey, Bitch. Who you think you're talking to? Who's your man?"

He gave her a break. He could have gone upside her head with his fists or made her move since she disrespected him. He still sent her and all the other girls on the track a message. He might be new, but he didn't deal in disrespect. He let them know it wasn't a game to him. He was serious about his business.

So was I. She not only disrespected me, but she also pitted me against another pimp. I gave her a tongue-lashing on the phone.

"It's going to be problems when I see you."

And there were. I slapped her around good when I got back to Boston.

Having a hard-headed ho is another occupational hazard. It's part of the game. You have to do some work for the money you're getting. Pimps put up with it when she brings in plenty of cash.

Luckily, I had girls like Dyna and Amazon who didn't cause me any trouble. They wanted to stay with me in LA. Dyna saw me as her insurance against more dog kennels, and Amazon grew up on the West Coast, so she didn't miss Boston like the other girls. Neither did I for about two years. Even the exciting life Rona provided me, though, couldn't compete with my business interests, and I hit a bumpy patch that ended my all-consuming romance with the Hollywood lifestyle.

The stroll suddenly got hot with girls going to jail frequently. More importantly, things got hot for me, too. Not with cops. With other criminals.

It started with a drug dealer I'd bought weed from multiple times. I arranged to meet up with him on the stroll as usual. I opened the door and let him in my car when he walked up. He carried the weed in his pocket and slipped his hand in to get it. Only this time, he pulled out a gun instead.

"Give me your money."

He said it in the same tone he used to talk about our drug deals, so I thought he was joking. I grabbed the gun out of his hand and told him to stop playing around. He lunged for it, and we tussled over it until his partner in crime walked up to my window with his weapon pointed at me.

"Let it go."

They weren't satisfied with the thousand bucks I had on me. The guy in the car with me reached over and tried to jerk the solid gold chain off my neck.

"You don't have to snatch it," I told him irritably. I was proud of that chain. I'd shelled out $2,000 for it. Its diamond-encrusted globe and the word "Daddy" hanging from it sent a message. Not just to the world. To my self-worth. It gave me a sense of identity that had been so elusive. I didn't understand at the time that *that identity* robbed not only my victims but me of our true worth and destiny.

I did come to understand very quickly they weren't playing around, though. I made enough money in one night to buy another ostentatious "identity," so I took off the chain and handed it to him. I couldn't believe they didn't at least give me the weed.

A few weeks later, one of the girls called and told me she had another girl, Rhedd, interested in joining the family. I picked them up on Sunset Boulevard and started interviewing Rhedd as we cruised the stroll. I only got a couple of questions out before a car pulled up beside me a few minutes later.

"That's my man! That's my man!" Rhedd yelled apprehensively.

I pulled over out of respect for the game. I got out of the car and walked over to talk to him.

"Yo, man. Rhedd hasn't given me any money, so you can get her." I motioned toward my car. It was the pimp thing to do. The girls weren't the only ones who could commit a violation. Pimps operate by unwritten rules.

He apparently didn't understand respect for the game or pimp violations. He not only yanked her out of the car, but he also grabbed my keys out of the ignition. He threw Rhedd in his car, smacking her as he peeled out.

My friend, Max Slim, pulled up and offered to take me to track him down. I ordered my girl back to work, and we took off in search of my keys. When we found him, he wouldn't talk to me.

"Look, man, you got your girl. I just want my keys."

"Get the fuck away from my car."

He ignored me while he pouted to Max Slim that I had been out-of-pocket because I had his girl in my car but couldn't get her money. I wasn't playing by the rules, he insisted. He didn't mention that he'd chased me down just a couple of minutes after she got in my car. Not that it mattered. If you get caught while interviewing, the interview is over. He finally begrudgingly told Max Slim he had thrown my keys in the bushes as he turned the corner.

I not only found my keys, but I also found a hot pistol on the streets. It was one thing for a drug dealer to pull a gun on me. It was a whole different game when a pimp jumped me because his girl got in my car.

"This is getting risky," I thought. "It's time to arm myself." I didn't bother getting a license to carry. If I had to use my new weapon, I'd throw it away.

I was glad I bought it when Smiley showed up at my motel with a warning a few weeks after that incident. A group of gang members hunted him down at his apartment, beat him up, and locked him in the trunk of his car before going upstairs to rape one of his girls and steal his money and jewelry.

"Tell your boy Daddy D he's next," they shouted as they made their getaway. Smiley banged on the trunk until passersby called police. He came straight from the trunk of his car to my hotel to tell me what they said. I especially appreciated that since B Money, the pimp I shoved Kayla out of the vehicle for getting out of pocket with, was his brother.

I blamed the girls for the first incident: "Here I was trying to get you some weed, and I got robbed." However, I decided I needed to protect my product from the competition after the last incident. I reiterated the rules and warned them not to get in a car with more than one person. I stayed watchful, as well, paying close attention to the vehicles and groups around me. It made me wary of where I went and who I hung out with. I grew tired of looking over my shoulder, so I had a talk with Rona.

"It's time for me to put my show on the road."

She was sad, but we both knew we'd stay in contact. Distance wouldn't stop what we'd developed. I'd traveled with her for a few of her son's out-of-town concerts and to her small Texas hometown to meet her family. She'd grown attached to my mom and Gina, as well, and she still adored me. I knew I wasn't saying a final goodbye to her world, so I had no qualms about turning my full attention to business for the time being.

I packed up the Benz with the girls, Holly, my snake and iguana, my black-market pistol, and a shoebox under my seat stuffed with almost $20,000.

As I watched LA fade from my rearview mirror, I realized Hollywood had produced a new leading man performing a new role. I'd arrived in LA two years prior as Derek, a guy from the hood playing around with selling girls for my profit and pleasure. I pulled out Daddy D, a hardcore, do-whatever-it-takes, career pimp.

The game was no longer a game to me. It was a lifestyle, an unequivocal way of life.

## Analysis With Dr. Deena Graves:
CSEC And Harm Reduction

Sparkle and Kayla had enjoyed their independence, but they were happy when the family reunited.

"Daddy's home!"

"Look, Daddy, how good we did while you were gone!"

"Yeah, Baby. Y'all did good."

They'd felt important running the Boston operation while I oversaw the West Coast division. It gave them more clout with the other girls on the track.

"Hey, where's your man? We've been seeing you but not him."

"Yeah, he's in California **with the rest of our family**, and we're here taking care of his business."

I stroked their ego while we were on opposite sides of the country, but I kept them in line, too, like with Kayla and Silk. That was as simple as my choice of words and my voice inflection. The word "bitch," for example, can be a term of endearment: "Yeah, this is my bitch right here." Or, a threat: "You maggot bitch. You'll answer for this."

It's important to understand that I had conditioned them to submit **to both**. I yanked those chains around their brains enough, and **they started thinking, talking, and acting like me**. That's what makes leaving your stable on automatic work – and it's what causes harm reduction to fail.

That chain extends from a trafficker's grip to their brains, whether they're sitting in the room with the pimp or in the room with you. Remember the statement I made in the last chapter? I methodically erased their identity until sex for pay became not only what they did but **who they were**. Think back to the buyers, too. Statements such as: *"She assumed the submissive* *position on her knees."* And, *"Unquestionable obedience. I mean that's powerful. Power is like a drug. The minute you walk in the door you are the lord and master until the minute you walk out the door."*

Do you see the pattern? Other people have dominated their bodies, minds, and souls. Traffickers and buyers alike bend the child's will to their will. How do they then fight for their own healing when they've been psychologically, emotionally, and physically beaten into submission? Let me answer that for you. They can't. They don't know how. It is almost impossible for them to get out on their own. We must help them.

If I were still a trafficker, I'd be rubbing my hands together and laughing a deep, menacing, arrogant laugh at harm-reduction principles applied to child sex trafficking. Let me give you a few reasons why.

1. Youth under the control of a trafficker – whether a finesse pimp or a guerilla pimp – ***do not*** get to make decisions about their safety. They don't have the luxury of telling their traffickers how much they will work or whether they will use condoms … unless they want to get severely beaten, thrown out of a moving car on the highway, or suspended over a third-floor balcony. It's not up for discussion. They don't get to sleep in, take sick days, vacation days, or any other kind of days unless the pimp decides to take them to a concert or Disneyland to screw that vice a little tighter. I can confidently assure you that you would not have wanted any child to come back to me.

2. Traffickers like I was protect their investment. I took my girls to the doctor every few months for an exam, birth control pills, and a supply of condoms. I didn't want to chance getting a disease myself, a buyer deciding not to hand over the money because of a foul smell, or passing things on to other girls because they shared a bathroom. I didn't want to shell out my hard-earned money for medical care for a girl with an infectious disease. That's not good business sense. It's called quality control. I rarely allowed my girls to have any kind of sexual contact without a condom. I made a few exceptions when the buyer paid extra money for a girl I knew wouldn't stick around long or who I knew I wouldn't have sex with. Some traffickers allow it anytime the buyer asks for it for an additional fee. That sentence has two crucial words for our understanding: ***Traffickers ALLOW***. Let me stress this point. Their victims don't have a say in the matter. Therefore, the harm-reduction practice of providing condoms to keep victims "safer" is a waste of time.

3. Harm reduction creates a vicious cycle that produces more victims. Just like I had more money to buy heroin when the government supplied me needles, traffickers have more money for themselves when we supply their victims with condoms, other supplies, and services. That creates a thirst for more victims.

4. Harm reduction sends children, especially those who already believe no one cares about them, a subliminal message that we don't care about their safety, and the trafficker plays that to his advantage.

"Really. They're all up in your face telling you they want you to be safer, and they know you're leaving out their door and going back to a pimp? And they're giving you condoms like that's some big deal? I give you all the condoms you need. They don't care about your safety. They just want to get you out of their hair. You're nothing but a case number to them. Or, worse, you're just a paycheck. Your foster mom wouldn't even give you time if she didn't get paid for it."

That kid is thinking things like, "He's right. They know I'm not safe if they're giving me things to keep me safer." Or, "They can't really care about me if they're telling me that it's not good for me, but I can go back. I bet they wouldn't let their kid go to a pimp. I am just a paycheck. He really is the only one who cares about me."

Chapter 16 touched on research that raises red flags about the success of harm-reduction principles applied to youth, so let's consider other research now. For example, researchers have posited that CSEC youth "may not have the maturity or power to break their victimization."[83] Further, "the trauma that a child experiences from being forced into prostitution and sex trafficking is *significantly likely* (emphasis ours) to cause death."[84]

The question becomes, then, can harm reduction keep them safer? As a former professional trafficker, my emphatic and unwavering opinion is no. It puts them at greater risk, not less risk.

Dr. Graves here. I want to add my emphatic, unwavering no to Derek's. I want to remind you about the study that found almost half of CSEC victims try to escape through suicide, and they "have a mortality rate 40 times higher than the national average."[85] With that fresh in our minds, I want to shift our focus to us for a moment. I propose that these kids are not the only ones who suffer when we let them walk out of the safety we can provide back into the waiting arms of their traffickers and dire physical, psychological, and emotional danger. It's not a question of whether they will face danger. It's a done deal the moment they walk out our door.

Let's look at it from a few different angles. First are the challenges researchers and professionals have raised regarding the ethics of harm reduction and if it can lead to life-threatening situations. One researcher argued that professionals are bound ethically to equip clients with coping mechanisms that work, calling it a violation of their legal obligation and a potential for malpractice when they fail to do so. Consider the Chapter 16 case of the person in prostitution who had injected heroin since she was 16. Despite almost a year of harm-reduction programming, she almost died in ICU. The researcher stated: "It is difficult to see how the health and interests of youthful users with rehabilitation potential are served by a harm-reduction system that supports them in their *self-destructive habits* (emphasis mine) for extended periods."[86] Perhaps if we look at it through a different lens, it would give us more clarity. For example, would we leave a razor in their hands if they were cutting themselves?

If I were an attorney, I'd be all over any situation that exposes them to danger. Harm-reduction policies and programs for youth have documented challenges. Coupled with recent and past legal challenges to care for system-involved children, your agency, your county, and you *personally* could be vulnerable to lawsuits. What happens if CSEC youth you equip with harm-reduction tools return to their traffickers and hurt or kill themselves or their pimp or a buyer seriously injure or murder them?

I would also look as an attorney at audits by the U.S. Department of Health and Human Services' Office of Inspector General, state attorneys general reports, and judicial rulings that lament care of children in the foster system. I'd take an even closer look if someone had flagged an agency in those reports. There is precedent from recent lawsuits alleging agencies could have prevented a child's death by not returning them to a *known* dangerous situation. Traffickers *are known* to be dangerous. I have no doubt harm-reduction lawsuits would prevail.

The bottom line is each person, agency, and county should consider how much risk they are willing to carry. It goes beyond ethical and legal challenges, though. I would encourage you to think about what it would do to you personally, both psychologically and emotionally, if you allowed a child to return to her trafficker, only for her to be murdered.

For a case study that brings the risks of CSEC harm reduction to life and provides a solution for breaking the cycle of returning to their pimp, see *Appendix D*.

## Two-Minute Introspection

What emotions, what regrets, would you experience if a child you allowed to go back to a trafficker committed suicide or was murdered?

# 29

# The Whole World's a Stage

I heard Pep bragging on the New York track about the money his girls made in Montreal.

"Yeah, they're letting them work up there. If your girl knows what she's doing, she can really make some money in Canada."

Sparkle always knew what she was doing, so I packed her up and headed across the border. Excitement welled up in both of us. More uncharted waters for me. A chance to be alone with her daddy for Sparkle.

Sure enough, she made good money. She also scored something I'd never had in my stable before: Someone who spoke a language none of us understood. Sparkle brought Zoe home a couple of nights into our visit. She spoke a little broken English she'd learned from American men on the track, but her native language was French.

I bought an English-French translation book so that she could choose me. We managed that, but I couldn't get her to tell me who her pimp was to serve him. We asked her several times to tell us her man's name; she kept insisting I was her man. I shrugged and went on. I'd tried. No man, no problem.

Most of the pimps I met on the track were American, from upstate New York, Cleveland, and border states. I ran into a couple of California pimps, too. I even met a White pimp there. Most of the girls, on the other hand, were Canadian, drawing in American and other tourists. Sparkle caught the eye of the Canadian men with her sharp contrast to the French-Canadian look.

She'd tell me, "I'd be getting in the car with one date and a guy in another car would say, 'I'm waiting here until you get back.'"

I stacked plenty of money between the two of them before the track got hot.

Zoe wanted to go with us when I decided to head back to the States. I knew it wasn't a good idea to drive an 18-year-old who I couldn't communicate with without the help of a book through Customs with me. I put her on a bus with Sparkle and told them I'd meet them at the first stop in Maine. Good choice because, sure enough, Customs flagged my car. They questioned me for a couple of hours after they found my trunk full of women's clothing.

After I picked up the girls, we stopped in a few cities to work, which proved a little more challenging than pimping Zoe in Montreal. She knew what to do there. She was like a turnout in the U.S., where the rules varied from what she had operated under. She didn't know, for instance, to hop off the sidewalk when a pimp walked up or that she needed to get out of earshot if a pimp tried to knock her. She could stand right next to the pimp in Montreal and simply ignore him.

The other girls weren't too happy when we got back to Boston. Zoe's French-Canadian accent gave her an exotic aura in Boston. Pimps and tricks stayed after her, and she made more money than them. Plus, Sparkle took pride in bringing her home with us, like our special project, so she showed her favoritism. And, I didn't want Zoe to think Sparkle was her pimp, so I spent extra time with her and the French-English translation book. I kept it tucked under the armrest of my car for easy reference. I didn't tell the girls that the communication barrier accounted for most of the extended time I spent with her. It didn't matter to them. The green-eyed monster reared its head, and they gave her the cold shoulder. They especially didn't like that I let her stay at my apartment. I didn't have sex with her, but I knew she needed extra attention because she was so far out of her element.

But they only had to sulk for a couple of weeks about the amount of attention I gave her. After that, we all feared our good ride was finally over. Zoe got busted, and one of the girls saw cops driving her around the track, presumably to point out her American trafficker. I sent Sparkle to bail her out. That's when the inconvenience of the communication obstacles became a pounding headache. I'd found the challenge enticing before because it broke up the routine we had settled into and added back in a little of the flashiness I'd relished in in California.

The fascination quickly paled at the thought of what could happen with this person I'd never had a real conversation with. Police told Sparkle they didn't have anyone by the alias we'd given her. I hadn't been able to give her my usual spiel about what to do when arrested, so I felt sure she had given them her real name. What other truths might she tell them? I knew they would understand her with the help of an interpreter.

I stayed on pins and needles a few days before learning they deported her. Maybe the rules were the same about not turning on your pimp. Or, perhaps, I was another notch in her belt. "You've never been out of Montreal? I had a Black pimp who took me to America. I paid someone who can't even speak my language."

She certainly was a notch in my belt. My ego was as big as the Empire State Building now. I didn't know how to say, "Where's my money" in French, but I'd gone into another country where a girl who couldn't understand me chose me and gave me all the money she made there. Not only that, but she left her country to work for me in the States.

Talk about notoriety with the other pimps. I worked it.

"Yo, Daddy D. You got some new work?"

"Oh, you talking about that White broad with my bottom? Yeah. Why don't you get at her?"

I encouraged their itch to go after the mysterious, exotic teen fascinating the tricks. I'd laugh when they'd get behind her, throwing all their best rhymes her way, not knowing their honey-dipped words sounded like mumbo-jumbo to her. I didn't fill them in until after police arrested her.

"Man, you had me sweating that broad all that time, and she didn't even speak English?"

It all fueled my arrogance. I knew what they were thinking. "That pimping is going to California messing with a popstar's mom, and now he's bringing back bitches from other countries who don't understand him?"

It didn't merely fuel my pompousness, however. It threw gasoline on my love for the game. I knew, and others recognized, that I was doing stuff most pimps never dreamed of. I was in a class of my own. I didn't bother going to pimp balls or other traditional events that they scampered to. I didn't have to meet flashy people. I didn't kick it with them as often at the bars and strip clubs. No one could tell me anything anyway, so why bother. I kept my California swag up in conservative Boston, wearing my Hollywood regalia and my hair fried, dyed, and laying on the side. I spread my wings like a peacock, enjoying how much I stuck out.

I went from thinking of myself as a pimp to thinking of myself as *the* pimp.

# Analysis With Dr. Deena Graves:
## First Encounters With Victims

I got caught up in the status of "international" pimp and broke my own rules. I had first ventured into trafficking with Lacy to avoid jail and almost let my fascination with Zoe send me there. I hadn't had time to forge a bond with her to keep her loyal, and I had no idea what happened in Canada when a girl got arrested. I left myself wide open to jail if she got arrested on either side of the border.

That wasn't usual for me or the majority of pimps. We need to jump on those opportunities when traffickers get sloppy.

As a rule, I meticulously taught the girls what to say and what to do if they got picked up. I had them befriend other girls on the track wherever we went to learn how to avoid cops and what to say and what to do if they got caught. Like pimp terminology, it depends on where you are.

Like in Hollywood. They learned they could usually get by a couple of times saying they were a tourist before the officer would say something like, "No, I've seen you standing on this same corner the past four nights. What more is there to see here?"

If we got stopped while traveling, I'd tell the officer we were passing through. I never told them our hotel name. "We just got here. We haven't found one yet."

I gave the girls false IDs with names I picked, or I'd let them choose. They always said they were at least 17, sometimes 18 or 19. I had juveniles who were held in adult jail.

I let them know I would never bail them out in person. "Sure, I could say I'm your uncle, but I'm not going to." I wasn't taking any chances on me. Didn't matter to me if they landed in jail except for the bail money it cost me. I wasn't making an appearance. Most of the time, they got out quickly and went right back to work. If I got arrested, I'd be there months or years. It was the lot they chose, in my way of thinking. They knew what the game was about. I'd tell them it was one of those occupational hazards. "Cooks burn their hands. Barbers cut their fingers. Hos go to jail."

This is another fact I want to be absolutely clear about – traffickers make youth lie to anyone who tries to help them. They teach them to hate law enforcement, social workers, foster parents, whatever you do and whoever you are. And, they're good at it.

Professionals and first responders ask us all the time what to do about that. My answer is the same as with many aspects of helping high-risk and trafficked youth: Think like a trafficker. Think back to the teen I met in the mall who liked music. I didn't walk up to her and jump into what I wanted her to do for me. I talked to her about *her*. I carefully observed and then used what I saw to make her feel at ease with me. I connected with her over music, which took her off her guard. I didn't mention my line of work during that first meeting. I kept the conversation focused on her. She believed I was into what she was into. I set up a second meeting where I built more "relationship" before turning the conversation to the game. Two short conversations, and she was in. Not only that, but I also had enough details filed away to continue building trust and relationship until I learned more about her.

In my experience, many of the youth in the system feel no one has ever shown a genuine interest in them. Whether true or not, trauma influences their thinking – and, again, so do the traffickers. That means we have to make an extra effort. *Everyone* who works with them should take the time to talk to them as a person before talking to them as a case. In fact, we recommend keeping the case file shut and the screening tools in the desk drawer until you establish a foundation that lets them know you care about them more than you care about filling out a report. It can seem like an impossible task with casefiles stacked up so high they're about to topple over like a Jenga tower. It's surprising, though, how much a little extra time invested in the beginning can save in the long run.

## Two-Minute Introspection

List three things children or teens might be afraid of when they talk to you the first time. How can you frame the conversation based on those insights?

# 30 Take The Show On The Road

Emotions started overwhelming Rona and Amazon about the same time.

I'd flown to the Midwest to join Rona on one of their tour stops. We talked on the phone frequently, but I hadn't otherwise seen her in the six months since we'd left California. She asked me to join them in New York City, so I took the girls with me. No need to pass up the opportunity for the additional money the New York game always yielded.

I hung out backstage, as usual, and went to eat with them afterward. I stopped short of staying with Rona in her hotel, though.

"I have to work." I shut her pleas down.

I broke the girls at the end of the night and took them to breakfast. Later that morning, we went shopping before I met Rona for lunch. She started in on me not long after we sat down.

"You didn't have to be there when you were in California, and some of them were in Boston. Why did you have to be there when you are in the same city?"

She was partially correct. I didn't have to be. I wanted to be. She had become clingy, and I needed to maintain my pimp persona. I'd seen one superstar's wife make him cry in the studio once, and I wasn't about to let some woman manipulate me. That was my game. I could still hear Uncle Danny's words about not getting emotionally attached. He might have been talking about the girls in my stable, but I applied it to all relationships. You can call the shots, or the shots can call you, I had decided. I wasn't putting my heart out there to get trampled or jerked around.

Besides, I was *the* pimp. I didn't need Rona. As long as I kept doing what I was doing, doors would fly open for me as they had with her and in Canada. I would not risk that or my bottom line by giving her more attention than I did my business. I didn't appreciate that she thought she could pull my strings by dropping names. Her son got discovered overnight by a music producer, and they flew to Hollywood. She might have discovered me in that beauty salon, but I'd worked my way across the country to get there. I wasn't throwing it all away to give her the level of attention she craved.

"I've told you this before. You're not going to stop managing your son and focusing on his career for me. And I'm not going to stop managing my girls and focusing on my career for you. You're only going where the record company sends you, anyway. I'm going wherever I want."

She didn't like it, but she knew I meant business.

I meant business with the girls, too. That required me staying attuned to their emotions rather than squashing them like I did Rona's. I noticed a few times when Amazon came back from calling her parents that she had tears in her eyes.

"What's going on with you?" I already knew. Her mom had been sick. We'd sent them money a couple of times to help them out with the medical bills.

"My mom's really sick, and my dad misses me," she hesitated. "I think I just need to go home."

"When do you want to go?"

"I don't want to leave you in a bad position."

"Oh, no. I'm straight. I have enough other girls, and you know Rona gives me money."

She was ready. I told her to pack up all her stuff, bought her an airplane ticket, and gave her a couple hundred dollars for the trip.

I didn't have time to replace her before Rona called and wanted me to fly to Europe with the tour. I immediately turned to the money.

"I can't go to Europe. Amazon just left, and I have a business to run."

She pivoted to her fallback: "You ran it from the other side of the country. Why can't you run it from outside the country?"

"I guess I could if I were getting paid for it."

"Let me check. I think I can get you paid for it."

The record company hired me as her son's personal assistant for the week-long trip. They paid me almost $1,000, plus a $200 daily per diem. Rona told me to charge anything I ordered in the hotels to my room, too.

I left the girls on automatic and jetted to Germany, London, and Amsterdam. Curious, I decided to check out the pimping scenes. In Germany, I met a guy from New York who took me to the bar where American girls worked. I noticed a young girl watching me and sent her a drink. I walked over when she started drinking it. She told me her pimp had left her there on automatic.

"Yeah, I'm over here handling some music business, but I've got girls back in Boston on automatic. I'm trying to spread my wings and do other things with the music business, but that's what I do."

I could tell she liked the swagger. I showed her pictures of my girls for good measure. The combination of music and pimping business intrigued her. She handed me her money and told me she'd be back. She showed up a few hours later and gave me more money for a total of about $700. I didn't see her again after that. She knew I was leaving, and I couldn't take her with me with Rona.

I didn't try my luck in Amsterdam or London. Prostitution was too prevalent in Amsterdam. I knew they were giving their money to whoever's window they were dancing in. In London, I felt out of my league. They were too sophisticated for my way of trafficking. I didn't have time to learn the appropriate vernacular to figure out how they played the game.

It didn't matter to me. I got on the plane home thinking, "I'm not taking a girl home, but I still have ho money in my pocket. The record company paid me, they covered all my costs, and I have ho money on top of it."

I bragged a little to Rona. There weren't any other pimps around, so she'd have to do. "You bring me here for one thing, and a bitch went to work and gave me her money. Everywhere I go, I put a charge on a ho."

I brushed her off when she asked me where she was if I was such big pimping.

"She didn't follow her money. That's not important. I got her money."

I reflected on what I'd seen in Europe, Canada, and across the United States as our plane taxied down the runway. Prostitution isn't just the oldest profession, I realized. It's the most widespread. I could get money anywhere from girls selling sex.

Armed with this insight, I could take my boasting to the pimps back home to a whole other level. I already bragged that I could go anywhere in the country. Now, I could tell them anywhere I went in the world, a bitch would give me her money.

"I've got squares paying me to go to Europe, and while I'm over there, I'm checking trap."

My heart grew colder, and my self-admiration grew hotter on the trip back across the ocean. I no longer simply believed I could make a living off selling girls' bodies. Now I was convinced I was invincible. I wasn't *the* pimp. I was a *super* pimp.

Daddy D, I had learned, translated in any language.

## Analysis With Dr. Deena Graves:
### Victims Exiting Prostitution

I hope this chapter exposes and destroys another falsehood. Many believe traffickers never let their victims leave. Some don't. That's more the guerilla pimps, gang members, drug traffickers. You might be shocked that I sent Amazon's parents money and paid for her plane ticket home. It might surprise you that I let her take all the clothes, jewelry, the cellphone, and other possessions I had bought her. Let me assure you that it wasn't out of the kindness of my heart. We've established that pimps don't have a heart.

I've pointed out several times now that I operated my stable like a business. Consider this a severance package. Amazon made me tens of thousands of dollars and did not cause any trouble. I left the door open for her to come back if she decided to return to work. Why have her leave with a bad taste in her mouth and risk her applying for a job somewhere else? She's going to come back to the company that provided her with a great severance package.

Think about what this kind of finesse pimping does to those who try to help teens exit the game. How can a minimum wage job flipping burgers and scrubbing toilets compare to the lifestyle Amazon grew accustomed to? I had ongoing contact with Amazon and other girls when they went home, and I always kept them thinking about the benefits, the fun we had, never the life-threatening, repugnant, destructive aspects.

Teens don't think about what multiple sex partners, six or seven nights a week, month after month, year after year, do to their bodies, emotions, and identities. We've talked about many of the consequences, such as suicide. Let's add a few more.

On the medical side, they can suffer communicable diseases, reproductive damage, or dental trauma, to name just a few. Think back to the buyer domination, which can include strangulation, resulting in asphyxia, suffocation, choking, or smothering. The list of medical ramifications is long.

Mental health concerns beyond suicide include depression, anxiety, eating disorders, Post-traumatic Stress Disorder, and Dissociative Disorder. The list of psychological and emotional ramifications is also long.

On the "career" side, as they age and their bodies wear out, buyers lose interest, leaving them with no retirement, no health care, no employability, and no future.

They don't think about these things as teenagers. All they see is what's in the moment, such as escaping foster care, a parent standing over their shoulder, or a guy who's telling them he loves them and taking them to concerts.

It's essential for us to understand, too, that if you grow up in chaos and confusion, all you know is chaos and confusion. It becomes normal, as routine as brushing our teeth in the morning. You don't see anything wrong with it. There's comfort in it because it's familiar. It's easier than the effort and pain it takes to heal. That's part of the reason they run back. Familiar is easier. It's also easier to let the trafficker do all the thinking and just go through the motions. Trauma exhausts you, and finding the energy to meet treatment plan goals and expectations can be overwhelming.

We have to help them see down the road to the wear and tear on their bodies, minds, and spirits, the damage to every aspect of their lives. The game drains you of your sense of value. It sucks it out of you little by little without you realizing the void it leaves behind. It's devastating when you wake up one day and realize it. It took me, Derek, two years of therapy to see I was still worth something, and I was the victimizer.

We must shed light on the long-term consequences while also engaging them in *effective* treatment plans that heal their inner trauma and help them learn to thrive without chaos and confusion.

## Two-Minute Introspection

How can we clearly communicate the long-term consequences in ways that make victims want more and better for themselves?

# 31 The Show Must Go On

My success consumed me; my arrogance ran out of control. I started telling people I was in the entertainment business – personal entertainment. I'd leave the door to my safe open and lie on the bed looking at the stacks of money. Or, I'd spread it on my bed and sleep on it. My pompousness must have worn on Dyna and Kayla's nerves because they both left a few months after I returned from my pop-star pimp European tour.

Dyna went first. I should have noticed the crack in the armor when her unfaltering obedience wobbled on a road trip. She committed a violation that enraged me. I had only rented one room for all of us, so I went to the front desk and rented another room on the other side of the motel. I didn't beat my girls in front of each other as many pimps do. Everything in my life was about keeping me out of jail, and I didn't want witnesses.

I marched Dyna to the other room, stomped her multiple times while I drove my point home, and then held her down with my foot while I threw in a few extra verbal reprimands for good measure. I got the point across. The sneaker prints still embedded in her body the next day made me confident of that. I'm sure that caused her flashbacks of the dog kennel, but she went on with business as usual for three or four months.

Then one day, she told me she didn't think she wanted to sell herself anymore.

"What's wrong?"

She couldn't pinpoint anything, so I convinced her to stay. Her demeanor grew gloomier over the next couple of weeks. She'd always been happy to go to work. She'd come back and want to talk about her dates. Now, she stayed sullen and standoffish even when smoking weed or spending time alone with me. I'd prided myself on, "Always by choice; never by force," and "Hos come going; they come to pay, not to stay," so I pulled her aside one day.

"You're really not happy, huh?"

"No. I keep telling you I don't want to do this anymore."

Kayla didn't lose her passion for the game. She was merely as into herself as I was myself, and she got tired of not getting the attention she thought she deserved. She started pushing the boundaries again – with everyone. She fought with her wifeys and other girls on the track. She pushed my buttons and subtly disrespected other pimps, enough to get under their skin but not give them a reason to break her or put their hands on her. She wanted to do what she wanted to do with the protection of a pimp's covering.

I didn't cover anyone's ego except mine. She kept me in money, but I couldn't stand the sight of her anymore. Our egos clashed one too many times, and I started putting my hands on her for the slightest violation. Her pride puffed up until it was about to explode, and she left in a huff early one morning without saying goodbye to anyone.

I called her when it was time to go to work.

"I don't have to put up with this. I make you money. I could be keeping all this money."

"You can't get out there and work on your own, Bitch. I better not see you on the track. I'll take your money and have every other pimp on the track take your money."

I didn't give severance packages to hostile employees. To make sure she understood I meant business, my business, I turned her phone off.

Their departures didn't faze me. I got a good run out of them. They had served me well. Now it was time to put them out to pasture like a race-horse owner retiring a prized, but worn-out, winner.

Sparkle and I both were skilled recruiters. I knew it would take no time to replace them. And it didn't.

After all, there's an endless supply of vulnerable kids in the United States.

## Analysis With Dr. Deena Graves:
### Recruiting Vulnerable Youth

I regularly cruised places I knew teens hung out, especially high-risk youth: Malls, bus stations, group homes, juvenile probation centers, juvenile courts. My approach depended on the situation and what I saw in a kid's eyes.

Take a bus station. I knew those girls were broke, starving, and scared out of their minds with no place to go and no way to get there. They ran away from their small or midsize towns to big cities like New York, Dallas, or Seattle. Runaways think they're stepping off the bus into an exciting new life but, instead, step into the middle of drug dealers, homeless people with mental-health issues, liquor stores, tattoo parlors, stores with bars on the windows, and harrowing noises in the middle of the night. Vultures perch around places like that waiting for a kid to disembark from public transportation.

I'd walk up to them in my slick clothes and expensive jewelry, with my fancy car parked nearby. I turned on the charm and the concern.

"You look hungry. When's the last time you had something to eat?" Or, "I noticed you haven't changed clothes in a couple of days. Let's go get you something else to wear, Baby."

I'd warn them about the bad people who hung out there, the people who would lie to them to get what they wanted. Let's say I was at the LA bus station.

"Now you know you have to be careful around here because people will say they have a part for you in a movie or music video. They'll take you up there in Hollywood Hills, and you'll never be seen again."

Typically, bad people don't tell you about bad people, so I must be safe.

If I was at a teen hangout like an arcade, a fast-food place, or the mall, I'd eavesdrop on their conversations to gather a little intel. Say I heard a girl mention her foster mom. I knew I could weaponize the trauma that landed her in that foster home and any tension between her and the foster mom. I felt out the situation and took it from there. I might give her my business card and tell her I'd take her to lunch. I jumped on the following scene more than once:

"We're going to buy shoes. You coming?" Her friends would be ready to move on from me. I saw her hesitation and played on that.

"Oh, you can't buy any? That's not right. Let's see what they buy, and we'll get you some."

The opportunity always presents itself, and traffickers are skilled at noticing the slightest opportunities. They pounce at the tiniest opening. It doesn't matter if adults are around, either.

I'd watch a bunch of girls and a couple of staff members on an outing from a group home, for example. I knew the ones constantly whispering or trailing behind the rest of the group were easy marks. I'd make my way close enough to whisper my own enticing word or slip them my number.

I even had girls jump out of a residential treatment home with staff wide awake to run with me. I met one of them, a 16-year-old, at the mall. While I was grooming her, they sent her to the treatment center. I stayed in contact with her, and when they gave her a weekend pass home, she ran to me. She worked for me a couple of weeks before they picked her up on the track. They sent her back to the residential treatment home, but she called me as fast as she could.

"That was my fault," I reassured her. "I should have gotten you out of town. I didn't know they were going to look for you like that. I would have gotten you out of town where you'd be safe from them."

"We can still get out of town." I had kept selling her the dream the couple of weeks she'd been with me, and she was still chasing it.

"Give me a couple of days to get my business together, and I'll come get you."

The next time we talked, she had recruited another girl without me asking her to. Teens work hard to make dreams come true.

"Did you explain what we do?"

"Yeah, she's down."

I told them both the same thing: "Be ready because we're hitting the high-way as soon as you get in the car."

I pulled up one night after dinner when the schedule wasn't as regulated and the staff wasn't as guarded. They dangled out the upstairs window and dropped to the ground. I was more afraid than them because I was driving the getaway car from a court-ordered placement.

A teen's still-developing mind doesn't get that the smooth-talking traf-ficker plays on their troubles. He actually adds to their problems, but they don't realize that until it's too late.

Those working with them don't realize until it's too late that they're not the only ones with a list of vulnerabilities to look for. Traffickers have their own list of red flags they look for in a potential victim. See lists for professionals in *Appendix E* and traffickers in *Appendix F*.

Once they spot one of those vulnerabilities or red flags, they zero in on it. I'll use me as an example again. If I met a girl starved for attention, I'd call her two or three times a day just to say hi. If I ran across a girl who thought her parents or foster parents were too strict, I'd call her the first day and then not again for two or three days. I'd give a girl looking for fame or fortune one of my business cards with a 1-800 number on it and say something such as: "Say, Baby. You come with me, and anything is possible."

They'd tell me about their sexual abuse within minutes of meeting me. Why when they hadn't told anyone for years? They wanted help. They wanted the abuse to stop. They wanted someone to understand their plight, but they were afraid no one would believe them or that no one would do anything about it. They knew I'd do both. They knew because I *listened* and had a "heartfelt" conversation based on *what I heard*.

I asked them questions that mattered to them or planted ideas in their heads, such as: "Do your foster parents make you feel like you're just a paycheck?" Or, I stated what I knew they were thinking, however invalid: "I bet they don't treat you the same as they treat their kids. Do they, Baby?"

We'd say, not coincidentally, that the common age teens enter sex trafficking[87] and the peak age for risk of running[88] are the same: 14-16. We can prevent runaways by also having intentional conversations with high-risk youth. Please see *Appendix G* for a ***Runaway Prevention Toolkit*** with a sample script and tools to de-escalate them when they trigger and spiral into flight mode.

I knew how to listen for the pain, the uncertainty, the unhappiness, the disgust. If we learn to not only think like a trafficker but to *listen* like a trafficker, we'll see different results with our at-risk and trafficked youth.

We must get to different results. Dyna and Kayla are two reasons why. Dyna and I crossed paths a few years after she left. She had gone in and out of the life, unable to get the help she needed to stay out. She had a beautiful baby girl, Miracle, with her. Tragically, Dyna didn't live to see Miracle grow up. I never learned why. Kayla, unable to find healing either, only managed to stay out of the game a short time before she went to work for an escort service.

## Two-Minute Introspection

What have you learned about how traffickers think and listen? How will this change your approach?

# 32

## All In The Family

Sparkle's close family member sexually molested her as a child and then exposed her to the life as a young teen without her mom's knowledge. He abused her right under her mom's nose, in fact. Like all kids, it shattered her identity and left helplessness and terror in its wake. She only went through the motions of life after that and other abuse, spiraling into harmful coping mechanics to try to dull the pain. She used prostitution as a weapon against the trauma she couldn't fend off. In her mind, prostitution was all she was worthy of.

Her mother, Peggy, thought Sparkle was worth more, but she lived in the projects without the needed resources to help her daughter. She didn't learn what her own relative had done to her daughter until years after he tired of her. Sparkle was an adult by then. Her mom tried to talk her out of the game, prayed for her, and regularly invited her to Bible study. Sparkle couldn't hear her pleas over the trauma echoing in her mind.

The thing about trauma is you can never outrun it. It eventually catches up with you. The game could not give Sparkle or me the long-term escape we had spent our lives searching for. It could only provide temporary "relief," a relief that buries people under multiple other traumas. The game is like a drug. Before you know it, you're addicted to it. Somewhere along the way, though, both of us lost the rush it had given us. We had to find a "high" – or something to blur our trauma – somewhere else, so we both turned back to drugs. Sparkle preferred cocaine. I missed the euphoria of heroin. I envied the dope fiends I ran across. I abstained as long as I could before making my way back to the projects in search of my first love. I fell head over heels again.

I craved the emotional high heroin gave me. I started second-guessing my decision, though, when my body also started craving it. They call it "chipper": Not far enough gone to spiral into full-fledged dope sickness without it, but I recklessly walked on the edge of it. I didn't want to live through that again, so I signed up for Narcotics Anonymous meetings. Sparkle decided to go with me.

They talked about God in one of the steps. What they said didn't make sense because I thought God was angry and out to get you. After all, the same teachers who taught me about God also hit my hands in anger. Sparkle's aunt had taken her to church regularly as a child, so she understood what they were talking about. She tried to explain it to me. When I still couldn't comprehend it, she called her mom to help. Peggy invited us to Bible study at her house, and I decided I had nothing to lose. I'd tried everything else I could think of.

Peggy knew what I did to her daughter, so it surprised me that she welcomed me into her home and her Bible study. The others didn't know what I did for a living, but they showed me as much hospitality as Rona's friends had. They offered me something I'd never had before, though. They prayed for me every week. I didn't know what to make of that, but it felt good. Their conversations didn't revolve around material things, either. They talked about things I'd never heard. The more I learned from them, the more I wanted to know. I mentioned to Sparkle that I felt better when I left Bible study than when I left a meeting.

"Yeah, when you go to Bible study, you're focusing on God. You're not hearing all the things drugs did to people or what the drugs made them do to other people."

That made me curious enough that I finally said yes to her mom's weekly invitations to church. The service wasn't what I expected. People seemed excited to be there. Their singing and clapping moved me. The preacher read out of the Bible and then broke it down where I could understand it. It shook me up a little that he came right down my street, talking about how getting involved in bad stuff grabbed you up and kept you in its grasp longer than you wanted to be there. Maybe he had been on my street because he even talked about how when you decide it's time to leave, it won't let you go. I identified with every word he said because I was living it. It was like he had met my father – the streets – and knew how much I idolized them.

I accepted Jesus as my Savior at the end of that service, but I had no idea what that meant. I voiced my doubt to Sparkle and Peggy as we walked to the car. I felt like it was the right path; I just didn't know what path I'd gone down. I gave them a rare peek into my emotions. They reassured me that it was normal, telling me the devil would try to make me believe that nothing was different, that I couldn't change. That wasn't true, they promised me. They tried to boost my belief in myself: "You have to know Jesus made you different."

I didn't feel any different. I didn't look any different. I still had the same desires swimming around my head. I wondered what they saw that I was missing.

Peggy could tell something was still eating at me, so she told me to keep coming to Bible study and asking God to show me.

"I'm allowed to talk to God?" I'd never been allowed to do that before.

"Just tell Him whatever is in your heart," Peggy told me.

I felt foolish, but I started to pray about everything – except myself. I thought that would be selfish. I prayed for things like my mom's doctors' appointments. I watched in amazement as God answered them. This works, I thought. I wanted to know more.

We worked hard during the week, taking tricks' money and recruiting girls, but we made it to church every Sunday. We'd always invite the girls to go to church with us. Some of them did. I'd give a generous offering from what I made off them whether they went or not.

As Sparkle and I grew closer to God, we grew closer to each other. I felt something for her I'd never felt for anyone, not even Kiara – emotions. I had searched my entire life for a belief in myself. I'd looked in burglarizing houses, robbing people, drugs, sex, pimping. I'd never caught a glimpse of it, but Sparkle gave me a close-up view. I could finally be myself. I could talk about what had hurt me. I could talk about my doubts and fears. I could cry. I could see something I'd never seen when I looked in the mirror – genuine worth.

I'd never understood love, but she had introduced me to the unconditional love of Jesus, and I loved her for that. The deeper our relationship got, the more I wanted to set things right. We quit drugs and got out of the game. Well, sort of. We didn't recruit other girls any longer. Sparkle sold herself enough for us to make ends meet. I spent my time talking to people on the track about Jesus.

About six months after we got out of the game, I served Kiara with divorce papers. She signed them and sent them immediately back. She probably hadn't known how to find me to do it herself. Sparkle and I went straight to the courthouse to get married and moved into a new apartment, where we settled into marital bliss. I could feel myself changing, slowly but surely. I didn't want to be in the street or as street as I had been for so long. This new life was becoming as much a part of me as drugs and pimping had been.

Sparkle was changing, too. She no longer was the same Sparkle I'd known all those years. It had bewildered me when she talked about believing in Someone Who hadn't kept her out of drugs and prostitution. She told me it was her choice, not His. He lets people make their own choices, she said.

"I can only stay off drugs when I keep my hand in His hand," she explained.

I guess she shook His grip free about two months into our marriage because she suddenly reverted to her old behaviors. She ran off when I confronted her with the cocaine use she was hiding. I was stunned. She had never run from me. I hunted for her for about a week. I finally found her hiding out in the projects, high. She was extremely apologetic. Too late. I was livid.

And crushed. I couldn't understand how she could help me see the light and then run headfirst back into the darkness.

"You can come get your stuff out of the apartment. I'm through with this. I don't need this crap. Later for you and later for this church crap."

She begged again when she came to gather up her belongings.

"I can't do this, Sparkle." My insides were in knots. More moments collided just like they had when I was a kid. I had promised myself I'd never let my guard down again, and I had. I let myself trust. I let myself love. I couldn't believe I had been so stupid as to get my hopes up again. Sparkle had crushed them, and so had God. They had both betrayed me. I blamed God that the person who led me to Him went back down the road she brought me up. He could have thrown up a roadblock. He was God, after all.

"Don't blame God for how I act," she insisted.

"How am I supposed to trust Him? This is your God that you led me to and now look. You trust Him, and He's not keeping you clean."

"We can work it out," she pleaded. "I've been there for you. Now, I need you to be here for me. We'll focus on recovery. I'll go back to work. Let's keep our marriage strong."

All the worth I'd discovered had stayed back in the projects where I found

Sparkle, but I still had the emotions that had come alive. I made an emotional decision: Yes, we would get back in the game. That's all that I had ever done that had worked.

We slid back in the game like we'd never been gone. I stacked money for a couple of weeks, and then we hit the road again.

I didn't take my ego with me this time. It was deflated. I didn't care any longer about being *the* pimp or *super* pimp. I'd found money, notoriety, expensive cars and jewelry, international hos, and friendship with superstars and movie stars with my magnetic pimp persona. I had thought if that guy invited enough girls to church and put enough of the money they made me in the offering plate, it would buy the one thing I'd really been chasing my whole life. It still eluded me.

Flamboyant pimping had failed me like everything and everyone else. I only had one option left – bad pimping.

I stayed with Sparkle, but I went on the rebound. I looked up my first love again. This time, heroin and I fully committed to each other.

## Analysis With Dr. Deena Graves:
### Familial Trafficking

Ninety-nine percent of the girls I trafficked had been sexually molested before I met them, just as Sparkle had. Prior sexual abuse is the single greatest "gateway" trauma for entry into trafficking.[89] Many people realize that.

However, they do not realize that familial trafficking is rampant in our country. They think that only happens in other countries. Tragically, it goes hand-in-hand with poverty, hunger, addiction, homelessness, and many other epidemics plaguing our country.

One research study found that illicit drugs were involved 82 percent of the time when a family member sold a child. Family members also traded their children for money, a place to stay, food, and other things. It sometimes involved producing pornography of their children to sell or trade.

The victims included very young children, both male and female. They endured threats, intimidation, bribes, physical force, use of weapons, parental authority, and forced drug use. Let us give you a trigger warning before you read the rest of this section. It often included a high severity of abuse, including object penetration. More than half of the children tried to commit suicide.

Trips to the emergency room and law enforcement investigations successfully uncovered some of the cases. However, multiple ER visits in six cases did not yield any suspicion of trafficking. All cases had child welfare involvement. Neglect findings were high, but only three cases had a sexual abuse finding. None specified CSEC. The children in the study were involved in multiple service systems during the time of trafficking, including behavioral health, health care, child protection, and juvenile justice.[90]

Families traffick their children in multiple ways, including word-of-mouth and online. For example, a Houston man sold his 4-year-old daughter on Craigslist five years after the site "permanently" shut down the prostitution section of its site in the United States. His ad read: "Come sleep with daddy's little girl."

An undercover detective exchanged more than 60 emails with the man before paying him $1,000 at his apartment, where he found the preschooler unresponsive and naked under the covers. The dad warned the officer, "It may not fit in." He reassured him, however, that he could "do whatever he wanted" to the little girl.[91]

If you work with high-risk families such as those listed above, it's crucial you know what to look for and what to do because many of these children are slipping through the cracks. For example, one youth in a juvenile hall wrote us a note after *The Traps of a Trafficker*© that read: "My mom pimped me out of our own home from ages 9-12. We moved around every year during that time."

Notice where the child was? In juvenile detention. She was crying out for help with negative behavior. No one had become suspicious despite years of involvement with multiple parts of the system. One dynamic that should cause you to take a more in-depth look, then, is children with multiple touches with the system. Another is children who enter care earlier.[92]

## Two-Minute Introspection

Think of a child you've worked with who fits the red flags in this chapter. What did you notice? What is it we're not seeing when working with high-risk families that could be indicators of familial trafficking?

# 33 This Isn't Going To End Well

Another old flame came back into my life about the same time I committed myself to heroin again. Lacy started pressuring my mom about Derek. He was now a young teen selling drugs out of her house. He'd tell her longtime boyfriend and father of her other children that he wasn't his father, so he couldn't tell him what to do. He needed his biological father, Lacy decided, and she'd never stopped insisting that was me.

My mom had never quit believing her, either. He looked and acted too much like me to doubt it, she insisted.

Curiosity finally got the better of me, so I headed to Lacy's one day. Derek wasn't there, but she pointed me to the Boys Club in hopes I could talk some sense into him. I think she was desperate since she knew I lived a life of crime myself.

I did a double take as I passed two boys walking down the road. One of them could have been me. I pulled over and called his name. I could see the same confusion on his face as I had had when I finally realized I was the spitting image of the dad I'd never known.

"It's your father," I tried to put him at ease. He had an advantage over me when I met my biological father. I didn't come as a surprise; he had known about me his entire life. He was standoffish, but I could tell he was curious, too. I'm sure it didn't hurt that I had my jewelry on and told them to hop in my fancy car.

We had an awkward conversation over lunch, but the longer we talked, the more his wall of resistance came tumbling down. And so did mine. This kid not only looked like me, but he also had all the same mannerisms and the same I-don't-care-about-anything-except-me attitude. Another generation of like father, like son.

I jumped full in. I went to his basketball games and hung out with him as much as I could. He wouldn't listen to me, though. Just like I was too old by the time my father came into the picture, Derek was too old by the time I decided to believe Lacy.

Ironic that I gave back into heroin shortly before I met my drug-dealer son. He could probably tell I was a junkie. Junkies can spot each other. The biggest difference between us was our crime of choice. I chose trafficking to stay out of jail. He chose to keep dealing drugs after he landed in juvenile detention.

I visited him in juvie and tried to talk him out of a life of crime every chance I got. He knew what I did for a living, and I tried to use that as leverage. I told him I understood the money and the power. I talked about how he was putting his life at risk of going to prison. I told him where else drugs would lead him. I did everything I could think of to steer him out of the dope game. The problem was I didn't try to steer him *into* anything.

I'm sure I didn't have any credibility with him. A short time after we met, when I decided to get out of the pimping game, he told me that was great. But, I'd be back, he nodded his head knowingly.

"That's not going to get it for you. You're not going to be good making in a week what you make in one night on a girl."

The "that" was a partnership in a barbershop.

I started getting my haircut by one of my cocaine buddies from barber school because I didn't like the wait and the limited parking at Uncle Danny's.

We picked right up as if all those years didn't stand between our last conversation, and I started hanging out at his shop. Sparkle didn't like the time it pulled away from our work or the attention it deprived her of. She wasn't just jealous of the shop. She turned green-eyed when I knocked other girls. That would be like your marketing manager getting upset when the sales director introduced a new product. She soothed her hurt feelings with cocaine and started disappearing for days at a time.

She still brought in a couple a thousand a week, but the headache started to outweigh the profit. I liked the tranquility of the barbershop and had an idea. I approached my friend about buying into his shop. I had spent too much of my profits to buy into Uncle Danny's chic salon, but I could swing investing in a shop in the hood.

I only worked weekends initially since I didn't have a clientele and depended on walk-ins, but that was enough to send Sparkle into another rage. I didn't care when she moved out. I didn't chase her around to make sure she went to work. I didn't bother calling her. She'd still drop by the shop occasionally, though, to give me money. I never refused it. It was kind of like retirement pay. She'd throw jabs my way, trying to get me back in the game – and our marriage – full-time.

"I don't know why you're living this square life. You're a pimp trying to be a barber, not a barber trying to be a pimp."

Others agreed, trying to pull me back into the life, but I blew them off. Rona stopped by the shop a couple of times when she came to town to visit my mom and Gina, but I'd lost my appeal in her eyes. Probably a combination of my now humdrum life and blowing her off on our trips.

My clientele grew, and so did my relationship with Derek, who lived 45 minutes out of the city. I spent all the time I could with him. We both made good money, so we ate at the finest restaurants and shopped for designer clothes together. I introduced him to my jeweler. And, he introduced me to his girlfriend's best friend, Jada.

I fell fast for Jada, a square. She tried to stay out of trouble like Kiara. Something drew me to that. I sent Sparkle a writ of divorce, but it came back. I didn't know if she rejected it or if it hadn't found its way to her. I learned, however, that I could get a divorce without her signature by posting a notice in the legal section of the paper three times.

I patiently cut hair while I waited for the required time to pass. I'd drive the Lincoln Continental she'd paid for to the shop each day and work hard, so I could get out of the game and be a good husband to Jada.

One day as I cut hair, I heard glass shattering and loud thuds. I ran outside to find Sparkle whacking my car with a baseball bat. I saw the brick surrounded by chunks of glass where it had landed on my front seat. I flew back into pimp mode, grabbed her, and drew my fist back. My business partner caught my arm before I could throw my first punch, yelling at Sparkle to get out of there. She jumped in her car and took off.

He tried to talk sense into me: "It's only a car. It's not worth the risk. You can get it fixed. You have insurance. Go get a restraining order instead."

He was right. Why risk a domestic violence charge after years of torturing women and girls while dodging jail time? She pulled one of her disappearing acts, though, and I couldn't track her down to serve her. I got a lucky break when she got arrested for drugs, and they called me. I served her the restraining order while she sat restrained in jail.

Jada and I got married as soon as the court granted my divorce petition. I felt good about myself for getting out of the game. I bought a condo with the money I'd stacked before getting out, and we settled into marital bliss. Jada and I had fun together. I didn't even mind the 45-minute commute to the barbershop.

My emotions started coming back to life again. I loved her as much as I knew how and liked her family. They liked me, too.

Before long, she got pregnant. This time, I wanted to be an involved father. I went to all her appointments and helped her prepare for the baby. Our excitement escalated as her belly grew more prominent and her due date drew nearer. We'd smile and laugh when the baby kicked or we got to hear the heartbeat. Our laughter faded away one week before her due date when the doctor couldn't find the heartbeat. They told us they believed our baby had died and to come back the following week for them to deliver him. Kered was born with the umbilical cord wrapped around his neck three times. Grief overcame us, and they suggested we take bereavement classes. They helped. Some.

It helped a little more when Jada got pregnant again soon after, this time with a baby girl whose due date the following year was one week before Kered's. Doctors erred on the side of caution and induced Jada two weeks early with our second baby. They had concluded that the umbilical cord had wrapped around Kered's neck when he made the final turn to prepare for birth.

We were glad they did. I saw the umbilical cord around her neck as she came out. The doctor did, too: "The cord. The cord." They cut it quickly and handed us a beautiful baby girl. They believed if they had not induced Jada, the cord could have tightened around Trinity's neck, just as it had Kered's.

We were overjoyed, and I loved every moment of being a dad, from burping her to changing her diapers to getting up in the night with her. I realized those were precious moments I'd missed with my other kids.

Things were good. I'd been out of the game almost two years. Well, kind of. Silver, who had been with me when I decided to get out, dropped by the shop occasionally for me to do her eyebrows. I'd tell her $15 when we got done, and she'd hand me $400 or $500 or so. Or, she'd ask me to go to lunch. I'd tell her no, but she could bring me lunch. She'd hand me a few hundred with the food. She'd tell me I didn't look right in there. I needed to be downtown. A few other people kept telling me that, too.

But, like I said, things were good. Not just at home or in the shop. When I wasn't cutting hair, I'd stand in the doorway and watch the drug deals and gang members causing trouble. A liquor store sat next to us, so we always had a lot of activity near our shop.

I always said "hi" to a high school girl who passed by on her way to class and friends' houses. She'd say "hi" back, and it quickly turned into flirting. Kammy and I eventually started dating. I only knew how to love Jada so much.

I had also grown my clientele, and our business boomed until the city decided to renovate the hood. They moved the Section 8 apartments to a new area, and we lost most of our customers who lived too far now. We lost the people who drove to their appointments when they tore up the street and sidewalk. We could barely keep the shop afloat. My partner's wife had a full-time job, so they kept their heads above water. I was drowning with a wife, baby, condo payment, and high-school girlfriend.

We'd sit in the shop for hours and not make any money. The stack I had from my time in the game and Silver dwindled daily. I finally told my partner I couldn't do it anymore. I had to have money to support my family. He tried to encourage me not to give up, but he couldn't afford to pay me or buy me out, so he understood.

I knew who could pay me, though. I headed to the track, where everyone warmly greeted me.

"Yo, Daddy D. We've missed seeing you."

Silver became my permanent girl, but I let her take charge. I didn't give her a quota or question how often she worked. I didn't have to; she handed me enough money the three or four times a week I'd go downtown to take care of my expenses. I'd only stay a few hours because I spent most of my time with my family and Kammy. Silver had my numbers if she needed me.

Jada knew what I did for a living when we met, so I told her I'd gone back to the game to support us. She was okay with it. I might not be there when they went to bed, but I was there when they woke up, and she liked having me around. Besides, she knew I wasn't recruiting, and Silver did all the heavy lifting. She knew the thousands of dollars I stacked in my night-stand allowed us to enjoy life, too.

With all that in my mind, I never could figure out why she exploded one night when Silver called the house.

I tried to get a few words in between her screaming and yelling.

"You know this girl has been paying our bills. You know this is where our money comes from. I didn't tell her to call. She knows I'm here with you."

She turned to stomp off, and I grabbed her arm.

"Don't walk away from me. I'm talking to you."

She shook my grip off, screamed again, ran to the phone, and called 911.

"So, you're going to call the police? I haven't hit you. I just want to talk to you."

She hung up. I explained again I didn't want Silver to call.

"You know I have to deal with her, though."

The doorbell cut through my words. I looked out the window and saw police standing outside the condominium.

"See that. Now police are here. I gotta get outta here."

"Where are you going? Are you going to see her?"

"You can go with me if you think I'm going to see her, but I'm not going to stay in here until police get inside the building."

She grabbed the baby, and we nodded at the officers as we walked past them to our car. We went to a restaurant and talked a couple of hours and then rode around a little longer to be absolutely sure the heat had left our house. We got a little sleep when we got home. When we woke up, I packed my bags, pulled enough money out of my stack to cover all the bills for a couple of months, and left.

Jada tried to get me to come back home, but I refused.

"Nope. You called police. That's a dealbreaker."

"I understand. I'll never do that again," she cried.

"I've spent my life trying to stay out of jail. I've thrown girls out of cars, left sneaker prints on their faces, locked them in the trunk. None of them called police. All I did was grab you to keep you from walking away. I made a commitment to you, and you called police. I'm done."

And, I was. I stayed involved in Trinity's life and visited both of them, but I couldn't live with someone who betrayed me. I could control who betrayed me as an adult, unlike my inability as a child to control what happened after my mother's betrayal. Jada had devastated me because I was trying to become square for her. I'd invested all of myself into her and our baby. I didn't see my relationship with Kammy as taking away from my investment. I'd married Jada. I provided for them. I'd never laid my hands on her.

I did what I always did when disloyalty stabbed me in the back. I hurt myself and others. I jumped into the deep end of trafficking and heroin without a life vest.

I knew where to find heroin in the projects and Silver on the track.

"I'm getting back in the game all the way. I need to stay with you until I find a place."

Just like that, I stepped back in as owner and operator of the operation, and Silver became my bottom. We made excellent money. We not only worked the tracks, but Silver also had a business idea for a startup. She named it Pure Platinum after her hair. She managed an escort service on Craigslist, Backpage, and the Phoenix. We got $100 for every call a girl went on. They decided how much to charge above that.

Girls came and went during the two years we worked together. Eventually, I let some of them stay with me to avoid a hotel bill. Silver didn't like that or when I'd drop them off at work instead of sending them in a cab. The last straw came when a couple of girls ran off with escort service money. Her enthusiasm for the game had been slowly waning, and without me giving her the attention she longed for, the money wasn't worth it to her anymore. She grew weary of sleeping with strangers and dodging the police. She quit the game, moved to the country, bought a horse, and got into a committed relationship.

I'd never understood someone tiring of the excitement of the game before. I'd try to get out to do the right thing, not for lack of excitement. Suddenly, I understood tiring of it. Because I was. I was weary of heroin, too, but it had its hooks deep in me again.

294

## Analysis With Dr. Deena Graves:
### Online Safety

I took all the money for the online escort service, but I considered it Silver's business, not mine. I never liked trafficking online. The track was easy work with multiple advantages. I could recruit. I could kick it with the other pimps. I could see what the buyers were up to. I could keep a watchful eye on the girls. In other words, I could keep a pulse on all aspects of the game without too much effort.

Online required too much expense and work for my taste. I had no choice but to rent a hotel room when we posted online ads. I had to buy laptops. The ad inches down the page with time, so the girls had to keep posting, so it stayed at the top of the list. First and foremost, to me at the time, I didn't like how it impacted my money. Money always came up short when we took the game online.

I didn't like hanging out in the room with them, so I'd check on them every few hours. The TV would be on, the bed a mess, but no money, so I knew they were sleeping and smoking instead of working. They got too comfortable sitting in a heated or air-conditioned room. They got too cold or too hot on the track, or their feet got tired, so they wanted to jump in someone's car. They didn't necessarily want someone jumping in their bed if they could hang out instead.

I hope it's become evident through this book that pimps operate their businesses according to their personal preferences. It's not a cookie-cutter game like is often portrayed in trainings and movies. I might not have liked online trafficking, but it was and is a thriving business – even with Craigslist and Backpage "shut down." Traffickers and buyers are just like any other criminals. Shutting down a website isn't going to deter them. Go back to when I burglarized businesses and homes. Most were locked down tight. Some had bars on the windows and doors. Locks, bars, and "permanently shutting down" a criminal enterprise doesn't stop hustlers. They find a new hustle. Remember how I'd go around to the back of the house to find another way in?

Traffickers have merely found other ways "in" to the online game. They'll hide ads in different sections; find smaller, lesser-known sites; post kids on social media; sell them through video games; or worse yet, traffick them on the dark web. Driving criminals to the almost impenetrable dark web makes it harder to find them and the kids they're torturing. It's also harder to find them when they're spread out across sites and platforms.

We could talk in-depth about each of these, but let's focus on social media since most youth hang out there. So do many predators. What parents and caregivers often don't realize, though, is how frequently youth unintentionally endanger themselves and how they cover it up.

First, let us give you another example of social media as a predator's recruiting ground in addition to the one we provided in Chapter 21.

A trafficker laid his trap for a 12-year-old Houston girl from a wealthy family by telling her she was pretty. He plied her with compliments while empathizing with her about how unfair her parents were. After gaining her trust, he talked her into him selling her. He set up two Snapchat accounts. He shared posts of the child completely dressed in the first account. Once it gained a following, he shared posts, such as: "Send $40 Snapcash if you want to see me naked." He housed the nude photos on a private account. Those who paid to access the private account received the photos and a description of sexual services they could pay for. Shortly after, law enforcement rescued her from a hotel when her parents reported her missing.[93]

Parents and caregivers must protect children on social media because the companies running them don't have a stellar track record doing so. TikTok, for example, has been accused of allowing known child predators to go unpunished. They have been known to remove a sexual comment to a child but allow the person to stay on the app, free to target other youth. People have found hundreds of predatory comments on videos posted by children as young as 9.[94] TikTok also has been accused of deliberately dangerous algorithms and dark patterns.[95]

It's not limited to social media, however. Youth and children face the same vulnerability with online video gaming. A Florida man, for instance, was arrested for empathizing with a teen over Fortnite to groom him for child pornography.[96] And parents have found sex torture rooms on Roblox, the No. 1 ranked game for children under 13 with more than 100 million players each month. Parents think the game is safe, clean fun, but the avatars of very young children have been gang-raped, with the predators threatening to kill themselves if the child leaves the game or tells.[97]

The still-developing brain of a teenager – or a child – can't think through the consequences of what seems innocent to them, especially when they are angry with their parents or caregivers. They not only fall for the predators' tricks and traps, though. They intentionally cover up their actions to keep their parents from catching on. Sometimes, the predators supply the tools to do that. Fake location apps, for instance, lull parents into believing they know where their child is, but the reality is they have NO idea. People publish step-by-step videos to help youth deceive their parents with such apps.[98]

There are many steps parents and caregivers can take to find what their teens are hiding online and do something about it. One example is identifying if the child uses an onion router or TOR browser, enabling them to use the internet anonymously. Youth don't realize it exposes them to such dangers as people running the servers spying on their activity. It also can draw the government's attention because it is highly encrypted.[99]

M³ Transformations offers a training for parents and professionals on what youth hide online, how to find it, and what to do about it. It also offers one for youth on how they unintentionally put themselves in danger and the unknown digital footprint they leave behind. Visit m3transformations.com for more information. Together, we can keep our children safe from predators.

## Two-Minute Introspection

Child sex trafficking, sextortion, cyberbullying, sexting, and teen pornography use are at epidemic numbers. For instance, the CyberTipline had a record-breaking 97.5-percent increase in reports of online enticement from 2019 to 2020.[100] Yet, the vast majority of youth say their parents don't need to know what they do online and admit to hiding it.[101] What conversations can you have with youth to help them understand the hidden dangers of social media and the internet?

# PART 4. LEAVING THE GAME FOR GOOD

# 34 Diamond in the Rough

I no longer had a bottom to run my organization, but I had a three-to-four-bag-a-day dope habit that ran me. I'd slipped back into bed with heroin because I was lying in bed beside a woman I didn't love. I loved my wife, but pride and feelings of betrayal wouldn't let me forgive her. I had mixed emotions toward Silver. If she had not called me, I'd still be with my wife. If she hadn't given me money, though, Jada and I would not have been able to keep our condo, two cars, and money stacked away in the night-stand.

Heroin was the only thing that had ever eased my confusion, so I turned to it more and more for comfort. Silver threw me into another bind with her departure, though. I couldn't chance waking up dope sick in an unfamiliar city, unable to find my next high, so I stayed close to Boston. At the same time, police buckled down on the track. Most pimps fled the city, but, once again, my addiction held me captive.

I had to do something quickly before my life spun out of control or I landed in jail. I checked into another weeklong detox program about two weeks after Silver left so that I could get my game back on. I didn't bother telling the stragglers I had left in my organization what I was up to. If they were there when I got out, great. If not, I knew where to find more. I had to get myself together for me. Detox was never a final goodbye – simply a "see you later." I wanted my dope. Only on my terms, not its. This time, it was failing miserably at its job, though. Pain often overpowered the euphoria; pimping failed to pump my ego back up. I had nose-dived into a dismal depression. I didn't understand what was happening to me.

I went through all the motions of the program and all the withdrawals of the addiction, like usual. I laid on that detox bathroom floor and puked my guts out as I had in all the other programs and in that jail cell so many years earlier. People always stirred clear of that. Not much they could do for an addict fighting his way through the harsh realities of withdrawal. This time, though, a nurse invaded my misery.

She stuck her nose right in the middle of my addiction and said something to me no one ever had.

"Come see me when you finish, and I'll tell you how you never have to go through this again." I'll never forget her words. At the time, I thought I might as well. I'd tried everything else. Maybe she had some kind of magic potion.

I picked myself up off the floor when I could and headed to find her. She didn't give me a magic potion, merely some commonsense advice.

"You need to leave heroin alone for good, and detox won't do it. You can't just stop using. You have to figure out what led you to use it in the first place."

"Yeah," I shrugged in my head. "This is getting old. It's not fun anymore, and I know what it does to me, so why do I keep ending up back here?"

It seemed so simple, yet no one had ever suggested I get to the root of the addiction. They'd simply glaze over the symptoms of it. I talked to her every chance I got during the rest of my stay. She not only encouraged me, but she also helped me register in a dual-diagnosis residential program that would address both my addiction and my depression.

That one superhero nurse rescued me from a lifetime of addiction. I never touched heroin again after the dual-diagnosis program. Unfortunately, the program didn't delve deep enough into my trauma to end my trafficking addiction. On the contrary, it introduced me to my next victim.

A judge ordered Diamond to the program to get her baby back. She struggled with depression and behaviors I wouldn't learn about until much later. She spilled all the traumas that drove her to that behavior to me, however. She told me about her sexually and physically abusive father, the gang she'd joined when she fled him, her addiction, her time selling herself to survive.

I, on the other hand, did not tell Diamond about my traumas or much of the behaviors I'd developed to deal with them. All she needed to know was I could help her make more money than she'd ever made on her own. The program didn't allow such exchanges of stories or the exchange of phone numbers, but we managed both. She called me as soon as she got out. I picked her and her 1-year-old up while her girlfriend was at work, and we got busy working ourselves.

I'd watch her little girl while she worked the track in Boston, and we'd leave her with my mom and sisters when we traveled to other cities on the East Coast. I didn't give Diamond a quota, but I did the other girls who came and went. I didn't feel pimpish as I did before I got out of the game with the barbershop, but I needed to pay for their housing, food, clothes, and medical care, so I mustered up enough of my old trafficker persona to get the job done.

A few months later, my mom retired and moved to Georgia, where two of my sisters had relocated, so we headed to Texas to visit Diamond's mentor, Julie, who wanted to meet the baby. Julie had taken Diamond under her wing as a teen during one of her stints in juvenile detention.

We worked the Dallas-Fort Worth Metroplex for a few weeks, picking up an 18-year-old to take back to the East Coast with us. We left the baby with Julie when she offered to keep her. In hindsight, I realize Julie wanted to keep the baby safe from the life we were exposing her to.

Even without the baby, I didn't frequent the track often. I'd sit in the bar occasionally, downing a few drinks, but I'd lost interest in the pimp hustle. I'd grown so detached that it barely fazed me when the Texas teen disappeared less than two weeks in. We never found out where she went. I tried to do better at keeping my head in the game after she vanished, but my heart hadn't been in it for some time.

Then something started messing with my head, too – excruciating headaches. At the same time, five of my family members died within three months of each other. That messed more with my heart. My blood pressure spiked, and I started having seizures.

Diamond and a few family members visited me in the hospital, but I had a lot of time to think in that sterile room. Depression and hopelessness engulfed me. For the first time since I was a teen, however, I didn't want the quick fix of heroin even though I couldn't escape my head or my heart.

My life played out in my mind like a bad rerun, and I couldn't change the channel. All the opportunities I'd let evaporate into thin air repeated over and over. My time in the Army, my marriage to Kiara, Sparkle and her mom introducing me to Jesus, the barbershop, Jada. I had a chance each time to reclaim my identity and destiny, but I forfeited them to the streets time and again.

When the going got tough, I admitted to myself, I defaulted to the easy way out. I never bothered making excuses about it, either, because I'd never cared. I just did it. Like when you drive somewhere and then realize you don't know how you got there. That's not an excuse. Simply the reality of how hardened I had grown over the years. The streets do that to you. So does the money the streets make you. I ate, drank, and slept trafficking for the majority of my life. It wasn't a way of life, either; it was life. I saw it as my right. But now, the thought of pimping left a bad taste in my mouth.

An emotion I'd never experienced washed over me – conviction. I'd toyed with Jesus off and on since Sparkle and her mom told me about Him, but I'd never gotten serious with Him. I'd never taken the time to get to know Him or His heart. I'd tried to control my relationship with Him like I controlled the girls … investing just enough in Him so that He'd do what I wanted.

I started reading the Bible and praying while recovering in the hospital bed. I really talked to God, and He had things to say to me. I'd never thought of pimping as immoral. I'd thought it was exciting, cool, fun, lucrative, my passage out of poverty, one of the only career choices for someone from the hood, my get-out-of-jail-free card.

God and the nurse who introduced me to the dual program helped me see things about myself I'd never seen. I'd never thought about using the skill and savvy I'd developed in criminal undertakings for good. It never dawned on me that the will it took to be a successful trafficker, drug addict, and armed robber could be used to transform things for the better. I didn't think I had it in me to do anything constructive, but they saw something in me buried deep underneath my trauma.

They gave me a belief in myself. I'd already conquered dope. Now, with God on my side, I felt I could overcome the hopelessness and despair. I believed I could find my identity outside pimping. I could find my self-worth in something other than manipulating and controlling other people. I had no idea how or what it would look like, but I knew I could no longer survive off hurting people.

I didn't know it at the time, but God was setting me up for my true destiny.

I didn't want to desert Diamond, so I filled her in on my plans.

"I can't keep doing this. I'm going to square up. I'm moving to Georgia to stay with my mom while I get my life together. I don't know what I'm going to do, but I'm not going to do this anymore. You're welcome to go with me if you want."

She decided to go. Jada had divorced me, and I wanted to start my new life off right, so I married Diamond.

My mom was elated, if not cautious, about me exiting the game again. She had every reason to have a wait-and-see attitude. So did all the other people who played it cautious around me for years. After all, I'd said I was quitting before. Thirty-two years is a hard habit to kick.

My mom had also recently developed a relationship with Christ, and I started going to church with her. Diamond went to appease me.

The only job I could find was as a groundskeeper at a different church. I'd told the senior ministry leader who hired me about my background, and he took a chance on me anyway. I was learning a lot of people could see something in me.

He hired Diamond, too. We found an apartment, and I thought I finally had my life on the right track. It was short-lived, though. My world came crashing down again when I noticed a wound on Diamond's arm. Then I saw more cuts. That behavior she'd hidden from me in the program where we met was self-mutilation. It scared me for her. My frozen heart had started to thaw, and, for the first time, I cared about the trauma someone else had lived. I finally cared about myself, which allowed me to care about others.

I found a day program that she agreed to enroll in. I'd drop her off and pick her up. One day when I went to pick her up, she didn't come out. I went in to get her when the parking lot emptied. They informed me she had left with another woman from the program.

She answered my calls after a few days, and I picked her up, but she still was in bad shape. My boss helped me find a residential program, but she walked out of it, too. She sold herself for the next five months to survive before she decided she wanted to come home.

I didn't long for heroin to dull the pain and the fear throughout those months. I didn't feel betrayed. I didn't fly into a trafficker's rage. My only emotions were worry and concern for my wife. I was thankful when she wanted to come home, so I picked up the pieces again, getting her into a program at church this time. She became close friends with the lady over the program, who became her mentor. Diamond stabilized, and we had a little girl, Persis. My biological and church families formed a support network around us to help us keep our lives on track.

And we did. Diamond stayed home with Persis while I continued to work as a groundskeeper. We still went to church with my mom, and I tried to get involved with a ministry there that started going to the prostitution track. The ministry could have worked with a different approach, but they got between the pimps and their money. Pimps won't listen to you when you do that. You can't beat them, or anyone else in the game, over their heads, either. That pushes them away. And it causes them to push you away. More like run you off. They threw stuff at the people from the church and chased them off the track.

I told my boss how disappointed I was, and he suggested I start my own ministry. My heart burned to do something to make amends for all the people I'd hurt, so I took his advice. I wasn't sure what to do, so Diamond and I packed up sandwiches, and we headed to the Atlanta inner city. We served people working the track, the homeless under the bridge, and the strung-out addicts on the streets. Before long, the church where I worked and a nearby fast-food restaurant started supplying food, and Back to the Streets Ministry was born. It blossomed as families and youth from the church got involved. Some of them asked me to speak in schools or at events, and I also started holding a Bible study before feeding people.

The ministry grew so much that we got a van and trailer. Tragically, something was growing inside Diamond, too. Something I was not aware of. She ran off again after Persis turned one. My family jumped in to help me with my baby, but I was overwhelmed. I'd never been an involved father, so I didn't know how to be a single dad. I kept my resolve and didn't turn to heroin, but I did turn to my younger sister, Sheri. She had a strong family and took custody of Persis, but I stayed heavily involved. We didn't hear from Diamond for almost a year. She popped back up then, wanting to see Persis. She was back in prostitution, and we knew her other daughter was still with Julie in Texas, so my sister told her no.

"You're not going to run in and out of this baby's life and mess her up." I was thankful she was protective of Persis. However, I blamed myself for Diamond, and I still struggled with what I had done to so many other people. The senior ministry leader I worked for could see my turmoil and helped me get into counseling. I thought I would go for a few days or a few weeks like I had in previous programs and hoped it might help me heal a little more. When I began to open up to my therapist, though, he thought I needed intense therapy to unpack all the baggage from my childhood, drug addiction, trafficking, and other criminal undertakings. He told me something similar to what the nurse had said – I had to understand where my problems came from to heal from them. They both were right.

This time, I spent almost two years in intense therapy. It was there that I came to understand the deep bitterness I had for my stepfather. It was also there that I was surprised to learn of my agonizing animosity toward my mom. I loved my mom, so I hadn't realized how acutely she had hurt me. Over the course of those two years, I was able to forgive her, my stepfather, my father, and others who had hurt me. I was also able to forgive myself, but that took longer. I'm deeply grateful to that therapist who helped me heal from my trauma and understand the trauma I had inflicted on others. That and God were the only way I got to a place to forgive any of us.

Thankfully, I had a strong foundation when the economy took a downturn and the church cut funding for my job and Back to the Streets. I knew it would all work out. Sure enough, my boss, who I'm sure you see by now was also my mentor, managed to keep me on as a private contractor, giving me enough odd jobs to make it.

Despite all the moments once again colliding in my life, the thought of returning to pimping didn't cross my mind once. Heroin didn't tempt me. I still didn't feel betrayed by Diamond. Instead, I felt sad for her. I held out hope for a couple of years before divorcing her. I didn't know how to find her, so I posted a public notice as I had with Sparkle.

About six months after my divorce, Kammy sent me a friend request on Facebook. Kammy had been a safe place for me when I tried to get out of the game the first time. She has always made me want to be a better person. She was one of the few people in my life who believed in me when I couldn't find anything to believe in. I respected her from the beginning because she respected herself. She was one of only three girls I became close to who I never tried to sell. Kiara and Jada were the other two. She continues to be an inspiration for me today.

Kammy and I dated, fell in love, got married on August 25, 2018, and moved to Alabama to get a fresh start. We have a little boy, Isaiah, and are raising him and Kammy's daughter. Watching Isaiah grow from a baby to a toddler has been a joy. I've gotten to experience things with him I never shared with my other children, which has caused deep feelings of regret. I got to watch him take his first step and be there when he potty trained. I'd never done those things.

While I will experience many firsts with Isaiah that I missed with my other kids, I'm working to make all of my kids and grandkids proud. I want them to see what you can become when you decide not to take the easy way out or the way that your environment says you should take. I want them to see what it means to live your destiny. And, I want them to know I believe in them like that nurse, my boss, and Kammy believed in me.

I've had the opportunity and the financial need to go back to the game during the more than 13 years I've been out, especially when I ministered to high-risk girls and women in the Atlanta hood. Through the ups and downs, though, I've never considered going back. Instead, I've worked construction. Kammy and I worked in a sandwich shop together. I've done other odd jobs. Long story short, I've done whatever it takes to make it without decimating another life. When I got on that plane on May 8, 2008, to exit the game, I didn't simply fly from Boston to Atlanta. I flew into a new identity. I set my face like flint, resolved to make amends for all the degradation and damage I caused so many. I can never undo the wrong I did, but I am unconditionally devoted to preventing others from being abused and exploited in the same way I abused and exploited people. And I'm determined to stop others from causing the pain and suffering I caused by preventing youth from becoming traffickers.

When I was a child, all those traumatic events collided to send me spiraling into a life *without* purpose. Now, all the trauma adults inflicted on me as a child and that I wreaked on adults and children I'm using for a life *of* purpose.

## Analysis With Dr. Deena Graves:
### Self-harm

Teens are inventive when trying to escape the pain of trauma. For instance, a teen who disclosed to us as a trafficking victim was placed in a CSEC residential care program. Knowing the high risk of self-harm, the program made any object with a potential for cutting inaccessible. I, Dr. Graves, visited her a few weeks later for her birthday and saw burn marks on her leg. She had found a way to use what was accessible – ice and salt – to harm herself. The one-two punch of the ice and salt, similar to frostbite, causes a tremendous amount of physical misery,[102] which diverted her attention from her mental anguish. She's not alone; trafficked youth, as well as other abused-and-neglected children, often turn to self-harm as a coping or self-soothing mechanism.[103] They are especially vulnerable to self-harm if they have a combined history of early childhood adversity and prevailing trauma; they frequently injure themselves in an attempt to outrun the agony.[104]

As susceptible as any highly traumatized child is to self-injury, trafficked youth have a heightened risk. Research has found statistically significant differences in trauma symptoms between trafficked youth and youth who have been sexually abused but not trafficked. Trafficking has a profound impact on them emotionally, developmentally, and psychologically. Trafficked youth have especially been found to have greater levels of avoidance, hyperarousal, dissociation, and PTSD.[105] Thus, they are highly vulnerable to many additional risk factors, including stunted development, drugs, suicide, subsequent sexual abuse, and reoccurrence of trafficking.[106,107,108]

With their risk of ongoing trauma and death, they need urgent and intentional intervention. However, they are not receiving that. As I discussed in the *Prologue*, research has overwhelmingly found youth across the country have received inadequate treatment strategies for their unique, complex trauma and have not been kept safe from traffickers.[109,110]

Consider the following statement carefully. Notably, trafficked youth not only had more post-traumatic stress symptoms when they came *into* care compared with those with no trafficking experiences, but more than one research study has found that *when they leave care*, they have a more deteriorated symptom profile compared to other youth in the child welfare or juvenile justice system. The gap between these two groups persisted almost five years later. That means they are leaving care not healed and, thus, continuing to spiral even years later.[111] Bottom line: They're not getting the help they need. At the same time, traffickers prey upon their PTSD to cut them off from their ability to exit trafficking. And the extreme violence, fear, shame, and numbness keep them trapped in risky situations and behaviors.[112]

That tells you we have to change what we are doing. We're trying to force-fit policies and practices not designed to deal with this level of complex trauma. That can lead to "solutions" that cause more damage, leaving us feeling that despite our best efforts, we are like a hamster running endlessly around that wheel. We find ourselves stuck in a vicious cycle that is almost impossible to break. That's because we're acting on what we see in front of us: Child sex trafficking. We have to do like Derek and get to the root of the problem. His problem wasn't heroin. The unresolved trauma kept him falling back on heroin as a pain reliever. He couldn't break his addiction until he dealt with the source of it, and we cannot solve one of the greatest atrocities on our planet until we deal with the source of it – for the traffickers, the buyers, and the youth who become their victims.

It's not as complicated as it sounds. We just have to quit falling back on our "pain reliever," also known as what we've done in the past. We must get to the root of the problem like Derek got to the heart of his addiction. He repeatedly failed until he did and then had immediate and long-lasting success. We know what that root is, yet we continue to respond to trafficking as an isolated event rather than as the explosive chain reaction that lands a child there, whether as a victim or a victimizer. Like Derek, we'll fail again and again until we get to the core issue.

That's the heart of this book – putting out the fiery powder train that leads to trafficking, as well as myriad other dangers for our children. When we do that with our treatment plans, programs, policies, procedures, mandates, and laws, we'll take our children back from trauma and traffickers. $M^3$ Transformations has a training with an innovative tool to help you do that.

For far too long, trauma and traffickers have had their way with our children. It's time to take them back with strategic, cutting-edge prevention and treatment strategies. It's time to design solutions with hope.

## Two-Minute Introspection

How has this book challenged your thinking about trafficking? What will you do differently as a result?

# A  Appendix A: Where Are They Now? An Update On My Family

## My Mom

My mom, Helen, is enjoying retirement and grandkids. She worked in the bereavement ministry at church until a couple of strokes forced her to step down. To this day, my mom and I have not had an in-depth conversation about my biological father, my stepfather's abuse, or my time as a trafficker. I'm thankful for the peace I made with that in therapy.

## My Sisters

All three of my sisters worked their way out of the inner city and moved from Boston. Two of them are property managers, and one works in a divorce court. My younger sister, Sheri, is still raising Persis.

They realize they played a role, as well. They learned from that, and none of us are proud of participating in any form. It's not an excuse, but we all operated in survival mode. I was the one bearing gifts and paying them for their help. Survival mode doesn't turn down gifts or money.

## My Father

My biological father, Jimmy, died in a hospital in 1988 from his alcoholism. His girlfriend at the time accelerated it by taking him a bottle of liquor as he lay dying. They found him on the bathroom floor with the empty bottle next to him. I had just left from visiting him, and they called me back. It was still at the height of my pimping days, and I was ready to hit her, but my aunt and uncle stopped me. Thankfully, we had a little more time with him before he passed away. I forgave his girlfriend with time and therapy.

My father and I developed a good, but distant, relationship over the years. I'd visit him at the liquor store when I was in town and would buy him food. I cut his hair for the funeral, and I have a tattoo of the date of his death on my arm.

## My Stepfather

My stepfather, Tyrone, lives with my sister Sheri, who is his biological daughter. He is on dialysis and not doing well. During the years I was on the road abusing women, he stopped abusing them. His mother, brother, and best friend all died, and that impacted him enough that he laid down his violence.

He can't fit in his shoes anymore because of the dialysis, so he gave them to me. Although I figuratively walked in his shoes for a long time, I am thankful that we both eventually decided to take a different path. It took a long time, but I also forgave him. I've been forgiven much, so I know he deserves my forgiveness, too. I see him regularly at my sister's and can honestly say I have developed a pure love for him since exiting trafficking.

## My Children

My oldest son, Derek, Lacy's child, has been in and out of prison for dealing drugs. At the time of this book, he is in prison. I tried to counsel him through the years, but it was hard for him to take me seriously when I was living my own life of crime. I hope he will follow my example now and get out for good. He is where I was for so many years, though – blinded by the amount of money he can make on one drug deal compared to what he can make for a week or more of hard work. It isn't easy to walk away from that kind of money, especially when you've been making it since you were 13. He's never had a square job and grew accustomed to raking in thousands of dollars a week. The thought of going from being your own boss to working for someone and bringing home $500 a week instead of $5,000 a week is unfathomable when you have a mind raised in the streets. Tragically, many young Black males do not see any way beyond the streets to make money. It's the only way they know to get up and out; they just don't realize what it gets them *into*.

I hold out hope for Derek, though. He knows my relationship with God and how it has changed my life. My prayer is that he'll find the same. His teenage son needs him to do that just like he needed me to when he was a teen. Derek is involved in his son's life when he is not in prison. I see him when I am in Boston, as well.

Lacy hates me for Derek's life of crime. She blames me because after we got close, I would take him riding around the track and exposed him to other bad influences. I haven't spoken to her in decades, but, if she would listen to me, I would tell her that I am sorry for the man I was when we were together. I am not proud of the things I did to her and with her because of my drug addiction. I also am sorry for not being involved in our son's life as a child and not being a strong role model for him when he was a teen. I hope one day she can find it in her heart to forgive me.

My other son named Derek, who I had with my first wife, Kiara, lives with my mom. He served 16 years in prison as a young adult for selling drugs and contacted my mom from there. She visited him in jail, and they developed a close relationship. I met him for the first time when he was in prison, as well. We also have forged a close relationship, and I am proud that he has turned his life around and now works as a physical trainer. He has two adult children who he is involved with.

My son, Tyrone, has gotten into some trouble, but he's turned his life around. He now owns a cell phone business and has one daughter who recently graduated and is headed to college. He's had a serious girlfriend for 12 years. He is close to my entire family, and I am involved in his life.

My daughter, Gina, works in the same state office that her mother did. I stayed involved in her life as she grew up, and we are very close today. We talk and text every day. She is married and has three kids, a teenaged boy, a pre-teen boy, and a little girl who is one year older than Isaiah. She stayed in contact with Rona for years. Gina, like all my daughters, never got into trouble with authorities.

My daughter, Trinity, and I have stayed in contact, but not as much as I would like. She works in retail and recently became engaged to her longtime boyfriend.

I stay involved with my daughter, Persis, and am thankful for Sheri's influence in her life. She is going into junior high and does well in school.

One of Kammy's daughters graduated high school recently and is going to cosmetology school. She loves to practice on her younger sister, who is in high school.

## Uncle Danny
Uncle Danny and I stayed close until he died of prostate cancer several years ago. I'd drop by his shop, and we'd catch up on life. He never tried to talk me out of the game, and I stopped asking his advice. I didn't need it any longer. I knew more about the game than he did.

## My Father's Family
My grandmother died, but I am very close to my Aunt Bernadette, who is retired and lives in Georgia now. We text every day and talk regularly. I occasionally go to church with her online.

## My Ex-wives

### Kiara
My first wife, Kiara, still lives in Kansas. She had more kids but never remarried. We lost communication soon after I left Kansas and haven't talked since.

### Sparkle
As you might have guessed from her foreword, Sparkle, or Denise, finally overcame her drug addiction and got out of the game. We remain friends, and I appreciate her writing the foreword for this book. We now work together, saving lives instead of destroying them. You'll hear much more from her in the coming days.

### Jada
Jada and I remain friendly and speak occasionally about Trinity. She is doing well. She never remarried and did not have additional children.

### Diamond
Diamond's mentor still has her older daughter, and, the last either of us knew, Diamond was in jail.

# B Appendix B: Notes From Derek's Wife, Daughter, and Spiritual Father

**Derek's wife, Camelia**

Like so many impressionable teen girls, I fell for Derek's bigger-than-life outward persona. Thankfully, though, I also got a glimpse of the real person deep down inside. I saw the struggle between who he was and who he wanted to be.

Oh, there's no denying he talked a good game. The difference between me and the other teens he targeted, however, was he smooth-talked me into falling for *his* game but not *the game*. He never even hinted at the idea.

In fact, he never told me he was a pimp. I figured it out myself after we'd been seeing each other for about six months. I'd hang out in the barbershop and talk to him between clients or wait for him to get off work. Despite being young and naive, it didn't slip past me that girls would occasionally come and go but never got their hair done. They'd whisper with him a few minutes and leave. Sometimes, they'd hand him money. I'd see him leaving the shop from time to time with a girl, too. I knew what the way they were dressed meant. You didn't live in our neighborhood and not understand that.

By then, I was too far gone to care. He was different from all the other guys I knew. His Sunset Boulevard appearance and mannerisms made him bigger than life, but how he treated me made me feel like I was his life. I felt safe with him, even after I figured out other girls were anything but safe with him.

I'm not naïve now. I know part of it was his innate mind manipulation. Even then, I knew enough to know that although he never rushed me into anything, he was rushing other teens into unimaginable things. I didn't doubt he told them he loved them, but I felt like he *genuinely* loved me. He physically opened car doors for me while psychologically opening car doors – and motel room doors – for them. He'd take me out of the hood to experience things I never would have; he'd take them out of the state to experience things they never should have.

He played his words like a violin, and I got lost in his song. That doesn't mean it wasn't hard. I'd lay awake at night crying because I knew what he was out in the night doing.

Despite all that, I'd see the genuine Derek when he'd forget to keep his guard up. I'd see who he wanted to be when he slipped out of his pimp mentality into the same mentality of the little boy who wanted to protect his mom. He'd insist I go to school. He steered me clear of the people in the neighborhood addicted to drugs or alcohol. He showed up to help whenever something went wrong. A callous pimp doesn't do those things; a man struggling to remember who he once wanted to be does. He treated me with more respect than any guy I had known.

I never told my family anything I'd figured out about Derek. My mom was the only one who knew him the first time we were together. She met him before I did, and she didn't know he was a trafficker, either. My mom was a pillar in our crime-infested neighborhood. People turned to her for hope when other people robbed the community of it. That was how she met Derek. A gang shot someone in front of the barbershop. She lifted up the yellow police tape and walked right into the shop to see how she could help.

My dad didn't meet Derek until after he got out of the game. I hid from him that he'd ever been in the game. Derek had come clean to me about all the horrific things he had done, and I had forgiven him, but I didn't think my dad or six brothers would understand or believe he'd changed, so I kept quiet. A family friend saw a story about Derek's work to prevent trafficking in the *Boston Herald*, though, and showed it to my dad.

I was right. In their mind, once a pimp, always a pimp. I was their daughter and sister, after all. My dad didn't like it. My brothers wouldn't tolerate it. They threatened to hurt him if I didn't quit seeing him. Derek held steadfast, though, determined to prove he was a changed man. Time won them over. So did my daughters. They always talked about Derek. He treats them as his own. He honors them and me, and he's teaching our son, Isaiah, how to respect women, as well. My family saw that actions really do speak louder.

We don't hide who Derek was from any of our kids because we're ending the generational trauma and poverty that manufactured a career pimp. And, I'm proud that Derek is working tirelessly to end this crime against other children. Derek isn't his past, and he doesn't want his past to become any child's future.

Kammy

**Derek's oldest daughter, Gina**

I'm incredibly proud of my dad. That wasn't always the case. In high school and as a young adult, I hid what he did from everyone except my closest friends. It wasn't easy, though.

It didn't take people too long to figure out what he did for a living when he'd show up at things. He made an impression wherever he went – the flashy clothes; big jewelry; expensive cars; long, meticulously coiffed hair. You've seen what I'm talking about – he was the spitting image of the movie version of a pimp. Regular blue-collar dads didn't look like that. And, if the dads in my neighborhood drove a car at all, it certainly didn't catch anyone's eye. So, when people asked what my dad did, I told them I didn't know.

That was true for a long time. As a child, I really didn't. As I grew older, I started noticing the similarities in music videos, TV shows, and movies. I was like, "Oh! *That's* where my dad gets all his money. It's not that my dad lied to me; he just didn't talk about it with me. I would have had an even harder time if he had lied to me about it, and I found out. He was always straightforward with whatever he did talk about – he even told me there wasn't a Santa Claus when I was in kindergarten. Not that I needed Santa Claus; my dad played that role without even donning a red suit. He always showed up bearing presents, a group of helpers, and a ton of cash. He'd drive up while I was playing outside, fan out money, and tell me to pick what I wanted. I'd pull out hundreds, fifties, twenties. As a kid, it was all exciting.

When I became a young teen, however, I started realizing how much it cost other people. I grew up in Roxbury, not far from where my dad grew up and where several of the girls who worked for him did. I realized it could have been me if circumstances were different. The thought of living that life made me ill. I struggled with a lot of mixed emotions. I loved my dad, but I knew he was exploiting females. I could tell they all thought they were deeply in love with him, but they suffered because of him. None of them – my dad or his girls – ever talked to me about what they did. And I never asked. I couldn't bear to know any more details than I had figured out on my own. It was easier as a kid to keep the movie version of a pimp in my mind. He was my dad, after all. It was enough knowing what they had to do, hearing them cry, seeing the sadness in their eyes, the wear-and-tear on their bodies and emotions.

They were so kind to me, and I felt like we were friends. I didn't know for sure if they liked me because of me or to make my dad care more about them, but I cared about their well-being. I felt awful for them when my dad got angry at them. I always knew because I'd get extra attention. He never told me why he was mad or what he did when he was, but he'd tell me they were in trouble and using me to get closer to him. I loved spending time with them as a kid, no matter their motive. They made me feel like I mattered in a world where poverty and hopelessness hung in the atmosphere. They took me shopping, horseback riding, to lake houses. Several of his girls came from the suburbs, so they exposed me to experiences kids in my neighborhood rarely got to do.

And then there was Rona. She exposed me to things that kids from my neighborhood could only dream of. I hung out with many legends during my years with Rona and went places only legends had access to. It was interesting to grow up with a pimp for a dad, to say the least.

It also made me wiser than I would have been at that age. I knew that after we went to a concert in matching outfits and the limo dropped me off safely at home, it dropped them off at work, where they never knew if they'd get raped or beaten. I also knew they made a lot of money but didn't have any money. They handed it all over to my dad; he decided what it was spent on.

Their situations always played in the back of my mind. I kept my eyes wide open when dating. I never wanted to be in the position I saw them in. I didn't want to be used. So, I always had my guard up. I'd wonder, "Is he trying to get something out of me?"

My mom certainly was more protective of me, and, ironically, I think it made my dad more protective of me, too. When I'd bump heads with my mom as a teen, he'd talk to me about how much my mom loved me. He'd tell me a lot of the girls who worked for him came from broken homes where no one loved them, and I needed to appreciate that she cared for me. He'd urge me to stay on the right path and not let some guy exploit me for feelings, money, or anything else. I knew he wanted to steer me clear of guys like him, so I listened to him.

My close friends, on the other hand, didn't see all that. They just saw the glitz and glamour. They thought my dad was cool. Girls and guys both. Pimping was in. Jay-Z's song *Big Pimpin'* landed on the Billboard Hot 100 and Rhythmic Top 40 charts. The culture glorified what my dad did, so my friends thought they were hanging out with some kind of legend, too.

That's probably why I'm honest about what my dad did with my teenage son and will be with my other two kids when they get a little older. Movies and music still idolize it, so I unglorify it. It's surprisingly hard to do that because people use the word "pimp" so lightly, so loosely. Like "Pimp my ride" or "Pimp my shoes." A man can be dating several women, and they call him a pimp. I guess that's why people think I'm playing when I tell them my dad was a pimp. I'm like, *"No. A real live pimp. A legitimate pimp. You need to listen to what I'm telling you."* I've seen what it does to girls from every culture and every demographic. It's not a game, and we **must** stop glamorizing it.

That's what I would tell any teen as a mom: "Don't fall for the glitz and glamour. You don't know the darkness underneath the surface. You can easily fall into something that looks appetizing but is decimating. Don't take everyone's promises to heart. A lot of guys will make promises they have no intention of keeping."

That's why I'm incredibly proud of my dad: He now tells teens about how he'd lure girls in with those kinds of promises. He doesn't hide anything, and he'll answer any question. A lot of people don't have the guts to do that. It's hard for anyone to admit the bad things they've done, let alone the horrific ones. Usually, parents are proud of their children. I'm proud of my dad because I've watched his transformation. I've seen him rise from the dregs of pimping and drugs to become a protector of children. He's incredibly passionate about protecting young girls from guys like he was – just like he did me – and stopping any youth from going down the path he did. I admire that.

I also respect him for not letting himself off easily. He went through a lengthy grieving process for what he did. He still regrets it, but he refuses to let it define his future. He's determined to use his dark past to give kids a bright future.

I know many people think it's a ploy to get close to teens; or get angry that he didn't serve any jail time for trafficking. I understand the concern because they didn't walk through the lengthy healing process with him. They didn't watch him one day lay down a life of luxury and never look back when he fell back into poverty. He's been out 13 years without any thought of returning to the game. He's fully committed to helping youth and equipping those who work with them. He did all that after he accepted Jesus Christ as his Savior and developed a close relationship with God. God is everything to him now.

As for me, he's always been my dad. He was the first man I ever loved. It hurt to share him as a child with a lot of girls who adored him for all the wrong reasons. Now, I have the honor of sharing him with a lot of people for all the right reasons. He can teach people things no one else can, and I hope you will open your heart to learning from him.

Gina

**Derek's spiritual father and Boston pastor**
On the outside, I could tell the person who took a seat at my kitchen table was a pimp. He had perfectly manicured hands and hair. He had a smooth swag about himself. At that time, I did not know for sure what he did for a living. However, unbeknown to me, one of his victims, who had visited our Bible study many times, brought him. I could tell he was curious about why some guy would invite people to his kitchen to talk about the Bible. He listened intently, trying to figure out what we were talking about. He was inquisitive, asking probing questions. Later he told me he thought it was strange to have a startup church in a house, but he was glad he came. More surprisingly, Derek talked openly about his life once he got more acquainted with me. As he opened up, I could see someone different on the inside – I saw a broken man, a man hungry to understand spiritual things, desperate to find his real identity.

A deep and lasting friendship started soon after. I became Derek's pastor and spiritual father, taking him under my wing because I saw something in him that he didn't know he had yet.

He came faithfully to Bible study, as well as the church services we had started in the basement of a community center. But it was our private conversations that convinced me Derek knew God didn't create him to harm other people but help them. Many people hide their struggles, the challenges of walking away from something lucrative. He talked about it frankly and transparently. He wanted out of the streets, but they didn't want to let go, and he knew it. The streets pulled him like a magnet. That's not surprising. He had found his identity there most of his life. He felt in control there. He felt needed by those he manipulated and profited off of. He'd never had any of that before the streets became his home.

The streets weren't the only magnet, though. The Holy Spirit kept yanking on his heart. Derek and I had a lot in common. We were close to the same age; we both grew up in Boston's inner city. We knew many of the same people, but we didn't meet until he walked through the door of my home. We also both were familiar with pimping and selling drugs. I wasn't involved in that lifestyle, but my brother, Deke, was. I watched helplessly as they destroyed his life. The pull of the streets was too strong for Deke, so I had a lot of insight into Derek's inner turmoil. For a while, my brother didn't want to hear about God. However, I'm thankful he accepted Jesus Christ as his Savior on his deathbed. Unlike my brother, Derek yearned to learn more about God; his heart was tender. He kept persevering even as the streets would pull him back.

I knew he was battling, so I created a position for him that is called an "armor bearer" in some church circles. He became a key person for my security. That kept him closer to me so I could regularly sow spiritually into him and walk with him through the process of deliverance. Through that, I've had the honor of watching him transform. He grew from a person who forced people to do it his way to one who realized his way didn't work. His lust for a lavish lifestyle evolved into a love for the finer things of life, and by finer things, I mean family, friends, and his relationship with Christ. He went through years of spiritual battles and challenges, but he kept turning back to Christ until he won freedom from pimping and drug addiction. We lost contact for years, but we later reconnected. Several years ago, he came to a New Year's Eve worship service at our church, and I was ecstatic that he looked great.

When his pursuit shifted from easy money to Jesus, God delivered him from pimping, but it was a conscious effort on Derek's part. This book has been in the making for more than a decade now because he's been working hard to share his story with others, so they can find their true identity as he did. He's had plenty of opportunities to go back to manipulation and fast money, but he's stayed the course. His powerful story of eventual triumph over childhood abuse, neglect, and the streets has the power to change the story of many of our vulnerable and at-risk youth.

Bishop William E. Dickerson II
Greater Love Tabernacle
Boston, MA

# Appendix C:
# Terminology Use In The Game

Because I limited my trafficking career to girls and women, we'll focus on vernacular used for them in the game. Specific terms also exist for boys. Keep in mind that terminology varies by region, and even city, and changes with time. This list gives you insights into their thinking, however. This list contains words and terms that are traumatic and graphic, especially in the sex-buyer terminology list. However, they are important for us to understand as we work with children who have lived them.

| Terms Related to Those Who Are Exploited For Commercial Sex Or Chose Sex Work | Meaning |
|---|---|
| Fresh | New girl. |
| Break In, Seasoning | Preparing new girls for commercial sex, typically through having sex with them or raping them, but can include other means, such as a "boot camp" where they are taught the tricks of the trade. |
| Turn Out | First time in prostitution. |
| Stable, Folks, Breezes | The group of girls under a pimp's control. |
| Bottom Bitch, Bottom Girl, Bottom | The highest-ranking girl in the pimp's stable or group of girls who controls and supervises the others. |
| Wifey, Wife-in-law, Sister-in-law, Sister Wife, Cousin-in-law | What the pimp makes the girls call each other or they choose to call each other. |
| Senior Citizen | A girl older than 24; see also *Trafficker-Related Terms*. |
| Lot Lizard | A derogatory term for girls at truck stops. They solicit customers by going truck to truck. Truckers might signal they want to purchase sex by flashing their headlights. Some truckers have signs in their windows that read, *"No Lot Lizards allowed."* |

| Continued: Terms Related to Those Who Are Exploited For Commercial Sex Or Chose Sex Work | Meaning |
|---|---|
| Rabbit | Girl who frequently changes pimps. |
| Outlaw, Renegade | A girl in prostitution without a pimp. Tiny was an example of a renegade. |
| Square, Square Up | Someone who tries to get out of the game to live a normal or "square" life. Silver is an example of someone who squared up, see also *Law Enforcement-Related Terms*. |
| Couch Surfing | Homeless youth's temporary use of the home of a friend, family member, or acquaintance for a place to sleep. A common situation for at-risk youth vulnerable to trafficking. |
| **Trafficker- or Pimp-Related Terms** | **Meaning** |
| Saucin' | Pimping. |
| Mack, Player | Pimp. |
| Romeo Pimp, Loverboy | Controls his girls through "love." |
| Finesse Pimp | Controls his girls mainly through psychological manipulation. Derek was a finesse pimp for most of his career. |
| Guerrilla Pimp | Controls his girls through extreme, frequent violence. Think prisoner of war. As Derek's pimp mentality grew, he turned to guerrilla pimp tactics when angered. |
| CEO Pimp | Offers potential victim a role in a music video, modeling contract, or similar opportunity for fame. |
| Catcher, Watcher | Usually a younger, "wannabe pimp" paid by an experienced pimp to watch his girls to ensure they follow orders. |
| Selling the Love | Boyfriend syndrome. |

| | |
|---|---|
| Daddy | What girls often are commanded or choose to call their pimps, as in Derek's case. |
| Facilitator | Person who "facilitates" trafficking, such as motel managers who take pay to turn their heads or a ride-share driver who shuttles the pimp's stable. |
| Tennis Shoe Pimp | A term pimps use for another pimp with only one or two girls he doesn't take care of well; low-budget pimp. Derek would have been considered a tennis shoe pimp when he was not supplying his girls with hotel rooms and other necessities as defined by the game. |
| Wannabe Pimp | Pimp in training as Derek was when he convinced Lacy to prostitute herself. |
| Recruiter | A person responsible for finding new people to work for the organization. Recruiters can include the pimp, the bottom or other members of the stable, or someone not part of the organization who the pimp pays. Both Derek and Denise recruited, as well as most of the members of his stable. |
| Tracker | A person who tracks and returns an escaped victim to a pimp for a fee. |
| Selling the Dream | The pimp sells girls the dream of making money and enjoying life together because of it. This was a frequent tactic Derek used. |
| Senior Citizen | A pimp in his 30s; see also *Victim-Related Terms*. |
| Choose Up or Down, Trade Up or Down | The status level of a pimp when a girl goes from one pimp to another. |

322

| Sex Buyer-Related Terms | Meaning |
| --- | --- |
| Trick, Date, Sex Buyer, John, Exploiter | A person who pays for a sex act. The act of prostitution. |
| Kerb Crawler, Curb Crawler, Curb Crawling | Driving slowly down the street with the intent to pick up someone to pay for sex. A driver checking out the "merchandise." |
| Hobbyist | The buyer who is serious about his "hobby," typically a frequent buyer and does such things as write online reviews of the person he bought. |
| Incall | An arrangement where the buyer comes to the person he is soliciting sex from, such as to the person's hotel room. |
| Outcall | The buyer takes person he solicited sex from to the location of his choice, which can mean increased trauma and danger for her. The girl or her pimp do not have any control in an outcall situation. |
| Peel a Trick, Hitting a Lick | When a girl steals money, checkbooks, credit cards, or other items from the sex buyer. The items may be sold or used by the pimp, the girls, or members of a prostitution ring. They might also be used for identity theft. It may happen before or after performing a sex act. |
| Roll a Trick | When a girl, pimp, or associates rob a sex buyer with force. Usually involves weak or intoxicated buyers. |
| Trick Roll | Getting as much money as possible from the buyer by means such as stealing his wallet. |

| Terms Used By Buyers In Reviews and "John Board" Discussions | Meaning |
|---|---|
| *Note: Ads for commercial sex also contain some of these terms, including willingness for fetishes and dominance, whether it's the person's willingness or the pimp forcing it for additional payment.* | |
| GFE | Girlfriend Experience. Soliciting sex more like making love than a typical commercial sexual encounter. |
| SYT | Sweet Young Thing. |
| PSE | Porn Star Experience. A buyer seeking a session that provides an experience like in a pornographic video or feels like a date with a porn star. |
| Dead Fish Experience | Describing the person solicited for sex as unresponsive and lying still similar to a lifeless fish. |
| DFK | Deep French Kissing. |
| Bag, Hat, Beret, Cover, Party Hat, Raincoat | Condom. |
| CBJ | Covered Blow Job; with a condom. |
| BB, Bareback | Without a condom. |
| OWO | Oral Without Condom. |
| BBBJ | Bare Back Blow Job; no condom. |
| BBBJNQNS | Bare Back Blow Job No Quit No Spit; oral sex completed with swallowing. |
| BLS | Ball Licking and Sucking. |
| DT | Deep Throat, entire penis "swallowed" by the victim. |
| Rimming | Oral sex on the anus. |
| Stealthing | "Rape adjacent" act where the buyer removes his condom without consent (natural right, male supremacy). |

| Continued: Terms Used By Buyers In Reviews and "John Board" Discussions | Meaning |
|---|---|
| MSOG | Multiple Shots On Goal; buyer climaxes more than once during a paid session. |
| Spinner | Very petite, so much so that she can easily spin around on his penis. Reminiscent of the Sit 'n Spin toy. |
| Poon, Kitty | Vagina and surrounding area. Buyer descriptions include "bold," "partially shaven," "trimmed," and "natural." |
| DATY | Dine at the "Y." |
| DDP | Double Digit Penetration of the vagina and anus. |
| Fisting | Forcing the entire fist in the vagina or anus. |
| BDSM | Bondage, Discipline, Sadomasochism. |
| Dominant, Dom | A buyer who exerts power and torture over the submissive in BDSM. |
| Submissive, Sub | At the mercy of the dominant buyer for BDSM. |
| Breath Control | Bondage play where access to oxygen is controlled. |
| Face Sitting | Dominant person sits on the face of the submissive person to force oral-genital or oral-anal contact as a form of erotic humiliation. |
| CG, Cowgirl | The victim is on top, facing the buyer. |
| Missionary | The buyer is on top. |
| K9 | Doggy style. |
| COF | Cum On Face; buyer ejaculates on the victim's face. |
| Pearl Necklace | Buyer ejaculates on victim to produce a white "necklace." |

| Squirting, Squirter | Female ejaculation. |
|---|---|
| 420, 420 Friendly | Will smoke marijuana with the buyer. |
| **Money-Related Terms** | **Meaning** |
| Doughski | Money. |
| Donation | Payment for commercial sex. |
| Quota | Amount of money a girl must give the pimp before she is done for the night. |
| Choosing Fee | The money a pimp requires from a girl to join his stable. Derek's typical choosing fee was $500. He wouldn't make the phone call to the other pimp until he got choosing fee. China is an example of a girl who paid him that fee. |
| Break | When a girl gives the money she has earned to her pimp; the pimp might break her several times a night. |
| Follow Your Money | A phrase a pimp uses when a girl who doesn't work for him gives him her money. He is urging her to "follow her money" to become part of his stable. However, she might give him money without choosing him as her pimp. For example, China gave Derek money several times before choosing him. |
| Charge, Put a Charge On | Penalty for getting out of pocket. If a girl looks at another pimp or talks to him but doesn't choose him, the pimp puts a charge on her, meaning he takes her money. D Money put a charge on Kayla. Derek beat her for getting out of pocket and losing his money. |

| Continued: **Money-Related Terms** | Meaning |
|---|---|
| Walking-Around Money, Fronts | Money a pimp gives his girls to use for transportation, drinks, condoms, bail, and other expenses. |
| Pimp Hard | Raising quotas, reducing rest time, or requiring a girl to accept dangerous sex buyers she would ordinarily avoid. |
| Buy and Sell | Pimps' disposal of girls who no longer match the profile sought by the pimp's regular clientele or who they consider problematic. |
| Automatic | The pimp's stable runs on "automatic," with the money continuing to pour in, when he is not present. The bottom usually runs the stable when he is gone, whether in a different town or in jail. |

| **Game-Related Terms** | Meaning |
|---|---|
| The Game, The Life | The people, rules, language, and hierarchy involved in prostitution. |
| Reckless Eyeballing | When a girl is engaged in eye contact too long with another pimp and appears interested in him, his car, clothes, girls, etc. Reckless Eyeballing gives the pimp the "right" to break her. Kayla engaged in reckless eyeballing when she was in Boston and Derek was in LA. |
| Campaigning, Sweat | Pimp targeting another pimp's girls to work for him. |
| Knocked | Pimp's girl chose another pimp. |
| Staying in Pocket | Staying loyal to the pimp. |
| Out of Pocket | When a girl speaks, looks at, or makes gestures to another pimp, suggesting she wants to work for him. |

| Make a Move, Make a Mad Move | When a girl chooses another pimp. A mad move is when she does it in anger and might go right back. That is one reason for the choosing fee. |
|---|---|
| Serve | Letting another pimp know that his girl chose you. |
| Lay Some Drag | The words and actions pimps teach girls to use when interacting with people not involved in prostitution. |
| Kiddie Stroll | Track known to have several minors. |
| Track, Stroll, Blade, Ho Stroll | An area well-known for prostitution, such as the Combat Zone in Boston, International Boulevard in Oakland, or Harry Hines in Dallas. |
| Circuit | Group of cities or states that traffickers move their victims around. For example, one circuit runs along the East Coast from Boston to New York to New Jersey to Washington D.C., down to Florida.<br><br>Traffickers rotate their victims around a triangular circuit in Texas from Dallas-Fort Worth to Houston to San Antonio to Austin to Waco and the cities between.<br><br>An example of a smaller circuit runs between Chico, Corning, Red Bluff, and Redding in California. |
| Holine | A loose intercity or interstate network of telephone communication among pimps used to trade, buy, and sell victims. |

| Violence-Related Terms | Meaning |
|---|---|
| Rufi | A slang term for a powerful sedative drug that is illegal in the United States. It is commonly known as the "date rape" drug because of its ability to cause semi-consciousness and memory blackouts. It is associated with unwanted sexual encounters. |
| Sponge | Victims forced to cut up pieces of kitchen sponges and insert them in their vaginas to absorb menstrual blood, so the buyer will not notice as he would with a tampon. |
| Head Cut | Banging the victim's head against cement, the wall, the floor, or another object as punishment. |
| Pimp Slap | Back of hand. |
| Bitch Slap | Palm of hand. |
| Pimp Stick | A steel whip made from twisting together wire clothes hangers with the hook used as a weapon to keep the girls compliant or punish them. |
| Branding | Tattoo, brand done with hot item, or carving on a victim that is a sign of the trafficker's ownership. |
| Pimp Party | When several pimps come together to rape, beat, and/or drug someone resisting being prostituted or who got out of line by trying to escape or talk to police. |
| **Law Enforcement-Related Terms** | **Meaning** |
| The Wire | A pimp "hotline" used to get the word around about which cities or hotels are hot with law enforcement. |

| Continued: Law Enforcement-Related Terms | Meaning |
|---|---|
| Izz, Izzn | Letters added to words of communication between pimps to make law enforcement surveillance difficult and evidence problematic in court cases. When presenting evidence using this slang, prosecutors could be required to provide expert witnesses to translate for the court. Pimps often also use changing slang and code words to confound law enforcement. |
| Caught Up, Caught a Case | Arrested. |
| Five-O | Law enforcement. |
| Square | Law enforcement and others who are not in the lifestyle; see also *Victim-Related Terms*. |

# D Appendix D: CSEC Harm Reduction Case Study

## CSEC Recidivism and Harm Reduction: Current State

Greetings, this is Dr. Deena Graves. I often ask myself, "What would it take to create a different future for our children?" To answer that in the case of CSEC and harm reduction, let me walk you through two causal loops. Don't panic. We're not going to go into all the technical details of the figures. Instead, we'll walk through these causal loops with the eyes of a highly traumatized child – a child who was sold not just for sex but bondage sex and videos, which includes dominance, submission, restraint, sadism, and extreme fetishes.

We'll call her Ariana for the purposes of this illustration. Let's begin Ariana's journey in the top left-hand side of *Figure 1*, where she first disclosed to me as a CSEC victim after seeing *The Traps of a Trafficker*©.

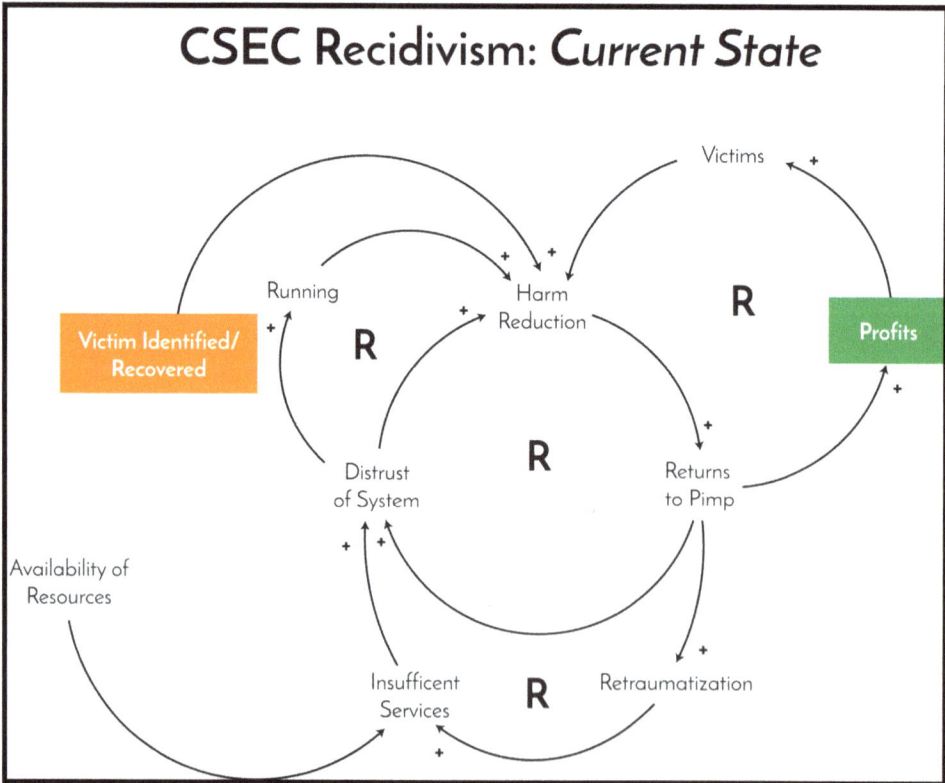

*Figure 1: CSEC Recidivism: Current State.*

Before we start her journey, let me give you a few details of the case so that you have the same view as Ariana. When she was 3, she witnessed her parents commit murder, and, when I met her at 16, she could still remember the sensation of the blood hitting her face. Her parents went to prison, and she moved in with her great-grandmother. She did not receive therapy. That is not uncommon for children that age. People assume they will forget. They don't. So, she found her own coping mechanisms, including sex at 10. That led to rape, and other adults started introducing their preferred coping mechanisms to her, such as drugs and pornography. It eventually led to hard drugs and bondage porn.

It's not that she wanted all that. It's that she couldn't escape the nightmares playing over and over in her mind. Recurring flashbacks cause victims to relive the trauma even decades later in a never-ending nightmare unless their brains are intentionally rewired.[113] Hers wasn't. Actually, that's not true. Trauma, drugs, and porn rewired it, which, not surprisingly, caused the wiring to short circuit.

She ended up in the arms of two homeless men who tattooed her with their symbol, promised her they would make her bondage fantasies come true, fed her meth, and let people rip her body apart for up to 37 days at a time while she was oblivious. When I met her, she was sitting in a juvenile detention center with dislocated bones, a disc in her back thrown out of place, and a rip so severe she had told her great-grandmother that she was on her period.

And so much shame that no one even knew any of this. None of it. Not even the dislocated bones.

That's what's on her mind as she enters our illustration. Literally. At least 13 years of trauma upon trauma – cruel, reprehensible, inhumane carnage of her body, mind, and soul – has free reign in her mind because the inner nightmare has never been healed.

Her exact words to me when she disclosed were: "I want help, but I'm worried about my mom disowning me and what it will do to my great-grandmother and this man who's like a dad to me if they find out."

And, then, a little later, she asked me why she wanted to stop fantasizing about bondage pornography but couldn't. Why she couldn't stop craving it despite the way it was destroying every fiber of her being.

That is an unmistakable cry for help. Obviously, she didn't want all that, or she wouldn't have clawed her way through the shame and humiliation to tell me her story and admit she couldn't stop thinking about bondage sex no matter how much damage it had done to her. Think about if you had to share those kinds of intimate details and desires with a stranger – especially while locked up in a detention center.

All the pain, humiliation, embarrassment, torment, and cravings are with her as she steps into the causal loop. Her vision is blinded by the night-mares and fantasies.

Despite that, details poured from Ariana like water from a dam that gave way under pressure. She gave me enough information in a 30-minute conversation to build a comprehensive, unique treatment plan and identify the two traffickers, as well as a trafficker who had done similar things to her friend. Let me pause and tell you that's because I built instant relation-ship and trust with her. There's an art to that. That's what traffickers do; that's why Derek keeps telling us to think like a trafficker. I also didn't use a screening tool. Traumatized kids notice that.

Even if those details had not poured out, I wouldn't have asked a bunch of questions since it wasn't the time for that ... YET. Let me stress that. It's not the time for questions or to fill in a form. She needed me to be some-one who cared about her in that moment. Nothing more. Keep in mind, too, that trauma had more control of that conversation than her or me. We don't want to cause unintentional additional trauma or trigger a flight response by inciting the trauma.

I only asked a couple of crucial things. Like the phone numbers of the two homeless men since she had told me she could always reach them by phone when she needed a meth fix. That question was for the protection of other children.

After mustering up the courage to tell me her story, she finally had a sense of freedom and hope as she entered this illustration. It wasn't easy for her to get that story out through the uncontrollable sobbing, but she had finally managed to let out a cry for help after 13 years of trying to work it out by herself.

And then.

Then, she got an unexpected offer. Not from me. Later. It goes some-thing like this: "We understand adults have exercised power and control over your life. We don't want to do that. We're going to let you make the decisions regarding your safety so that you can gain your own sense of power."

She takes that in for a moment. She holds the power. That's a new concept. It felt good. For a few minutes. Maybe even a few days. Then they come back. Not the predators. The nightmares. The fantasies. *They* hold all the power. They merely give predators easy access. She doesn't have the strength to fight them off – the nightmares, fantasies, or predators who can make them temporarily go away. Neither does she have the stage of brain development or coping mechanisms. The only coping mechanisms she knows are sex, drugs, and pornography.

The freedom and hope she felt just died a quick death. Harm reduction doesn't stand a fighting chance against her lived experiences.

With no relief in sight, she has to get back to her traffickers to get a meth and bondage fix. That's why when I asked for the homeless guys' phone numbers, she told me they had changed their numbers right as she got detained and sent to juvenile detention. They were the only ones who provided her an escape from the torment holding her mind captive. She couldn't hand over her only relief until she knew she had another way to get rid of the pain. I didn't tell her I knew she was lying. She knew I knew. But it wasn't the time for that conversation.

Her life to that point had been a vicious, self-perpetuating cycle. Since the comprehensive, unique treatment plan she gave us the detailed strategy for never happened, it's likely we'd find her stuck in that cycle now *if we went looking for her. But we often don't.*

I can assure you more predators did.

Although she provided us insights for a unique treatment plan, that cycle is not unique to her. It's scattered with a trail of dangerous, life-threatening coping mechanisms because the inner terror holds all the power. That's the cycle Derek was caught in. And his victims. And countless other children.

That cycle typically has four possible outcomes:

- She continues to move around it as a victim, trapped in a hopeless existence.
- She follows it down the path of predator, as Derek did.
- She overdoses, commits suicide, or is murdered.
- Someone disrupts it again.

She might not ever work up the courage or trust to tell someone again. Even if she did, our job is harder, her road to recovery longer. The hope of help for all the trauma she'd dealt with herself as a child and teen got buried in a landslide of more trauma, however unintentional and well-meaning. Her brain does its job and locks it up tighter than a bank vault after a robbery. That makes it more exhausting for her to dig herself out or us to help her to.

There is some good news in all this. *For the traffickers*. It means more money for them. Triple profits, in reality. From:

1. Selling her drugs.
2. Selling her body.
3. Featuring her in porn flicks.

That's as intoxicating for a trafficker as more needles for a heroin addict, fueling their lust for more victims to line their greedy pockets. And, it is there that we again encounter harm reduction with both new and old faces. Self-perpetuating cycles birth self-perpetuating cycles.

**CSEC Recidivism: Desired State**

Derek discusses in length how traffickers recognize a deep need in abused-and-neglected children. They respond to it with overwhelming effectiveness. We don't *HAVE* to let them outthink us. We're smarter, and we genuinely *CARE* about our kids. They care about their profits and their pleasure, as he stated multiple times. That gives us a strategic advantage if we choose to use it. I suggest that we do not have time to wait. The time to replace harm reduction with harm elimination is *now*. There are different ways to get there, but let's look at one way based on our current case study.

Let's start back on the far left of our causal loop when Ariana first disclosed.

This time, instead of harm reduction tools, let's do what the nurse did with Derek and tell Ariana we believe in her and her pain doesn't have to continue. Let's do as we discussed and help her understand we care about her as a person, not a case or form. We want to provide her with an empathetic but non-invasive human connection during the hours immediately following disclosure or recovery. This sets the stage for short- and long-term adaptive functioning and coping and a willingness to engage with therapy.[114] If we follow Ariana around the causal loop, we see it increases her likelihood of staying in placement, too.

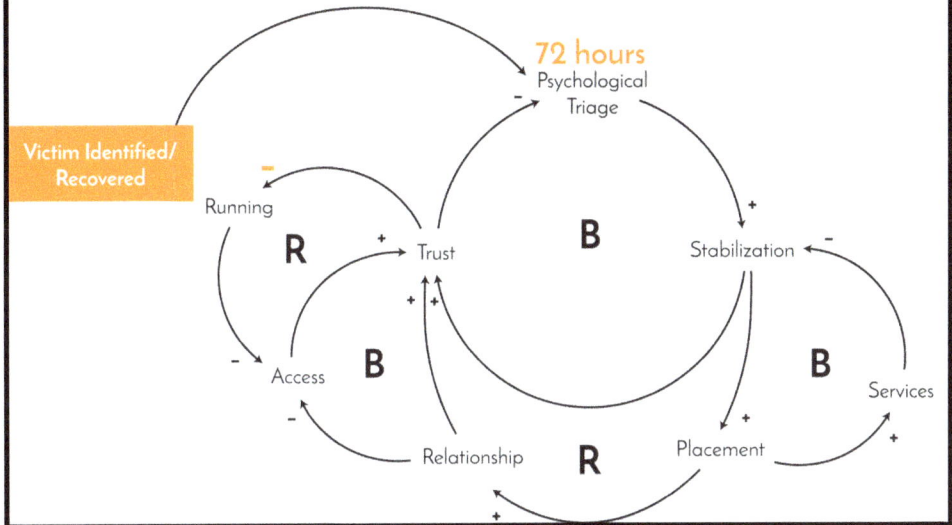

*Figure 2. CSEC Recidivism: Desired State.*

Let's also spend the first 72 hours grounding her instead of overwhelming her with goals that her locked-up brain cannot yet comprehend. Our goal is to help her in the "immediate aftermath" of the trafficking to curtail the distress. We'll call it psychological triage and equip her with positive self-coping tools. There's one right for her, and we want to help her find it. You'd be surprised at how many children have never been armed with positive self-coping tools, so they turn to destructive ones like Ariana. Sex, drugs, pornography, alcohol, self-harm. You know the list. They don't have the right weapons to win the war for their well-being and destines, so they lose on the battlefield of dangerous coping mechanisms.

Once we get her grounded or stabilized, we can develop our comprehensive, unique treatment plan based on the in-depth, informative disclosure she gave. We don't have to risk unintentional additional trauma with invasive questions. At this point, she would have a hard time putting words to what she is experiencing because trauma hasn't loosened its grip yet.

Let's make a hard stop for a word of caution. Both Ariana's hard work and ours will crumble underneath us if we do not have the resources for and knowledge of complex trauma to connect her to the ***right*** kind of services. Don't let the vivid reminder of that vicious, self-perpetuating cycle dim in your memory. We cannot forget we already have a system serving more children than available resources. If we do not plan ahead, it could desta-bilize our ability to stabilize victimized youth. We must develop a strategic protocol for what is needed at this intersection ***before*** we hit it if we want any chance of keeping Ariana in a mindset where she wants our help.

We also must ensure her entire team has a common understanding of words, tools, and processes we use. We often assume people have a shared definition of words like "trauma-informed," but they don't.

With our strategic protocol and needed knowledge, let's head back left now, moving up the bottom loop. The more time Ariana spends in a nur-turing placement, the more relationship and trust – and opportunity for healing – she builds. The more we're chipping away at the trauma bond she's formed with traffickers, drugs, and other harmful coping mecha-nisms. Turn left, and you see that reduces the impulse to run, snatching access from the arms of the traffickers. It lessens their profits while putting a solid case with decision-makers for more funding in our hands.

The facts, insights, and strategies from these two diagrams, plus some of the other tools M³ Transformations offers, provide your team with the power and potential to develop a protocol that slashes the recidivism rate and prevents new victims. That, in turn, will reduce the number of victims committing suicide and other harm to themselves. It also will divert youth off the path of trafficking and other predatory actions.

Don't delay. Protect our kids from becoming victims or predators. And protect yourself and your organization.

# E Appendix E:
## CSEC Red Flags And Warning Signs

*Note: The following indicators could signal a victim. You typically will want to look for a combination of these warning signs. This is a general list of red flags. Understanding the red flags or warning signs specific to your profession is essential to identifying victims; lack of understanding is why we often miss them.*

- Truancy.
- Running away.
- Gang involvement.
- Seems disoriented; drugged.
- Inappropriate clothing for weather; situation.
- Malnourished or eats as if ravenously hungry.
- Sudden change in attire, behavior, possessions.
- Withdrawn, depressed, fearful, crying frequently.
- Suddenly more confident and boasting about travel or gifts she's received.
- Older, controlling boyfriend/friend.
- Branding, tattoos, carvings.
- Scripted answers, inconsistent stories, won't or not allowed to talk or look at you.
- Travels to other cities frequently.
- Varied stages of bruising; clumps of makeup covering bruising.
- Burns, scars, mutilations.
- Signs of self-harm.
- Motel room cards; escort service cards, condoms, large amount of cash, gift cards.
- Uses terms common to the sex industry.
- Poorly formed or rotted teeth.
- Stunted growth.

# F

# Appendix F: CSEC Vulnerabilities And Red Flags Traffickers Watch For

- Bored.
- Fearful.
- Hungry.
- Runaway.
- On probation.
- Nowhere to stay.
- Low self-esteem.
- Unhappy home life.
- Doesn't like school.
- Wants independence.
- Lonely/doesn't feel belongs.
- In the same spot two-three days.
- Wearing same clothes multiple days.
- Thinks parents/caregivers do not trust.
- Goes in the restroom to wet hair down.
- Doesn't feel important/sense of self-worth.
- Parents/caregivers too strict/feels smothered.
- Can't buy things like other kids hangs out with.
- In foster care/group home/residential treatment.
- Believes not as loved as the other kids in the house.
- Tears.
- Poor or no hygiene.
- No cell phone.
- Substance or alcohol abuse or dependency.

# G Appendix G: Runaway Prevention Toolkit

Greetings Valued Caregiver,

Thank you for the thoughtful and nurturing care you provide children living in your home. Your passion and commitment make a tremendous difference in the lives of highly traumatized youth, and we are grateful for your dedication. We also understand it adds pressure to your already full lives. Therefore, we wanted to equip you with ***cutting-edge runaway prevention tools*** to use in conversations with the youth in your care. After the discussion, give the youth a copy, so they can go on the offense against their traumatic memories rather than merely reacting to them. In the following ***Runaway Prevention Toolkit***, you will find two tools.

***Short-term Coping Handout***. Many times, youth run from care or spiral into other adverse behaviors because they do not have ***any*** positive self-coping mechanisms. They also often do not understand that their reactions are normal after living through a traumatic experience, so they feel guilty, ashamed, worthless, helpless, or similar emotions. The memories of the trauma are free to assault them again and again unless they learn how to shut them down. The first handout in this toolkit (*Dealing with Bad Memories*) helps them understand their reactions are normal and what they can feel like. The second handout, *Short-term Coping Techniques*, teaches them how to take their brains off the emotional roller coaster. Make a copy for youth in your care. When you give it to them, you can say something such as:

> *"I know you have lived through some painful things. Sometimes, the bad memories can play over and over in our minds like a movie on rewind. Those feelings are normal. This sheet will help you understand what you are feeling and some things you can do to help when it feels like you can't get that movie out of your head. I use some of these, too, when I'm feeling stressed. What if we practice a few of them together? I want you to know you can always talk to me when you feel anxious. I want you to feel safe here."*

***I've Got This: My Safety Plan Handouts***. The subsequent two handouts (*I've Got This: My Safety Plan* and *We Care: Our Commitment to Your Safety Plan*) are additional proactive prevention tools. These handouts will help youth think through **why they run** and **how they can fight the impulse**. They also will help you have an effective conversation about how you can work together to defuse the things that make them want to flee. Use this sample conversation starter when the youth is calm, in a good mood, and settled in in your home:

> *"We talked about how a bad memory can feel like a movie playing over and over in your mind. Sometimes, no matter how hard we try, it seems like the only way to make it stop is to run away from it. When we do that, though, it can cause more bad things to happen and even put us in extreme danger. I want you to know I mean it when I say I want you to feel safe here, and you are the only one who knows what does make you feel safe. Would you mind thinking about these questions and writing out your answers to them so that we can talk them through? Then, we can work together to develop a plan that makes you feel safe. It'll be a contract between us. We'll both sign it and hold each other accountable. In the beginning, we'll look at it every week to see if we need to change anything.*
>
> *After you start feeling comfortable, we'll look at it every couple of months. I'm going to write it on my calendar for us to do that, so we make sure it happens."*

# DEALING WITH BAD MEMORIES

When something reminds you of a bad memory, emotions can flood your brain like a massive wave coming up from the ocean and engulfing you. No matter how hard you try, you can't "swim" back to the surface. It feels as if the wave became part of you.

## YOU CAN FEEL ANXIOUS AND FEARFUL...

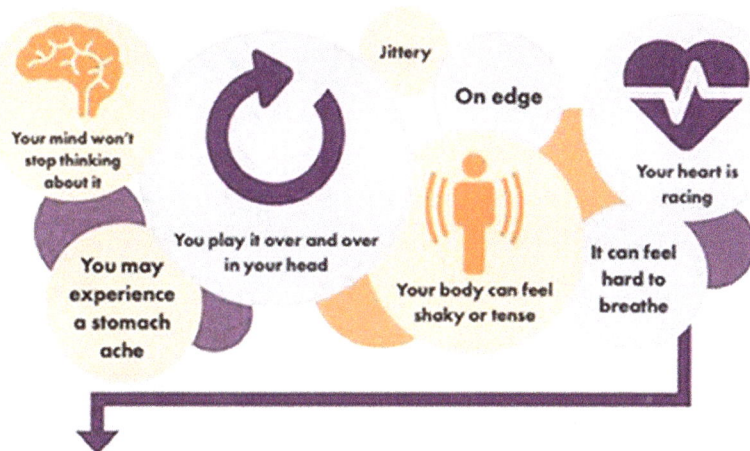

Jittery

On edge

Your mind won't stop thinking about it

You play it over and over in your head

You may experience a stomach ache

Your body can feel shaky or tense

Your heart is racing

It can feel hard to breathe

## THERE IS ACTUALLY A REASON FOR THIS.

Your brain has a part called the Amygdala – it's an emergency alarm. When something triggers that alarm, it begins to tell your mind and body you are in danger, and your body begins to feel unsafe.

## BUT HERE ARE SOME WAYS TO HELP CALM YOUR ANXIETY DOWN:

**Breathe.** Place your hand on your stomach and breathe in to make your stomach full (as if you are watching a balloon fill up) then slowly breathe out. Repeat that several times until you start to feel calm.

**Visualize a safe place.** Imagine yourself in your favorite place and let your body experience the feelings you get when you are safe.

**Take control of what your body feels.** Take a walk; take a bath or shower; jump rope, ride your bike or do other exercise.

**Listen to music or do art.**

**Get it out.** Journal what you are experiencing. Yell into your pillow.

**Talk to a trusted adult.**

TRAPS OF A TRAFFICKER

M³ Transformations

# Short-term Coping Techniques

- Place one hand over your heart and your other hand over your stomach and press lightly. Now switch hands. Either way works. Do whichever feels most comfortable.

- Press 10 places on your palm with the thumb of your other hand. Hold a few seconds. Press the center of your palm last and hold it 10 seconds.

- Breathe in deeply for four seconds, hold it four seconds; blow out a dandelion for four seconds.

- Tap your fingers on table or leg.

- Blow a cotton ball across the table or floor with a straw or just your mouth.

- Shuffle or tap your foot on the floor.

- Visualize a safe, calm place.

- Look around and name five things you see, hear, or feel.

- Journal.

- Exercise.

- Hit your pillow with whiffle ball bat.

- Bang a drum.

- Dance to loud music.

- Laugh out loud.

- Kick a ball against a wall; throw a tennis ball against the wall.

- Eat a peppermint.

- Write a letter about what you are angry, fearful, or ashamed about and then tear it up.

- Remind yourself of a time you were strong. What gave you strength then?

- Creative activity such as chalk art, drawing, clay, or finger painting

- Go outside. Nature and daylight reduces the bad, increases the good.

### What coping skills do you already use?

TRAPS OF A TRAFFICKER

M³ Transformations

# I'VE GOT THIS: MY SAFETY PLAN

In the moment, running away can feel like the safest option. However, leaving or not
returning can lead to many life-threatening situations. For example, sex traffickers intentionally
target teens who run. Sadly, research is showing almost 50 percent of trafficked teens try to escape through
suicide because the trauma eventually becomes more than they can handle. Think through the questions below
to come up with a safer alternative than taking off. Sign and date it to hold yourself accountable to what you
believe is a safer plan. Use more paper if you need it.

1. I would feel safe here if...

2. What's happening when I start to feel I need to leave or not come back? In other words, what makes
me want to run?

3. When I start to feel I need to leave, what can I do to stop the urge?

4. When I start to feel I have to run, what can someone else do to help me stop the impulse? Who do I
feel comfortable talking to about not leaving?

5. What **ARE** the possible dangers if I do go?

6. What am I running **TO**?

7. Where is a safe place I can go if I feel I absolutely cannot stay?

8. How can I stay connected to people in my life if I do leave?

9. If I run, what would make me feel comfortable coming back?

10. If I were to make my own missing-person flyer, the main thing I would say is...

11. After I run, I feel...

Signed:                                          Date:

TRAPS OF A TRAFFICKER                    M³ Transformations

# WE CARE: OUR COMMITMENT TO YOUR SAFETY PLAN

You matter to our family. It is important to us that you feel safe here and that you feel you belong. After discussing your answers with you, we commit to the following:

*Family member signatures:*          *Date:*

TRAPS OF A TRAFFICKER

M³ Transformations

# Acknowledgments

We are deeply grateful for our families. They've supported our work in so many ways, which often comes with great sacrifice for them.

A special thank you to Derek's wife, Kammy; daughter, Gina; and long-time spiritual father, Bishop Dickerson, for their contributions to this book.

We also would like to thank the professionals, first responders, foster parents, and others who pour into the lives of abused-and-neglected children. They, too, make many personal sacrifices that impact them and their families. We appreciate all you do for children and all we've learned from you over the years.

A huge thank you to Cheryl R. Welch for editing this book. She is a meticulous copy editor whose brilliant and insightful suggestions we knew would make the book a hundred times more meaningful and impactful.

Finally, we are incredibly grateful to Denise Williams for writing the foreword and providing crucial insights for other sections of the book. You might have noticed a teaser in it about her finding her true identity. That's our next labor of love. Denise's book will unpack the journey from innocent child to sex trafficking victim at 11 to complicit bottom and recruiter. The three of us will unpack the dynamics of a trafficker/bottom relationship and the added depth of psychological warfare that means for our children. Denise rose from the ashes of extreme childhood trauma and trafficker torment to now preventing other children from going down that path.

# About the Authors

## Dr. Deena Graves

Passion that inspires action is where Dr. Deena Graves' anti-trafficking story started. She could not sit back and do nothing when she first learned of the atrocity of child sex trafficking in 2009. She left her corporate leadership job and founded a nonprofit, Traffick911, in Dallas to combat one of the world's greatest atrocities, and they quickly found "M" tucked away inside a juvenile hall.

The tiny cell strained with the 16 years of relentless trauma crammed inside "M" from not only the abuse of her mom's boyfriends but of the notorious MS-13 gang. Pieces of "M's" story came tumbling out in relief – for the first time ever – when she heard the hope in Dr. Graves' personally copyrighted *Traps of a Trafficker* child sex trafficking youth prevention-and-identification program.

"M" was the first child to live at the safehouse founded by Deena. The experience with "M" inspired the name $M^3$ Transformations when she stepped down from her nonprofit and moved to California, where she carried on her work for the most vulnerable among us. Her experiences with many other children who have lived their own stories of torment at the hands of transnational crime syndicates, local gangs, street-level traffickers, and their parents inspire and influence $M^3$'s unique solutions.

She believes our children are worth our Biggest Ideas and works diligently to bring $M^3$'s clients Big Ideas that restore hope in both the children they serve and their organizations. She creates hope through cutting-edge research, the latest brain science, and strategic foresight. She believes so strongly in strategic foresight that she earned her doctorate in it.

Deena led employee communications, consulted with Fortune 500 corporations, and was a reporter before beginning her journey with abused-and-neglected children. She is an international award-winning communicator, Dallas Communicator of the Year, and adjunct professor of Communications who uses that expertise to give a voice to kids whose voice and hope have been stripped away by those preying upon them for their own pleasure and profit.

**Derek Williams**

For more than 13 years, Derek Williams has been working to get pimps, buyers, and their victims out of the game. Derek is passionate about helping people understand how traffickers prey upon our youth, the vulnerabilities they target, how they manipulate and control them once they are under their control, and how they keep them coming back. He speaks from an in-depth knowledge and understanding of how they do this after first selling his girlfriend when he was 16, and she was 14. From there, he spent 32 years as a pimp, trafficking more than 150 people in all 50 states, Canada, and Europe.

He left the game after a life-changing experience. He comprehends, acknowledges, and takes ownership of the predator he was without any excuses. Although he did not spend time in jail for trafficking, he served another kind of sentence – living with the knowledge of the decimation he caused others. He spent two years in therapy and went through an extended grieving process as he came to terms with what he had done. His deep remorse for the hurt and pain he caused so many led him to dedicate his life to getting people out and educating others about the horrors and realities of what traffickers do and how they do it. Derek puts it this way: "By unpacking my story, I hope to give you strategies to combat the hopelessness that holds many of our children captive, making them easy prey for a skilled predator or an incubator for a beast in the making. While I can never make retribution for all the lives I ravaged, I long to prevent the destruction of more of our children."

He also is passionate about teaching professionals, first responders, and caregivers how to keep our youth off the path of becoming recruiters or traffickers. He works with M$^3$ Transformations to train and consult.

# Notes

**Prologue**

[1]L. Griffin, "The Developing Teenage Brain," *Education Digest* 83, no. 7 (2018): 10-15.

[2]R.M. Hartinger-Saunders, A.R. Trouteaud, and J.M. Johnson, "Mandated Reporters' Perceptions of and Encounters With Domestic Minor Sex Trafficking of Adolescent Females in the United States," *American Journal of Orthopsychiatry* 87, no. 3 (2017): 195-205.

[3]N. Lanctot, J.A. Reid, and C. Laurier, "Nightmares and Flashbacks: The Impact of Commercial Sexual Exploitation of Children Among Female Adolescents Placed in Residential Care," *Child Abuse & Neglect* 100 (2020).

[4]C. Hounmenou and C. O'Grady, "A Review and Critique of the U.S. Responses to the Commercial Sexual Exploitation of Children," *Children and Youth Services Review* 19 (2019): 188-198.

[5]S. Tzu, *The Art of War* (Boulder, CO: Westview Press, 5th Century BC): 3.18.

**1. If These Walls Could Talk**

[6]D. Blankenhorn, *Fatherless America: Confronting Our Most Urgent Social Problem* (New York: HarperCollins, 1995).

[7]J. Block, *Lives Through Time* (New York: Psychology Press, 1971).

[8]The National Fatherhood Initiative, R. Lerner, principal investigator, *"Family Structure, Father Closeness, & Drug Abuse,"* (2004).

[9]N. Scunza, A. Allen, and C.C. Lo, "Drugs, Guns, and Disadvantaged Youths: Co-Occurring Behavior and the Code of the Street," *Crime & Delinquency* 58, no. 6 (2012): 932-953.

[10]S.L. Nock and C.J. Einolf, "The Costs of Father Absence," *National Fatherhood Initiative Report: The 100 Billion Dollar Man* (2008).

[11]G. Corneau, *Absent Fathers, Lost Sons: The Search for Masculine Identity* (Boulder, CO: Shambhala Publications, 1991).

[12]Y. Zia, S.D. Li, and T.H. Liu, "The Interrelationship Between Family Violence, Adolescent Violence, and Adolescent Violent Victimization: An Application and Extension of the Cultural Spillover Theory in China," *International Journal of Environmental Research and Public Health* 15 (2018): 371-386.

[13]The Annie E. Casey Foundation Kids Count Data Center, *"Child Population by Gender,"* (2019): https://datacenter.kidscount.org/data#USA/2/2/3,6,5,4/char/0.

[14]Infoplease, "United States Demographic Statistics," *Sandbox Networks, Inc., publishing as Infoplease* (2017): https://www.infoplease.com/us/census/demographic-statistics.

## 2. Road to Nowhere

[15]T.P. Jeffrey, "The Welfare Generation: 51.7% Kids in 2017 Lived in Households Getting Govt Assistance," *CNS News*, November 8, 2018.

[16]S.Y. Kim, "The Impact of Family Economic Status and Parental Commitment on Children: An Economic Approach to Children's Outcomes," *Purdue University Dissertation*, (1999).

[17]O. Lewis, "The Culture of Poverty," *Scientific American*, 215, no. 4 (1966): 19-25.

[18]M.M. Chilton, J.R. Rabinowich, and N.H. Woolf, "Very Low Food Security in the USA is Linked with Exposure to Violence," *Public Health Nutrition* 17, no. 1 (2014).

## 3. Betrayal of Trust

[19]A.K. Buduris, "Attachment Style and Emotion Dysregulation as Serial Mediators of Betrayal Trauma Experiences and Level of Satisfaction in Romantic Relationships," *Iowa State University, Doctoral Dissertation*, (2019).

## 4. Character Assassination

[20]R. Whitley, "How DNA Ancestry Tests Can Turn Your World Upside-Down," *Psychology Today*, March 27, 2019.

## 5. Name-Dropping

[21]Shatner Method, "'Peanuts' Teacher Calls Out Charlie Brown & Linus' – Wah Wa Wa Wah Wa Wa," YouTube Video, November 19, 2016, https://www.youtube.com/watch?v=CxC_AjFxS68.

[22]U.S. Department of Justice Office of Justice Programs, "*Children Exposed to Violence*," n.d.: https://www.ojp.gov/program/programs/cev.

[23]J.D. Osofsky, "Commentary: Understanding the Impact of Domestic Violence on Children, Recognizing Strengths, and Promoting Resilience: Reflections on Harold and Sellers (2018)," *Journal of Child Psychology and Psychiatry* 59, no. 4 (2018): 403-404.

[24]O. Paul, "Perceptions of Family Relationships and Post-Traumatic Stress Symptoms of Children Exposed to Domestic Violence," *Journal of Family Violence* 34 (2019): 331-343.

[25]W. Bunston, T. Pavlidis, and P. Cartwright, "Children, Family Violence and Group Work: Some Do's and Don'ts in Running Therapeutic Groups with Children Affected by Family Violence," *Journal of Family Violence* 31, no. 1 (2016).

[26]Ibid.

## 6. Following in His Footsteps

[27]T. Foroud, H.J. Edenberg, and J.C. Crabbe, "Genetic Research: Who Is At Risk For Alcoholism?" *Alcohol Research and Health* 33, no.1-2 (2010): 64-75.

[28]C.R. Colder, K. Shyhalla, S.E. Frndak, "Early Alcohol Use With Parental Permission: Psychosocial Characteristics and Drinking in Late Adolescence," *Journal of Addictive Behaviors* 76, no. 82 (2018).

[29]S. Sharmin, K. Yypri, M. Wadolowski, B. Raimondo, M. Khanam, et al., "Parent Characteristics Associated with Approval Of Their Children Drinking Alcohol From Ages 13 To 16 Years: Prospective Cohort Study," *Australian and New Zealand Journal of Public Health* 42, no. 4 (2018): 347-353.

[30]D.B. Pincus and A.G. Friedman, "Improving Children's Coping With Everyday Stress: Transporting Treatment Interventions to the School Setting," *Clinical Child and Family Psychology Review* 7, no. 4 (2004): 223-240.

**7. Lead by Example**

[31]C.M. Fratto, "Trauma-Informed Care for Youth in Foster Care," *Archives of Psychiatric Nursing* 30, no. 3 (2016): 439-446.

[32]R. Wamser-Nanney and C.E. Steinzor, "Factors Related to Attrition from Trauma-Focused Cognitive Behavioral Therapy," *Child Abuse & Neglect* 66 (2017): 73-83.

**8. Happy To Indulge**

[33]R.K. Payne, *A Framework for Understanding Poverty* (4th ed.), (Highlands, TX: aha! Process, 2005).

**9. Always On My Mind**

[34]J.C. Ball, L. Rosen, J.A. Flueck, and D.N. Nurco, "Lifetime Criminality of Heroin Addicts in the United States," *Journal of Drug Issues* 12, no. 3 (1982): 225-239.

[35]S.C. Brighthaupt, K.E. Schneider, J.K. Johnson, A.A. Jones, and R.M. Johnson, "Trends in Adolescent Heroin and Injection Drug Use in Nine Urban Centers in the U.S., 1999-2017," *Journal of Adolescent Health* 65, no. 2 (2019): 210-215.

[36]Substance Abuse and Mental Health Services Administration. "Results from the 2013 National Survey on Drug Use and Health: National Findings," *NSDUH Series H-34 DHHS Publication No. SMA 14-4863*, (2014).

[37]Z.P. Hohman, J.R. Keene, B.N. Harris, E.M. Niedbala, and C.K. Berke, "A Biopsychological Model of Anti-Drug PSA Processing: Developing Effective Persuasive Messages," *Prevention Science* 18, no. 8 (2017): 1006-1016.

[38]Griffin, *Developing Brain.*

**10. What's Love Got To Do With It?**

[39]D. Roe-Sepowitz, "A Six-Year Analysis of Sex Traffickers of Minors: Exploring Characteristics and Sex Trafficking Patterns," *Journal of Human Behavior in the Social Environment* 29, no. 5 (2019): 608-629.

[40]L.C. Miccio-Fonseca, "The Anomaly Among Sexually Abusive Youth: The Juvenile Sex Trafficker," *Journal of Aggression, Maltreatment & Trauma*, 26, no. 5 (2017): 558-572.

[41]I. Nyklíček, A. Vingerhoets, and M. Zeelenberg, *"Emotion Regulation and Well-Being: A View from Different Angles. Emotion Regulation and Well-Being,"* (New York: Springer, 2011): 1-9.

[42]S. McMain, A. Pos, and S. Iwakabe, "Facilitating Emotion Regulation: General Principles for Psychotherapy," *Psychotherapy Bulletin* 45, (2010): 16–21.

[43]A. Aldao, S. Nolen-Hoeksema, and S. Schweizer, "Emotion-Regulation Strategies Across Psychopathology: A Meta-Analytic Review," *Clinical Psychology Review* 30, n. 2 (2010): 217–237.

[44]Payne, Understanding Poverty.

**11. In The Money**

[45]Griffin, *Developing Brain*.

[46]Ibid.

[47]D.J. Siegel, *Brainstorm: The Power and Purpose of the Teenage Brain*, (New York, NY: Penguin, 2015).

[48]D. Graves, *"The Traps of a Trafficker©,"* (2021): https://www.m3transformations.com/protect.

**12. The Silence is Deafening**

[49]S.J. Cecchet and J. Thoburn, "The Psychological Experience of Child and Adolescent Sex Trafficking in the United States: Trauma and Resilience in Survivors," *Psychological Trauma: Theory, Research, Practice, and Policy* 6, no. 5 (2014): 482.

[50]Siegel, *Brainstorm*, 8.

[51]Dahl, *Affect Regulation*.

[52]Casey and Caudle, *Brain, Self-Control*.

[53]Galván, *Brain, Rewards*.

[54]Siegel, *Brainstorm*, 67.

**13. The Thrill Of The Ride**

[55]M. Farley, E.S. Matthews, J.M. Golding, N.M. Malmuth, and L. Jarrett, "Comparing Sex Buyers with Men Who Don't Buy Sex: New Data on Prostitution and Trafficking," *Journal of Interpersonal Violence* 32, no. 23 (2017).

[56]M.R. Di Nicola, A. Cuaduro, M. Lombardi, and P. Ruspini, *Prostitution and Human Trafficking: Focus on Clients*, (New York: Springer, 2009).

**16. Worth The Price of Admission**

[57]Substance Abuse and Mental Health Services Administration, "Harm Reduction," *U.S. Department of Health & Human Services*. https://www.samhsa.gov/find-help/harm-reduction.

[58]M. Hawk, R.W.S. Coulter, J.E. Egan, S. Fisk, M.R. Friedman, M. Tula, and S. Kinsky, "Harm Reduction Principles for Healthcare Settings," *Harm Reduction Journal* 14, no. 70 (2017).

[59]J.L. Taylor, S. Johnson, R. Cruz, J.R. Gray, D. Schiff, and S.M. Bagley, "Integrating Harm Reduction Into Outpatient Opioid Use Disorder Treatment Settings," *Journal of General Internal Medicine* 36, no. 12 (2021): 3810-3819.

[60]B.L. Paterson and C. Panessa, "Engagement as an Ethical Imperative in Harm Reduction Involving At-Risk Youth," *International Journal of Drug Policy* 19, no. 1 (2008): 24-32.

[61]S. Satel, "When Harm Reduction Harms Heroin Addicts," *Forbes*, March 24, 2016.

[62]N. Bozinoff, W. Small, C. Long, K. DeBeck, and D. Fast, "Still 'At-Risk': An Examination of How Street-Involved Young People Understand, Experience, and Engage with 'Harm Reduction' in Vancouver's Inner City," *International Journal of Drug Policy* 45 (2017): 33-39.

[63]A. Farrugia, "Assembling the Dominant Accounts of Youth Drug Use in Australian Harm Reduction Drug Education," *International Journal of Drug Policy* 25, no. 4 (2014): 663-672.

[64]J. Prochaska, "Failure to Treat Tobacco Use in Mental Health and Addiction Treatment Settings: A Form of Harm Reduction?" *Drug and Alcohol Dependence* 110, no. 3 (2010): 177-82.

[65]N. McMahon, K. Thomson, E. Kaner, and C. Bambra, "Effects of Prevention and Harm Reduction Interventions on Gambling Behaviours and Gambling Related Harm: An Umbrella Review," *Addictive Behaviors* 90 (2019): 380-388.

[66]Bozinoff et al., *Still At-Risk*.

**17. College Or (Pimping) Career?**

[67]B.L. Castleman and L.C. Page, *Summer Melt: Supporting Low-Income Students Through the Transition to College*. (Cambridge, MA: Harvard Education Press, 2014).

[68]S. Carr, "The Real Reasons Many Low-Income Students Don't Go To College," *The Hechinger Report*, February 26, 2013.

**18. You're In The Army Now**

[69]J.F. Kennedy, "Inaugural Address," *John F. Kennedy Presidential Library and Museum*, (1961).

[70]M.L. King, Jr., "I Have A Dream," *The Martin Luther King, Jr. Research and Education Institute Stanford University*, (1963).

**19. Nice Try**

[71]E., Pougnet, L.A. Serbin, D.M. Stack, J.E. Ledingham, and A.E. Schwartzman, "The Intergenerational Continuity of Fathers' Absence in a Socioeconomically Disadvantaged Sample," *Journal of Marriage & Family* 74 (2012): 540-555.

[72]C.A. Harriman "The Parenting Cycle of Fatherless Men," *California State University Dissertation*, (2003).

[73]K. Kost, "The Function of Fathers: What Poor Men Say About Fatherhood," *The Journal of Contemporary Human Services* 82, no. 5 (2001): 499-508.

**21. Who's The Boss**

[74]U.S. Immigration and Customs Enforcement, "*HIS Special Agent Featured in Human Trafficking Documentary*," (2016).

[75]A.F Levy, "Innocent Traffickers, Guilty Victims: The Case for Prosecuting So-Called 'Bottom Girls' in the United States," *Anti-Trafficking Review* 6 (2016): 130-133.

## 24. We Are Family

[76]H.A. Hargreaves-Cormany and T.D. Patterson, "Characteristics of Survivors of Juvenile Sex Trafficking: Implications for Treatment and Intervention Initiatives," *Aggression and Violent Behavior* 30 (2016): 32-39.

## 25. The Clock is Ticking

[77]D.L. Espelage, J.S. Hong, and A. Valido, "Associations Among Family Violence, Bullying, Sexual Harassment, and Teen Dating Violence," in *Adolescent Dating Violence*, eds D.A. Wolf and J.R. Temple (Cambridge, MA: Academic Press, 2018): 85-102.

## 27. Yank My Chain

[78]U.S. Department of Health and Human Services Office of Inspector General, *"States' Prevention of Child Sex Trafficking in Foster Care,"* (n.d.).

[79]K. Casassa, L. Knight, and C. Mengo, "Trauma Bonding Perspectives From Service Providers and Survivors of Sex Trafficking: A Scoping Review," *Trauma Violence Abuse*, (2021).

[80]D. Dutton and S. Painter, "Emotional Attachments in Abusive Relationships: A Test of Traumatic Bonding Theory," *National Institute of Health* 8, no. 2 (1993): 105-120.

[81]K. Kurst-Swanger and J. Petcosky, *Violence in the Home: Multidisciplinary Perspectives*, (New York: Oxford University Press, 2003).

[82]M. Aguilar, "Creating Safe Families: Resource Parent Awareness of Commercially Sexually Exploited Children (CSEC)," *California State University, Fresno, Master's Thesis*, (2017).

## 28. Risky Business

[83]Hounmenou and O'Grady, *U.S. Responses to CSEC*.

[84]Cecchet and Thoburn, *Psychological Experience CSEC*, 482.

[85]Cecchet and Thoburn, *Psychological Experience CSEC*.

[86]Satel, *Harm Reduction Harms*.

## 31. The Show Must Go On

[87]Shared Hope, *"What is Sex Trafficking?"* www.sharedhope.org, (n.d.).

[88]M.N. Jeanis, B.H. Fox, and C.N. Nuniz, "Revitalizing Profiles of Runaways: A Latent Class Analysis of Delinquent Runaway Youth," *Child and Adolescent Social Work Journal* 36 (2019): 171-187.

## 32. All In The Family

[89]J.A. Reid, M.T. Baglivio, A.R. Piquero, M.A. Greenwald, and N. Epps, "Human Trafficking of Minors and Childhood Adversity in Florida," *American Journal for Public Health* 107, (2017): 306-311.

[90]G. Sprang and J. Cole, "Familial Sex Trafficking of Minors: Trafficking Conditions, Clinical Presentation, and System Involvement," *Journal of Family Violence* 33, no. 3 (2018): 185-195.

[91]T. Salinger, "Houston Man Offered Sex with Sedated 4-Year-Old in Craigslist Ad Saying, 'Come Sleep with Daddy's Little Girl': Officials," *New York Daily News*, November 16, 2015.

[92]Aguilar, *Creating Safe Families.*

**33. This Isn't Going To End Well**

[93]M. Murphy, "Sex Trafficked on Social Media: The Children Sold on Snapchat and Instagram," *The Telegraph*. November 30, 2019.

[94]M. Silva, "Video App TikTok Fails to Remove Online Predators," *BBC News*, April 5, 2019.

[95]H. Zapal, "How TikTok Predators Are Interacting With Kids," *Bark*, July 24, 2019.

[96]G. Detman, "Man Used Fortnite to Recruit Child Pornography Victim: Attorney General," *WSBT News*, January 17, 2019.

[97]H. Schreiber, "Mom Warns of Popular Family-Friendly Video Game Where Her 7-Year-Old's Character Was 'Violently Gang-Raped,'" *Yahoo! News*, July 5, 2018.

[98]D. Thomas, "Fake Your Location if Your Parents Installed a GPS Tracker on Your Android Phone," *Gadget Hacks*, July 31, 2018.

[99]McAfee, *"The Digital Divide: How the Online Behavior of Teens is Getting Past Parents,"* June 25, 2012.

[100]B. O'Donnell, "Rise in Online Enticement and Other Trends: NCMEC Releases 2020 Exploitation Stats," *National Center for Missing Children*, (February 24, 2021).

[101]McAfee, *"The Digital Divide."*

**34. Diamond in the Rough**

[102]C. Deziel, "Why Do Ice & Salt Together Burn the Skin?" *Sciencing*, (March 13, 2018).

[103]S.R. Grant, *"EKG: Resuscitating the Bodies and Hearts of our Children,"* hard copy PowerPoint, (2018).

[104]A., Bernegger, K. Kienesberger, L. Carlberg, P. Swoboda, B. Ludwig, R. Koller, M. Inaner, M. Zotter, N. Kapusta, M. Aigner, H. Aslacher, S. Kasper, and A. Schosser, "The Impact of COMT and Childhood Maltreatment on Suicidal Behavior in Affective Disorders," *Scientific Reports* 8, no. 692 (2018).

[105]J. Cole, G. Sprang, R. Lee, and J. Cohen, "The Trauma of Commercial Sexual Exploitation of Youth: A Comparison of CSE Victims to Sexual Abuse Victims in a Clinical Sample," *Journal of Interpersonal Violence* 31, no. 1 (2016): 122-146.

[106]B. Brakenhoff, B. Jang, N. Slesnick, and A. Snyder, "Longitudinal Predictors of Homelessness: Findings From the National Longitudinal Survey of Youth," *Journal of Youth Studies*, (2015).

[107]H. Meltzer, T.J. Ford, P.E. Bebbington, and P. Vostanis, "Behavior and Substance Misuse," *Journal of Adolescent Health* 51, no. 5 (2012): 415-421.

[108]V.J. Greenbaum, K., Yun, and J. Todres, "Child Trafficking: Issues for Policy and Practice," *The Journal of Law, Medicine, & Ethics* 46, no. 1 (2018): 159-163.

[109]Lanctot et. al., *Nightmares and Flashbacks.*

[110]Hounmenou and O'Grady, *U.S. Responses to CSEC.*

[111]Cole et al., *Comparison of CSE and Sexual Abuse.*

[112]Cecchet and Thoburn, *The Psychological Experience.*

**Appendix D**

[113]B. Van der Kolk, *The Body Keeps the Score*, (New York: The Penguin Group, 2014).

[114]B. Keyes, L.A. Underwood, V. Snyder, F.L.L. Dailey, and T. Hourihan, "Healing Emotional Affective Responses to Trauma (HEART): A Christian Model of Working with Trauma," *Frontiers in the Psychotherapy of Trauma and Dissociation* 1, no. 2 (2018): 212-243.